Imperial Charade

OTHER BOOKS BY ALYN BRODSKY:

The Kings Depart
Madame Lynch & Friend

Imperial Charade

A Biography of Emperor
Napoleon III
and Empress Eugénie,
Nineteenth-Century Europe's
Most Successful Adventurers

by Alyn Brodsky

The Bobbs-Merrill Company, Inc.
Indianapolis   New York

Designed by Rita Muncie
Manufactured in the United States of America
First Printing

Library of Congress Cataloging in Publication Data
Brodsky, Alyn.
  Imperial charade.
  1. Napoleon III, Emperor of the French, 1808–1873.
  2. Eugénie, Consort of Napoleon III, 1826–1920.
  3. France—Kings and rulers—Biography.
  4. France—Queens—Biography.   I. Title.
DC280.B87   944.07′092′2 [B]   78–55665
ISBN 0–672–52346–9

for
Adeline and Lowell Burton
and
Gloria and Jack Herson

Contents

Part III: Exile

Foreword

It all began with the Empress Josephine, but for whom Napoleon III would never have been born, Eugénie would never have reigned, and the nineteenth century would never have known its most extraordinary pair of adventurers.

The marriage of Napoleon III and Eugénie is the most disastrous in the annals of dynastic history. Not only were they unfit for the throne of France, they were unfit for each other. Their marriage and accession have often been called a double miracle.

Actually, they were a double triumph of innate talent over historical implausibility.

Palmerston said of Napoleon: "The Emperor's mind seems as full of schemes as a warren full of rabbits." His scheme to make France the preeminent European power resulted in the collapse of France, the unification of Italy, and the rise of modern Germany; a continent that had enjoyed forty years of peace was plunged into a generation of war because he wanted peace.

Napoleon was indeed a schemer, but an embarrassingly mediocre one.

"I never form distant plans," he once said. "I am governed by the exigencies of the moment."

He was, though never in the way he anticipated. He was a gambler, but a gambler without a system; a gambler who left too much to blind luck. He labored hard, but found it difficult to make decisions. He liked everyone, but trusted no one. He preferred to surround himself with, in Karl Marx's words, "vagabonds, disbanded soldiers, discharged prisoners, fugitives from the galleys, professional beggars, sharpers, jugglers, pickpockets, conjurers, gamesters, pimps and brothel-keepers."

He felt more secure in such company.

In his *Fragments historiques 1688 et 1830,* Napoleon wrote: "March in the vanguard of the ideas of your century, these ideas will follow and support you; march in the rear of them, they will drag you down; march against them, they will destroy you."

Napoleon marched in the vanguard of the ideas of his century— and they dragged him down. The thesis was a sound one. The inconsistency was in the man. He was too decent a human being to be a dictator, yet a dictator he became; he was basically a utopian socialist, yet an autocratic emperor he became.

With all his faults, Napoleon III had but one vice: lechery.

With all her faults, Eugénie had but one vice: excessive pride.

She did not love her husband and was sexually frigid into the bargain; hardly the ideal consort for a man congenitally incapable of remaining monogamously loyal to any woman. Periodically, the Tuileries rang out with bitter recriminations on Eugénie's part and, on Napoleon's part, the cry "Ugénie, you go too far!" (He could not pronounce her name correctly. She resented that too.)

On one occasion they both went too far. The Emperor had established his mistress of the moment, Marguerite Bellanger, in a little love-nest in Passy, to which he would sneak of an evening, accompanied only by a detective to stand guard. On the evening in question, the Emperor—whose health was by then in a rather precarious state—suffered a fit in la Bellanger's bed. The panicking detective summoned the Empress, who went to bring him back home.

According to one of their courtiers, "Violent scenes in the Imperial ménage followed this scandalous adventure, and they went so far that the Emperor, tired of constant reproaches, talked so seriously of divorce that . . . influence was necessary to convince him that a great wrong would be done to the dynasty if the scandal became known."

The scandal became known; there were no secrets at the Napoleonic Court. But there was no divorce. The Emperor would never let her go; he had by then come to admire his wife, after a fashion. And, though she often threatened to do so, the Empress would never abandon the exalted position to which the Emperor had raised her because it was, simply stated, the only way he could bed her down.

Eugénie was one of the most beautiful women of her age; but she was more—infinitely more—than merely, as her enemies called her, *"La Belle Reine Crinoline."* She was, in fact—and this was about the only thing she and Napoleon had in common—a mass of contradictions.

She was acutely sensitive to the feelings of others, yet she could reduce people to tears with her caustic tongue. She presided with ease and grace over the nineteenth century's most brilliant Court, yet she functioned best only in the secluded company of the ill-chosen few. She stood at the epicenter of a morally disgusting society, yet she never slipped from grace; though she flaunted her sexuality, Eugénie was probably the only Second Empire woman of consequence who never took a lover. She was philosophically a libertarian, yet she marched with proud defiance in the forefront of reaction. She was a rabid Ultramontane, yet she was free of all religious prejudice and, even more inconsistently, was obsessively superstitious; her preoccupation with table-turnings, galloping stools and associable hokus-pokus was such that during one period the Empire stood in danger of being ruled by planchette.

On the eve of becoming Empress, Eugénie developed an almost ghoulish obsession with the memory of Marie Antoinette. The obsession was well advertised. Relics, miniatures, furniture, old dolls, slops jars—anything that obtained upon Marie Antoinette found its way to Eugénie's apartments. One of her courtiers said that "the desire to resemble Marie Antoinette was a kind of mania with her—but that which fascinated her in her model were Marie Antoinette's faults and foibles, and she made an effort to copy them."

That effort met with success. Like her royal predecessor, Eugénie was obtuse and foolish, incontestably arrogant, and inherently incapable of appreciating that there were limits to her intelligence. Furthermore, she sought to push her consort into deviating tragically from political reality, arrogating to herself power to which she was not entitled and which she abused mercilessly.

In addition to being sexually incompatible, Napoleon and
Eugénie were politically and philosophically incompatible. Once on
the throne, Napoleon moved to the left as Eugénie moved to the
right. Paradoxically, as Eugénie's emotional and physical hold on
him lessened, Napoleon allowed her political influence to increase.
And this at a time when France faced a number of problems with
which neither could cope simply because both were hopelessly out-
classed.

Both sovereigns wanted the same things: peace and prosperity
for France and a strong inheritance for their son. But they could not
agree on how these should be realized. Eugénie regretted that
Byzantine-like concatenation of activity Napoleon always brought
into play, only because she considered such activity unnecessary
and thus demeaning to anyone holding the Imperial dignity.

Indubitably it was; but—and this Eugénie could not perceive—it
was the only kind of activity Napoleon was capable of bringing into
play. She believed complex problems could be resolved with simple
solutions simply arrived at. Such a belief is probably understandable
in a woman whose grasp of the political realities was—there is
simply no other way to put it—simpleminded.

Nowhere is this more evident than in Eugénie's tenaciously held
conviction that Europe could exist in harmony if only all nations saw
the wisdom of living under the Temporal Power. Said she: "The
representative of God must have a visible power on earth and an
earthly authority in order to fulfill his Divine mission. Without this
earthly power, the concept of the Church cannot be realized. And
the maintenance of this power—in other words, of the Church-
State—involves the honor of France under the rule of Pius IX and
Napoleon III."

Such a "rule"—for which Eugénie strived in direct contravention
of her consort's will—was palpably impossible as well as totally
unrealistic. Pius IX proclaimed (in his *Syllabus Errorum*): "It is an
error to believe that the Roman Pontiff can and ought to reconcile
himself to, and agree with, progress, liberalism, and contemporary
civilization." Napoleon III could not subscribe to Pius's thesis on
what constituted *errorum*.

It was Napoleon's favorite cousin and Eugénie's *bête noire*, the
redoubtable Princess Mathilde Bonaparte, who wrote of the Empress: "She and she alone has been the cause of France's misfortune.

This woman has ruined the best and most generous of men and with him our poor country."

Actually, that best and most generous of men ruined himself, with a capable assist from this woman; together they ruined Mathilde's poor country.

But then, what other country would have tolerated so horribly mismatched—and incompetent—a pair in the first place?

Part I: Exile

Chapter 1
Louis-Napoleon:
1808–1831

The Bonapartes were a motley crew whose public squabbles, mostly amongst themselves, prompted Napoleon Bonaparte (Napoleon I) himself to lament: "I do not believe that any man in the world is more unfortunate in his family than I am!"

Louis-Napoleon (Napoleon III) inherited many of the Bonaparte family traits. Fortunately, to offset them, he inherited from his mother a few of the more salubrious Beauharnais family traits—most notably kindness, compassion for his fellow man, and an inchoate conscience. His mother was Hortense de Beauharnais, the Empress Josephine's daughter by her first marriage. The Bonapartes, Napoleon excepted, detested Josephine and her children (there was also a son, Eugène). Napoleon loved the Beauharnais youngsters; they were not only more capable but more loyal to him than were his own siblings.

Fearful that her inability to give Napoleon an heir might prompt him to divorce her for someone who could, Josephine suggested a marriage between Hortense and the youngest Bonaparte brother, Louis. It was a brilliant move; not only was Louis available, he was Napoleon's favorite brother.

He was also Napoleon's one blind spot. Said he, "Louis has none of the defects of his brothers." That was true. Louis had defects even his defective brothers never dreamed of. He was a bitter, suspicious, morose, misanthropic valetudinarian who, in his spare moments, wrote a number of novels, poems and plays that ran the gamut from the dreadful to the abominable.

3

In addition to being an emotional wreck, he was a physical wreck. Among his myriad afflictions were a mild paralysis on one side, occasional bouts of vertigo, periodic constriction of the throat and bowels, quotidian headaches, and chronic depression. He loved to sit in dark rooms and brood, and was given to monthly outbursts of clinical paranoia. Louis also suffered from locomotor ataxia, presumably the result of a stray encounter with a syphilitic, which left him without the use of the fingers on his right hand. (He ground out his literary gems with a special glove to which a pen had been riveted.)

When the marriage was decided upon by her mother and step-father, the eighteen-year-old Hortense accepted her fate without demur. The twenty-three-year-old Louis, on the other hand, reacted by fleeing to Bordeaux. Informed by Napoleon that the matter was decided, he then set about courting his bride-to-be.

It was an extraordinary courtship. Along with a covering note— "Either you are all good or all bad. There can be no in-between"— Louis sent her a twenty-four-page résumé of his erotic adventures to date and a demand that Hortense reply in kind. Hortense wrote in all honesty that she had nothing to "confess." Louis refused to believe her. He preferred to believe Hortense was Napoleon's mistress.

They were married on January 4, 1802. (Recalled the bridegroom dolorously: "Never was there such a ceremony so sad.") In March, Louis departed for the south of France to take a cure. In October, he returned to Paris in time for the birth of his and Hortense's first child, Napoleon-Charles—whose paternity he promptly refused to acknowledge. The child was born prematurely. Louis assumed that his brother Napoleon was the true father.

When Napoleon made himself Emperor in May 1804, he made Louis Constable of France. The Constable bought an estate at sub-urban Saint-Leu and turned it into a veritable fortress. High walls were erected around the mansion; sentries were posted in near contiguity to watch Hortense's every move; spies were hired to read her and her attendants' correspondence. He boarded up all the doors save one that led to Hortense's suite—and then moved his bed into her bedchamber. Their second son, Napoleon-Louis, was born later that year.

It was the only one of his three children whose paternity Louis would acknowledge unequivocally.

In June 1806, the Emperor put the Constable on the throne of Holland. As at Saint-Leu, Queen Hortense's every movement was overseen by sentries, her (and her attendants') every letter read by spies. Her bedchamber was a lugubrious dungeon—the walls were decorated with a horrific frieze of black and white skulls—that had formerly served as a way station for condemned criminals en route to the gallows.

Hortense spent most of her time back in Paris.

Louis determined to be first and foremost a Hollander; it is unclear whether he did so in order to antagonize his wife, who sided with the Emperor on all matters, or to antagonize the Emperor himself for having compelled him to make an unsought marriage. He went so far as to encourage wholesale smuggling when the Emperor's embargo on British trade threatened to wreak havoc on the Dutch economy.

For her mother's sake, Hortense sought to make a go of the marriage, but by 1807 it had degenerated into a public scandal. Louis sent her an insulting (and highly imaginative) eight-point bill of particulars demanding a dissolution of their union. The demand, which was ignored, earned from the Emperor a stinging rebuke. This sent Louis into a dark room for a week.

A few months later the couple was reunited by tragedy: the death of their four-year-old eldest son. Forgetting he had denied paternity, the repentant Louis joined Hortense at Toulouse, whither she had gone after mitigating her sorrow in the Pyrenees, and sought a reconciliation. Hortense agreed. Though now in love with another man, she was still determined to make the marriage work. Not only did the Emperor will it, the Empress demanded it. By Napoleonic fiat, the sons of Louis were now in the direct line of succession after the sons of Joseph, eldest of the Bonaparte brothers; and Joseph had no sons. Louis returned to The Hague in September. Hortense, who was pregnant, insisted on remaining in Paris until after the child's birth.

In the early hours of April 21, 1808—in her house at number 8 Rue Cérutti (now Rue Lafitte) and not, as Second Empire chroniclers claimed, the Tuileries—Queen Hortense gave birth to the future Emperor Napoleon III. The babe's birth, like that of his eldest brother, was premature. On hearing the news, Louis counted backward to the Toulouse reconciliation and then wrote snarlingly by way of congratulations: "It is a consolation to live so far from you, to have nothing to discuss with you, nothing to expect from you! Adieu, Madame! Adieu forever!"

Louis refused to set eyes on the boy for fourteen years.

Louis was not alone in denying paternity. Many of Louis-Napoleon's and his mother's enemies—most notably the Bonapartes—would agree that the King of Holland was not his father. None, though, could agree on who was. Knowing fingers were pointed in all directions. High on everyone's list (including most present-day historians') was a Dutch collaborationist, Admiral Verhuell, who had helped Hortense mitigate her sorrow in the Pyrenees.

Interestingly, the one man never charged with the deed was Talleyrand's bastard son, Count Charles de Flahaut—Hortense's only historically documentable lover.

At the end of 1809, the King of Holland came to Paris to seek the family's permission for a divorce. (He went out of his way to avoid seeing either Hortense or her infant son.) The timing could not have been more inopportune.

Only ten days previously, the Bonapartes had gleefully consented to the Emperor's divorcing Josephine so that he might marry the Austrian archduchess, by whom he suspected—with remarkable prescience, as it turned out—that he might sire a legitimate son. (He had already sired a brace of illegitimate ones.) It would not look right, in the eyes of the Church, for the Imperial family to have two divorces. With typical Bonaparte inconsistency, the family were sticklers for Church dogma at the very time they were condoning the Emperor's arrest and years-long imprisonment of Pope Pius VII.*

Nor did the clan's Catholicism inhibit them from laughing uproariously when the Emperor, on entering Milan, commanded a ballet troupe to dance a Papal Consistory that featured a chorus of cardinals doing stumble-bum bourrées, a comic pope doing pratfall entrechats, and a

Louis fled back to his favorite dungeon in the outskirts of The Hague to brood. Hortense followed after him (April 1, 1810) at the insistence of the Emperor. ("Louis is a good man, though nobody seems to be able to live with him.") Two months was the limit of her endurance. The Dutch climate was unbearable. The Dutch monarch's conduct was worse. One of his favorite gambits was to crawl into Hortense's skull-lined bedchamber on all fours, awaken her from a deep sleep with a loud "Boo!" and inform her that she was killing him.

Hortense rushed off to Plombières for a much-needed cure; she was compelled to leave her eldest surviving son behind in Holland. Five weeks later, outraged by the Emperor's criticism of his outrageous conduct on the Dutch throne, Louis abdicated.

It was a colorful abdication. First he secretly slipped a fortune out of the country, then he slipped himself out of the country; he left behind his favorite son, but took along his favorite dog. Characteristically, while walking to his carriage Louis stumbled into a ditch and almost broke his neck. He took refuge with his Imperial brother's father-in-law and archenemy, the Emperor of Austria.

Hortense, who had been named Regent for the abandoned heir, asked the Emperor what she should do. The Emperor replied, "Now you are emancipated," and that all else was academic. The regency was ended a week later, when Holland was annexed to France. The Emperor settled a handsome annuity on Hortense and told her she was now free to live apart from her husband.

She lived apart with Charles de Flahaut.

Charles-Louis-Napoleon (he would drop the Charles) was the first of the second-generation Bonapartes to be born an Imperial Prince. It would seem the infant, so frail that he had to be bathed in wine and swathed in cotton, could not have entered the world at a more propitious moment. The nation over which he would one day reign—though not even the Delphic Oracle could have foretold the

---

chimney that belched real smoke and almost asphyxiated the appalled audience.

circuitous route by which he would reach the throne—was at the apogee of its Napoleonic *gloire*.

Its Emperor held in thrall a France that stretched eastward to the Rhine and southward over the transalpine Habsburg provinces of northern Italy. Naples, the former Spanish Netherlands (the present-day Benelux countries), and the non-Prussian German states west of the Vistula were ruled by cowed satellites. Imperial troops were even now overrunning Spain and Portugal. Except for England, Russia and the Scandinavian countries, all of Europe had been subdued. And in France itself, the people were too busy hailing the "Little Corporal's" military and political victories as steppingstones to perpetual peace and prosperity to perceive that he was draining the nation's (and the continent's) lifeblood in the process.

It would take another four years for the French to suspect what the rest of Europe already realized: Napoleon Bonaparte, like Othello, had sowed the seeds of his own—and their—destruction.

Prince Louis's state christening took place in November 1810, when he was two years old. By then not only was his mother an ex-Queen, his grandmother was an ex-Empress. Josephine's scheme to assure her own position through Hortense's sons had been shattered by the Emperor's marriage to Marie Louise of Austria, a functional illiterate who devoted most of her waking hours to gorging herself on rich pastries until she literally retched. Within the year, Marie Louise—who stood godmother to Prince Louis—would bear the Emperor his long-sought legitimate heir, thus revoking the major justification for her godson's having been born.

Notwithstanding his altered status, Louis was indulged as if he were one step from the throne. The Emperor, who spoiled all members of his family outrageously, was particularly fond of Hortense's children. The young princes, but especially Louis, were the alpha and omega of their grandmother Josephine's existence.

The ex-Empress was now living in exile at Malmaison with little to do but tend to her famous flower beds and curse herself for having failed to bear "Puss in Boots" (as she called him) an heir. For Hortense, it was a mercy that this adored sorrowing mother seemed to have found in her grandsons a new lease on life.

It was also fortunate for Hortense. Protean when it came to loyalties, she was busy at court cultivating her mother's successor.

Also, she was given to occasional travel. It was a comfort to know that Josephine was available to play the doting grandmother-babysitter.*

The Emperor served as the young princes' surrogate father. Louis would recall at the end of his life how he and his brother "often went to breakfast with the Emperor." And then there were the weekly dinners at the Tuileries, when the Emperor would regale them with the fables of La Fontaine, breaking off from time to time to chat with officials come to discuss affairs of state.

When the Emperor was off to the wars, Hortense took the children out to Malmaison. That Louis was Josephine's favorite—she called him "Oui-Oui" because he was so affable and accommodating—is attributable in equal measure to the sanguine disposition he inherited from his mother and his initially precarious health. (When Louis helped Josephine tend her gardens, care was taken that the contents of his watering can were warm.)

More than half a century later, Louis would recall fondly "the Empress Josephine at Malmaison covering me with her caresses." Till the day he died, Louis venerated his grandmother's memory. When, as Emperor, he proclaimed Josephine to have been the most "virtuous" queen in French history, he actually believed what he was saying. He was the only one who did.

A perceptive analysis from the pen of Madame Cornu has survived and is worth quoting. Hortense Lacroix Cornu was the daughter of Hortense's *femme de chambre*. A year Louis's junior, she was his goddaughter as well as surrogate sister. According to Madame Cornu,

> He was a charming child, as gentle as a lamb, affectionate, caressing, generous (he would even give away his clothes in need), witty, quick in repartee, and with the sensibility of a girl; but easily puzzled, and intellectually lazy. . . . He had not a trace of arrogance, and would throw himself unreservedly into the arms of the first person he met, overwhelming him with caresses beyond rhyme or reason, so that people said

---

* *Hortense's most momentous journey—prior to her expulsion from France in 1815—was the secrecy-shrouded trip she made across the Alps in 1811 to bear Charles de Flahaut's bastard. After bearing the child, she farmed it out; she would never see him again. He was, of course, the future Duke de Morny, without whose help Louis might never have become Emperor of the French.*

he must have a warm and loving heart. But there was nothing in it: he forgot you as soon as you were out of his sight.

Louis-Napoleon would possess those traits till the day he died.

The Empire was crashing with a thud. Bonaparte's invasion of Spain, the failure of his Continental System to bring England to its knees, his political miscalculation in imprisoning Pius VII, the invasion of Russia, the defection of Austria (one wonders why they waited so long to defect)—all led inexorably to the grand climax at Leipzig, the so-called Battle of Nations. All else was anticlimactic. The Allies raced toward Paris. Hortense fled with her sons to the Eure Region, where Josephine had taken refuge at her château in Navarre.

When word came that Napoleon had landed at Elba, Hortense returned with her mother and sons to Paris. The First Bourbon Restoration was under way in the person of the murdered Louis XVI's eldest surviving brother, Louis XVIII, a mentally stagnant corpulent mass of unbridled conservative ineptitude.

Tsar Alexander I, ever the chivalrous autocrat, empathized with both the ex-Queen of Holland and the ex-Empress of France. Alexander set the tone for his fellow-royals, all of whom converged on Paris. Hortense set her cap for Alexander. She was one of nature's born survivors.

At Alexander's suggestion, Hortense moved with her sons to Malmaison, which in short order became the unofficial rendezvous of all the sovereigns gathered in Paris. There were dinner parties, rustic *fêtes*, and heady evenings of heavy dancing and light conversation, all punctuated by moonlight strolls among Josephine's flower beds. While the average Parisian was making do on what comestibles he could steal from his neighbor, mother and daughter were making do on champagne, caviar and other exotic goodies. All appeared with regularity at Malmaison, thanks to Hortense's illustrious benefactor.*

---

* *Also appearing at Malmaison with regularity was King Frederick William III of Prussia. One day—and such are the little ironies of history—he brought his two sons to play with Hortense's two sons.*

A month after the revels at Malmaison began, they were terminated tragically. Ever given to diaphanous gowns, Josephine fell victim to the capricious May weather that often catches tourists unawares, went to bed, and died of pneumonia. After burying her mother and bidding good-bye to her royal guests, who were departing for Vienna to begin their celebrated Congress, Hortense returned to Paris.

Louis XVIII, with a hint from Alexander, granted Hortense the patent title Duchess de Saint-Leu. The Treaty of Fontainebleau allowed Hortense and her sons a handsome settlement, which the Allies failed to hand over. She was not in dire financial straits, though. She and Eugène shared the proceeds of Josephine's estate, which came to a rather handsome sum, especially when Tsar Alexander, out of fond memories of the ex-Empress, willingly purchased many of her choicer belongings at outrageously inflated prices.

Word came from the ex-King of Holland that Hortense had to surrender his two sons to him. Given the nature of the beast, it is probable that his motives were rooted in abject malice; mourning her mother, Hortense could not have been more vulnerable. When she refused to surrender the boys, their father had no recourse but litigation. Because Hortense and the boys had been exempted (at Alexander's insistence) from the Bourbon proscription on all Bonapartes, the elder Louis had to sue in the French courts.

The courts rendered a Solomonic decision: the elder prince, Napoleon-Louis, must be given to his father; the younger, Louis-Napoleon, might remain with his mother.

Before the verdict could be carried out, the Emperor had fled Elba and was marching on Paris. Prince Louis would recall decades later: "When the first news of the Emperor's return . . . came, there was great irritation among the [Bourbons] against my mother and her children—the rumor ran that we were all to be assassinated. One night our governess . . . took us . . . to a little room in the boulevards where we were to remain hidden . . . but our young years prevented us from understanding the meaning of events, and we were delighted with the change."

Fifty-seven years later, the younger Hohenzollern prince and the younger Bonaparte prince would meet again when the former received the latter's sword in surrender on a hill above Sedan.

What was delight to a child was panic to a mother. The Bourbons, if not quite prepared to assassinate them, were quite prepared to seize them as hostages. Fortunately, Louis XVIII was too busy running for his own life to bargain for Hortense's. Napoleon rushed into Paris a week later, and thus commenced the so-called Hundred Days.

In the absence of his son, whom the Allies vowed would never return to France, the Emperor began to look upon Hortense's sons as his legitimate heirs. Louis would always remember those marvelous occasions when the Emperor took him and his brother to the Tuileries and allowed them to look on as he issued directives, interviewed officers and officials, and otherwise planned the reconstruction of his palpably unreconstructable Empire.

Then it was time for the Emperor to move on. History was converging at Waterloo. Hortense's sons were sent for to bid their uncle farewell. It was then that Napoleon I charged the future Napoleon III with his destiny.

At least, that is how legend has it; a legend that was first set down in print by Napoleon III's chief henchman, the spurious Viscount de Persigny, following their mind-boggling 1840 cross-Channel invasion of France on a chartered English paddlesteamer.

On entering his uncle's study and seeing him and Marshal Soult deeply engrossed in maps and plans for the coming battle—so the legend goes—the weeping seven-year-old Louis flung his arms about the Emperor and lamented hysterically: "Sire, I do not want you to go to war; those wicked Allies will kill you!" Whereupon the Sire, overcome with emotion, kissed the tot tenderly and, turning to Soult, said: "Embrace the child, Marshal; he has a good heart. Perhaps one day he will be the hope of my race."

On June 14, Napoleon crossed into Belgium. On June 18, he fought the Battle of Waterloo. On June 21, he crossed back into France. A few days later he was at Malmaison.

"The French are no longer worthy of your care, since they have forsaken you," Hortense told the Emperor. The Emperor agreed, and abdicated. This time there would be no Return.

The Second Bourbon Restoration was commenced on July 7, when Louis XVIII returned to Paris "in the baggage of the Allies," as Prosper Mérimée felicitously put it. The Bourbons found Hor-

tense's having remained on in Paris during the Hundred Days un-
forgivable. Frantic letters were dispatched to Tsar Alexander.
They elicited no response. Alexander and his fellow-royals believed
the rumors that Hortense had not only colluded in Napoleon's return from Elba, but was plotting with underground Bonapartists
against their collective majestic safety.

Early in the morning of July 17, Hortense was advised that the
Allies had added her and her sons to the proscription on all
Bonapartes. They had to be out of Paris within two hours and across
the nearest border with all possible dispatch. That night—with an
officer appointed by the chivalrous Austrian chieftain, Prince
Schwarzenburg, to escort them safely through the howling mobs
thirsting for Bonaparte blood—Hortense and her sons went into
exile.

The First Empire was at an end. If there was to be a Second
Empire, it seemed improbable that any of the Bonapartes could
bring it about. The true heir, the King of Rome, was doomed to
spend the remaining sixteen years of his pathetic life as a pampered
prisoner in his Austrian grandfather's Court.

There were, of course, the fallen Emperor's four brothers, any
one of whom might theoretically raise the standard. But the Allies
took elaborate measures to ensure against such a calamity; international police saw to it that all Bonapartes stayed out of France, and
kept an omnipresent surveillance over them wherever they lived
and traveled.

It was a case of overkill. The last thing any of the Bonapartes had
in mind was a Napoleonic revival. All were content to lie low, living
handsomely—and, by and large, scandalously—off the booty and
plunder of a continent, bestowed on them by a brother who had
demeaned the very concept of fraternal loyalty. As one of the clan's
nephews lamented symbolically: "All the Bonapartes are dead."

Not all.

There still remained Hortense, who—perhaps out of some desire
to give her Bonaparte in-laws the comeuppance they deserved for
having rejected her mother, perhaps because it was a reflection of
her true convictions—carried with her out of France a sacred vow.
She would form within her the cultus of the Emperor's memory—a
cultus in which her youngest son would progress, through natural
stages, from acolyte to high priest to patron saint.

As testimony to Hortense's success, the following is offered in evidence. In 1821, learning of his uncle's apotheosis at St. Helena, Louis wrote his mother: "Whenever I do wrong, I think of the Great Man, and I seem to feel his spirit within me, urging me to keep myself worthy of the name Napoleon." At the height of his own Imperial glory, he wrote to a Bonaparte cousin: "How can pygmies like ourselves really appreciate at its full worth the great historical figure of Napoleon? It is as though we stood before a colossal statue, the form of which we are unable to grasp as a whole."

Bonapartism was not a political ideology; it was a religion. And like all religions, its popularity derived less from its theology than from the richness of its martyrology. The exiled Emperor would have had this in mind when, on arriving at St. Helena, he said, with what some might call cynicism, others empiricism, "If Jesus had not died on the cross, he would never have been worshipped as God."

Jesus left the chronicling of his earthly ministry to those who came later. Napoleon Bonaparte's evangelists—a miniscule congeries of true believers—accompanied him into exile. It was to them that he dictated his gospel: an extraordinary pseudo-messianic brew compounded, in equal doses, of self-idealization, convenient departure from historical fact, exploitation of the brevity of human memory, and egregious gall.

The Napoleonic legend was created by one man on a small island in the South Atlantic who, in the six-year twilight of his incredible life, calculatingly became the first martyr of his faith.

Even as the fallen Corsican was being transported to St. Helena, the nephew to whom that legend would become an all-consuming *raison d'être* was beginning to play out his Bourbon-inflicted destiny as Ishmael to his mother's Hagar.

The three refugees made their first stop at Dijon. It was almost their last stop. The carriage was surrounded by a rabble shouting "Down with the Bonapartists!" with appropriate menacing gesticulations. As the three made their way fitfully to a local inn for a few hours of rest, Count Von Voyna, their Austrian escort, went off to raise a detachment of Austrian troops billeted in the city. While the anxious exiles cowered in bed, fearful for their very lives, outside the inn the Austrians managed to hold off a mob of French soldiers who strutted around in circles, drinking, swearing, brandishing their swords, and otherwise demonstrating that there is nothing quite so chivalrous as a Gallic mob holding three innocents at bay. When these gallants were joined by the civilian riffraff of the neighborhood and it seemed that a bloody collision was inevitable, Von Voyna gathered his three charges and sped them out of the city and on to the Swiss border.

They were ordered to pass through Geneva without stopping, but Von Voyna managed to obtain permits for them to remain on a day or two while he awaited further instructions from Paris. The Geneva citizenry gave themselves over to proving how militantly anti-Bonaparte they had never really been. In the very inn where Von Voyna's charges were huddling, a battalion of Swiss army officers held a roisterous banquet to celebrate the defeat of Napoleon Bonaparte by almost every other European army but their own.

Now abandoned, on Allied orders, by Von Voyna, and expelled from Geneva, the pathetic trio holed up in Aix-les-Bains. There the elder Louis Bonaparte's emissaries compelled Hortense to surrender her eldest son, as decreed by the French courts. The boy was taken off to join the father who had left him behind in Holland in favor of a mongrel dog.

Hortense's and young Louis's grief was assuaged by the arrival from Paris of Mademoiselle Louise Cochelet, Hortense's *lectrice* (reader), with whom she had left her jewels and funds, lest they be stolen during the flight from Paris. Mademoiselle Cochelet brought not only the jewels and funds; she brought in her wake other loyal friends and family retainers. All succeeded in restoring some semblance of balance in Hortense.

She was again thrown off balance a few days later, when word came from Paris: the Allied leaders had convinced Louis XVIII that the continued residence at Aix of a thirty-two-year-old woman and her seven-year-old son posed grave peril for the peace of Europe. On they moved—Morat, Berne, Zurich—arriving at Constance in the Duchy of Baden on December 7. To the minds of the Badenese authorities, encouraged by the various Allied constabularies, the arrival of a mere handful of pitiful Bonaparte refugees constituted a

Napoleonic invasion. Hortense quickly got off an urgent appeal to her cousin and erstwhile best friend Stephanie de Beauharnais, who was now the Grand Duchess. Permission to stay on at Constance was denied.

Whereupon Hortense reacted with an attitude that was almost Napoleonic in intensity. She simply refused to leave. Her brother Eugène, son-in-law to the King of Bavaria, arrived for a reunion. Eugène interceded with his Badenese relatives and arranged for permits for the party to stay on; he also arranged a credit account for Hortense with the Frankfurt branch of the House of Rothschild (her jewels were put up as collateral).

Hortense was now able to concentrate on restoring a sense of normalcy to her life and, of greater import, overseeing the education of her favorite son.

Louis was slow at learning and reluctant to improve his speed. A gentle, rather timid child who spoke little but thought volumes, he was one of nature's underachievers as a youth. The senior Louis—at whose mercy Hortense was, given her refugee status, France's chauvinistic laws, and the 6,000 francs he begrudgingly granted the Prince as a yearly allowance—maintained an epistolary presence in the household. He wrote insisting that young Louis's education be put in the charge of Philippe Le Bas.

Le Bas was the kind of man who, on entering a strange town, would collar the first person he met and demand directions to the local library. The young Prince was locked into a fixed schedule: from six in the morning to nine at night, he was taught grammar, Latin, mathematics, German, Greek, history, geography; there were also horseback riding, general calisthenics, and swimming. For an hour or so each day, Louis was permitted to partake in the talk within his mother's drawing room.

Le Bas considered it "the most dangerous hour of the day." Being the scion of a Jacobin family, he did not appreciate his pupil's exposure to the Bonapartist philosophy in which Hortense and her companions fairly wallowed. But, to his credit, Le Bas eschewed politics for pedagogy. Though he remained on for seven years, it is impossible to trace the extent, if any, of Le Bas's influence on Louis, though of two things we can be certain: the Emperor Napoleon III was neither a Jacobin nor a savant.

Winters were spent in Rome, the yearly gathering place of the Bonapartes in their diaspora. Hortense took pains to assure that her son enjoyed a close relationship with the former Imperial family. Regardless of what she thought of them—which was precious little—they still had the magic name Bonaparte.

The family had nothing against Louis, but wished his mother would abandon her fixation. The last thing any of them wanted was a possible renaissance of European ill will aimed in their direction. But Hortense was nothing if not a woman of determination. Though only one of those first-generation Bonapartes would survive to appreciate it, that determination paid off handsomely.

Hortense established a Napoleonic Court-in-exile to which flocked, among others, a number of die-hard veterans of the *Grande Armée* who, unlike the majority of their surviving compatriots, refused to swear allegiance to the Bourbon regime. Hortense was the magnet for their loyalty to the Martyr's memory. They willingly became her satellites. Notable among these was Colonel Parquin, a veteran of the *Grande Armée*, whose reminiscences of service under *l'Empereur* lent an added touch of validity to the Napoleonic bibelots and relics Hortense collected by the cartload.

More than flattering Hortense's feminine vanity, helping her relive the good old days, and otherwise sharing the sorrow of her banishment, the satellites performed a vital function: they helped to keep alive—indeed, to magnify—the memory of the late Napoleon I for the benefit of the future Napoleon III.

A year after defying the Allies, Hortense was told she must leave Constance. Thanks to brother Eugène's royal connections, she was permitted to relocate at Augsburg. There Louis, with Le Bas in tow, was entered into the St. Anna Gymnasium. The eight years he spent there constituted his entire formal education.

Given the school and its curriculum, it was inevitable that Louis become Germanic in his orientation. He preferred German poetry to French poetry—Schiller was a particular favorite; he could (and would) quote long stretches verbatim, and with feeling, at the feeblest encouragement. To the end of his life, he enjoyed swapping

German beerhall songs and students' memories with any and all comers. Too, Louis mastered German to the degree that ever after he spoke his mother tongue with a pronounced Teutonic flavor.*

Meanwhile, Hortense was creating a permanent home in Switzerland, whose alpine air she considered vital to her health and peace of mind. In 1821, the Swiss allowed her to purchase a small two-storied mansion in the Canton of Thurgau; situated on the Swiss shore of Lake Constance, Arenenberg—the name means "Fool's Hill"—would be Hortense's home for the remaining sixteen years of her life.

Here at Arenenberg, while Louis moved through his pre-teens and on toward young adulthood, Hortense indulged a nascent talent for painting landscapes and composing banal songs. Her most successful effort was *En Partant pour la Syrie,* the popularity of which was fixed when it became the official anthem of the Second Empire.

When not sketching and composing, Hortense concentrated on the writing of her *Mémoires.* They remained unpublished until this century, not because they reveal so much but because they reveal so little; the *Mémoires* are blatantly self-serving and reveal that the authoress enjoyed a remarkable talent for occasionally allowing historical fact to play handmaiden to piquant mendacity. Included are interminable hagiographical passages revealing that dedication to Bonapartism which Hortense passed on to her son. One in particular, in which the martyred Emperor is celebrated as "the Messiah of the people's interest," is absolutely priceless.

The relationship between mother and son was extremely close. Hortense encouraged Louis to go when, on rare occasions, the ex-King of Holland invited him for a visit. She knew Louis resented his father because of the way he treated her. Such treatment continued even after the marriage had, to all intent and purpose, ended. The elder Bonaparte literally bombarded Hortense with endless letters

---

* *When Napoleon III congratulated Bismarck on the latter's impeccable French—"I have never heard a foreigner speak our language as you do!"—the man who would destroy his Empire replied suavely, with the delicious sarcasm that was his wont: "Sire, I can return the compliment: I have never heard a Frenchman speak his language the way Your Majesty does!"*

loaded with unsolicited advice and disapproval of her as a mother and as a person. Hortense learned to live with it. His pitiful and constant yelps of poverty notwithstanding, the ex-King of Holland was an extremely wealthy man. Hortense intended that no obstacles be put in the path of her youngest and favorite son's getting his full portion.

Louis's first visit with his father, in 1823, set the pattern for future ones—which Louis tried to keep to a minimum. Le Bas, who went along in his capacity as tutor, described it as "one of the most disagreeable months of my life." Soap and eau de cologne were proscribed; washing was done only with dry bran. Other children were forbidden to call. A quarter of a square of chocolate, measured with consummate precision, was allowed daily. Laughter was forbidden. The use of a shoe designed by the elder Bonaparte, made to fit either foot indiscriminately, was encouraged. The reading of the elder Bonaparte's latest contribution to literature was mandatory.

The visits did have one positive result, however. They brought Louis and his elder brother closer together.

The Prince entered manhood at a time when wars of liberation were endemic on the Continent. Like Lord Byron, he believed in the right of national determination; and as a Bonaparte—and as a future emperor—he felt obliged to learn war firsthand. He sought his father's permission to assist the Russians in liberating the suppressed nationalities within the carcinomatous Ottoman Empire. The elder Bonaparte withheld permission; it was his conviction that all wars are barbaric save wars of national defense. Disappointed, Louis settled for a temporary career with the Swiss artillery. (The Emperor had been in artillery.)

In 1830, the "July Revolution" swept Louis XVIII's ultra-reactionary brother-successor, Charles X, from the throne. In its wake came the so-called Bourgeois Monarchy in the person of that eminently bourgeois Orléanist, Louis-Philippe. Prince Louis felt the time had come to inject himself into the political cauldron. An Allied precondition to the Orléanist's enthronement was a renewal of the proscription on all Bonapartes. Since he could not go westward into France, Louis went southward into Italy. In October, he accompanied Hortense on her annual visit to Rome.

It was the first step on the road that would lead to his assumption of the Imperial dignity.

The gospel set down at St. Helena was slowly gaining currency, due to the political turmoil in France and a concomitant desire to return to the good old days (and a willingness to forget the bad old days). The operative phrase was *la gloire*. No one understood this better than the Martyr himself. "Just speak to the French of *la gloire* and they are seduced at once," he said. (He also said: "For a man like me the lives of a million soldiers are just so much shit.")

There was as yet no organized Bonapartist movement. Even had there been, Louis was only fifth in the line of succession, behind his uncle Joseph, his father, his brother, and the imprisoned King of Rome (or, as his Austrian captors preferred, Duke of Reichstadt), none of whom had formally renounced his claim.

Therefore, Louis's leap into Italian politics—to his way of thinking, the best route to follow since he could not leap into French politics—was predicated on hopes of gaining himself a reputation. When his time came—and he knew his time was coming—Louis wanted to be known.

What sort of man was the Prince as he stood on the threshold of history? According to Lord Malmesbury, who first met him at Rome in 1829,

> Nobody at that time could have predicted his great and romantic career. He was a wild, harum-scarum youth, or what the French call *un crâne* [a swaggerer], riding at full gallop through the streets to the peril of the public, fencing and pistol-shooting, and apparently without serious thoughts of any kind, although even then he was possessed with the conviction that he would one day rule over France. . . . at that time he evinced no remarkable talent nor any fixed idea but the one which I mention. It grew upon him with his growth and increased daily until it ripened into a certainty. He was a very good horseman and a proficient in athletic games; although short [stubby legs were a genetic trait among all Bonapartes] he was very active and muscular. His face was grave and dark, but redeemed by a singularly bright smile.

Physically, he was remarkably unprepossessing. The once pretty child had evolved into a singularly unattractive, some would say downright ugly, young man. His long torso reposed somewhat precariously atop a pair of thoroughly inadequate legs; his too prominent nose stood guard, as it were, over a wide-flung moustache which, soon to be complemented by a modified Vandyke beard, would make the Emperor Napoleon III a caricaturist's delight. In profile, he looked like Mephistopheles in a road production of *Faust* by a troupe of well-fed midgets.

What people would most remark upon, however—other than his hypersexuality—were those heavily lidded eyes, the curious opacity of which emitted a hue that many called dullness, others called mystery. His cousin the Princess Mathilde remarked: "If I had married him, I should have broken his head open to see what was inside!"

By 1830, the dry rot of Europe's 1815 reorganization by the Congress of Vienna was manifest. The Italian peninsula was a conurbation of Bourbon kingdoms, duchies and principalities, Austrian-dominated provinces in the north, and the Papal States centered on Rome. None had much in common with the others, save a determination to stem the avalanche of republicanism that had flowed down over the Alps following the French Revolution.

Throughout Italy—indeed, throughout Europe—revolutionaries looked to a Bonaparte to lead them as the Emperor had led them. They remembered how he had overthrown the old dynasties (and forgot how he had replaced them with his own laughably inept brothers). Any Bonaparte would do.

In December, the clan gathered in Rome to weigh the pros and cons of heeding the cries of the revolutionaries by exploiting the dead hero's charisma. After much heated debate, they came to a firm decision: they would do nothing. The by-now-aging first-generation Bonapartes were behaving realistically.

As much could not be said for the second-generation Bonapartes. Prince Louis, having come down out of Switzerland a revolutionist in search of a revolutionary movement, encouraged three or four of his cousins to dream the impossible dream. They would capture the Vatican—for openers!

The *coup* was set for the middle of December, while Rome was caught up in the unsettled status of an interregnum: Pius VIII had died on November 30, and the conclave to elect his successor could not meet for two weeks. Details of the harebrained scheme need not detain us here. Suffice it to say that the young rebels planned to bribe the Papal Dragoons, seize the armory adjacent to the Castle St. Angelo, seize the Bank of Sancto Spiritu, arrest the leading cardinals, throw open the prisons, and march on the Capitol, atop which Prince Louis would proclaim himself Regent of France for his imprisoned Imperial cousin the Duke of Reichstadt.

It is extremely improbable that, as some believed, the Prince's grandmother, Madame Mère, financed the whole ridiculous affair; the last thing she, along with the rest of the Bonaparte clan, wanted was to antagonize the Vatican, under whose protection they were living in Rome. But the intriguing question of who put up the money is only one of many that remain unanswered.

Did Louis *really* believe the Austrians would permit the Duke of Reichstadt to leave the Schönbrunn and ascend his "throne"? What did Louis hope to accomplish by proclaiming himself Regent of France in *Italy?* How did Louis believe that seizing the *Vatican* would help his cause? And—most intriguing of all—why did Louis allow himself to be seen galloping about Rome in the days prior to the projected *coup* brandishing a cavalryman's saddlecloth in the revolutionary colors of red, white and blue—colors that were anathema to the Church?

On December 12, Louis was seized by the papal secret police and escorted to the border that separated the Papal States from Tuscany. The ex-King of Holland, reflecting the clan's severe embarrassment over the whole episode, snarled his contempt of the manner in which Hortense had raised "*your* son" and then rushed off to sit in a dark room. Hortense was not sorry to see her son expelled from Rome. A nationalist uprising against the Temporal Power was imminent; she was thankful Louis would not be a part of it.

In fact, he would be smack in the middle of it.

On February 2, 1831, the ultraconservative Pope Gregory XVI was elected, and insurrection broke out in Bologna; it quickly spread throughout the Romagna as the secular *Carbonari* nationalists hoisted the tricolor of liberty amidst much blood and papal embarrassment. Hortense rushed to Florence where Louis had gone to stay with his brother. There she learned that her sons had gone off to join the *Carbonari*.

Hortense was frantic, doubting the success of the entire enterprise. She met with her estranged husband, who, acting his usual considerate self, came up with a plan for getting their sons home: Hortense was to pretend to be seriously ill; this would compel her loyal sons to hasten to her side—at which point they would be arrested. Hortense refused to go along with the plan; she suspected her husband would turn the boys over to the papal authorities. The ex-King of Holland peevishly told her to go get the boys herself.

Meanwhile, in the field, Louis's and his brother's presence was an embarrassment to the insurgents, who entertained hopes that Louis-Philippe might intervene on their behalf—and fears that he would not if it was learned there were Bonapartes involved. Louis and his brother reluctantly resigned their commissions, but stayed on to fight in the capacity of simple volunteers.

They had little choice. They were banned from returning to Florence by the Tuscan authorities; worse, they could expect short shrift from the approaching Austrians. In line with Metternich's belief that the world simply had to be made safe for reaction, Gregory XVI's invitation to put down the rising had been accepted; a strong Austrian army was already on the move.

Ominously, its commander had omitted from his published promised-amnesty list the names of the two Bonaparte brothers.

Hortense prepared to smuggle her sons out of Italy. She secured two passports from the British ambassador in Florence; one was in her own name (Duchess de Saint-Leu), the other in the name of a "Mrs. Hamilton traveling with her two sons William and Charles." The passports were valid only to the degree that their bearers were permitted to enter England by way of France.

Arriving at Foligno on March 14, Hortense learned her boys had fled north in the wake of the advancing Austrians. She followed their trail, arriving at Forli five days later. There she learned that her eldest son had succumbed two days previously to measles. Louis had also caught the measles and was approaching delirium. Taking along a refugee named Zappi (since the "Hamilton" passport indicated two sons), Hortense managed to get the invalid to Ancona, the usual embarkation point for refugees, where a nephew by marriage owned a townhouse.

Their arrival at Ancona was followed two days later by that of the Austrian army, whose commander established his headquarters in

the house. Hortense gave out word that Prince Louis had fled by
sailing packet to Corfu, and that she was merely pausing for a few
days as her absentee nephew's guest before continuing home to
Switzerland.

The ruse was a success. For eight days, Hortense nursed her
feverish son at a room's remove from the excessively polite Austrian
commander's desk.

On Easter Sunday, after profusely thanking the Austrian commander for countless courtesies shown, the Duchess de Saint-Leu
stepped into her coach. Atop the box, meretriciously garbed in the
Saint-Leu livery, stood Louis and Zappi in the guise of the
Duchess's valets. Pausing only long enough to discharge a characteristic Beauharnais act of charity—selling off some land she
owned in the area, the proceeds to go to refugee relief—the
Duchess de Saint-Leu and valets headed north at a fast gallop.

They embarked at Genoa for Cannes and made their way to Paris
under the Hamilton *nom de voyage*. (Louis somehow managed, with
what can only be described as a curious command of the English
language, to convince customs officials and local constables that his
mother and "brother"—whose combined command of the language
was limited to what was written in the passport—were either terribly fatigued, unfortunately indisposed, or congenitally mute.)

On April 23, having taken rooms at the Hôtel de Hollande on the
Rue de la Paix, Hortense asked formally to be received at Court.
Thus did King Louis-Philippe learn that Paris was playing host to its
first Bonapartes in sixteen years.

Word had not yet spread of the Bonapartes' return; King and
ministers preferred to keep it that way. Hortense was secretly escorted to the Palais-Royal and shown to a bedroom barely able to
accommodate its bed and two chairs. Presently the obese Orléanist
waddled in somewhat conspiratorially, umbrella in hand. Hortense
came right to the point: Would His Majesty permit her and her son
to live again in France?

The "Citizen King" was in a quandary. (He would in fact spend
the entire eighteen years of his reign in a quandary.) Louis-
Philippe had begun to capitalize on the burgeoning Napoleonic
legend. Claiming that the First Empire and his own already wob-

bling regime shared a common denominator—the opportunity to reconcile the principles of the French Revolution with the stability to be found in a constitutional monarchy—he had taken to surrounding himself with some of the Empire's less obstreperous survivors. It would have suited his purpose to adorn his Court with the Emperor's favorite survivors.

But Prince Louis's activities in Rome and with the *Carbonari* were by now common knowledge; already rumors were rampant that Hortense and her son were directly implicated in a plot to depose Louis-Philippe in favor of the Duke of Reichstadt. Hortense was unable to convince her host that those rumors were without foundation. So far as the King was concerned, Prince Louis's presence in France would be intolerable. Perhaps, he suggested, the lad might eventually be permitted to return.

But not at this time. The Chamber of Deputies had decided to reinstate the statue of the Emperor on the Vendôme Column. Great celebrations were planned for May 5, the tenth anniversary of his death. With Prince Louis residing in a hotel that just happened to overlook the Place Vendôme, the celebration might possibly get out of hand; there could be no accounting for the actions of the radical anti-Orléanists, who were proliferating like rabbits run amok, when word got around that the Emperor's firebrand nephew was in town.

The King cordially invited Hortense to live in France—alone. Hortense thanked him, declined the offer, and returned to her hotel—to find that Louis had suffered a relapse and would be unable to travel. In her *Mémoires*, Hortense claims the relapse was authentic. We are entitled to our doubts.

The French government became overly solicitous of the Prince's health; that solicitousness turned to grave concern when, a few days later, Hortense was recognized on the street and cheered lustily. Punctiliously for five days running, the King sent around to Hortense's hotel for the latest medical bulletin. As May 5 approached, governmental anxiety over Louis's health gave way to near hysteria. On the afternoon of May 4, the King sent around his aide-de-camp to insist that the Prince's departure could no longer be postponed.

Next morning, as great crowds trooped into the Place Vendôme to festoon the base of the *Colonne de la Grande Armée* with garlands of flowers, the Prime Minister of France practically broke down the door of Hortense's suite—from the balcony of which she and her son were beholding the great spectacle below—and screamed, "Madame! You must depart at once! I am ordered to tell you that not another hour will be allowed unless the doctor is prepared to state that Prince Louis's health will be absolutely endangered by a journey so sudden!"

Hortense knew there was not a doctor in France who was prepared to state *that*.

Clio, that easily amused Muse of History, must surely have chuckled as she looked down on the future Emperor Napoleon III leading his mother to one of the Channel ports, unaware that across the Pyrenees the great beauty who would contribute so much to his Empire—especially to its miserable collapse—was that very moment celebrating her fifth birthday.

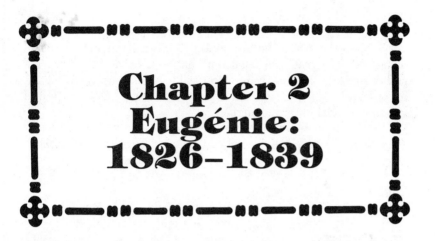

Chapter 2
Eugénie:
1826–1839

She was born during an earthquake on the fifth anniversary of Napoleon Bonaparte's death and never let anyone forget it. "What would the ancients have thought of such an omen?" she demanded rhetorically and often. "Surely they would have said I was destined to unsettle the world!" She would have liked to, but did not know how. It never stopped her from trying, though.

Claims would be made that Eugénie saw her Destiny as a child, it having been divulged by a particularly perceptive gypsy crone in some odiferous Andalusian encampment. The claims are rubbish. Only Cassandra might have foreseen the infant grandee rising to and falling from Imperial heights, condemned, like Hecuba, to mourn her loss and bury her dead.

Eugénie's parents shared the conviction that Bonaparte would fulfill his promise of eternal *liberté*, *egalité* and *fraternité*. When he failed, they preferred to believe, like Cassius, that the fault lay in the stars. Don Cypriano Montijo learned to live with his disillusionment. Doña Maria-Manuela de Montijo, *née* Kirkpatrick, kept the faith. Like a man who daily scans the northern horizon for first signs of the advancing floe that will herald the next Ice Age, she kept her eyes peeled for the paladin who would pick up the dead martyr's mantle.

William Kirkpatrick—Eugénie's maternal grandfather—was one of nineteen children born to a Closeburn, Scotland, family that was deep into politics and deeper into poverty. In 1788, while still in his teens, he left home and went to Málaga, at the time Spain's leading port. There he made the acquaintance of an immigrant Walloon named de Grévignée who had fled his native Liège and established a rather respectable wine trade. After talking Monsieur de Grévignée into giving him a job, William talked Monsieur de Grévignée into giving him a daughter in marriage.

Mademoiselle de Grévignée was one of those terribly gentle, terribly pious, terribly dull women who move through this life without attracting much notice outside a severely constricted circle. About all we know of her is that she was an ancestress of the Empress Eugénie. That should suffice.

By the time his youngest and favorite child, Maria-Manuela, was born in 1794, William had become the epitome of solid bourgeois affluence. The most prosperous merchant in a city where prosperity in trade was the rule rather than the exception, he had taken out American citizenship, which helped to increase his business (George Washington was one of his best customers), and had gotten himself made American consul at Málaga, which helped to increase his income.

We have no way of knowing from which parent Doña Manuela inherited the myriad talents that made her an international hostess and an international joke. She was beautiful, witty, well read, adept at music and conversation, multilingual; her *salon* attracted everyone of importance who chanced to visit Spain. Also, she was brassy, opinionated, raucous, strident-voiced, socially over-aggressive, and incapable of concealing a mildly disgusting determination to peddle her daughters in marriage to the highest bidder. She was one of those women who start out pleasantly and age dreadfully.

Doña Manuela possessed an extraordinary talent for bringing out the emotions of whoever hoved into her orbit. Washington Irving, while serving as American minister to Madrid, was quite taken with her. Prosper Mérimée, whose closest confidante she became, absolutely adored her. Lord Clarendon, the British statesman, loved her. Her husband could not live with her. Her Queen could not trust her. Her daughter Eugénie could not stand her.

The Kirkpatrick heiress was sent to Paris for her education, arriving shortly after Napoleon Bonaparte's coronation; she lived with her maternal aunt, the Countess Mathieu de Lesseps, mother of Ferdinand, the Suez Canal builder. It was at this aunt's house that

Doña Manuela met her future husband. The year was 1813; the twenty-seven-year-old Spanish grandee, a volunteer in the armies of the Emperor, was in Paris being hailed for his contributions to the Napoleonic cause. (He contributed one eye and the mobility of a shoulder and an arm.)

For the two, it should have been love at first sight. Both were physically beautiful, socially connected, and ideologically compatible. (Their temperamental compatibility is another story.) But Don Cypriano was at the moment more concerned with settling the affairs of his tormented homeland than with settling into matrimony. Doña Manuela did not push it. Although the dashing officer with the eye patch and game arm was a scion of one of Spain's leading families, he was, given the archaic laws of primogeniture, practically penniless. Doña Manuela liked to keep her options open.

Scanning the Montijo genealogical charts is like scanning Spain's political, military and ecclesiastical history. Whenever her Bonaparte in-laws carped about "*cher* Louis" having married a commoner—and they carped about it with the regularity and avidity of a postulant reciting her beads—Eugénie would remind them that *she* could trace *her* antecedents back a millennium, whereas "*cher* Louis" and the rest of his family had a hell of a time going back beyond a generation or two.*

Don Cypriano saw in Napoleon Bonaparte the defender of the principles of the French Revolution; he looked to Napoleon to deliver Spain from the grip of the incredibly weak Bourbon monarch Carlos IV. In 1808, Don Cypriano's brother Don Eugenio, Count de Montijo, to whom he was heir in default of a son, led the rebellion that deposed Carlos IV and brought to the throne his heir, Ferdinand VII. Whereupon Napoleon Bonaparte committed his greatest blunder: deposing and imprisoning the entire Spanish royal family, thereby bringing Great Britain into the Napoleonic wars. He then compounded this lunacy by putting his eldest brother, Joseph Bonaparte, on the Spanish throne. The Montijo brothers separated politically.

---

* *Eugénie would occasionally get carried away with herself. One evening, shortly after she became Empress, she informed a group of Bonaparte in-laws that her descent could be traced in a direct line to Saint Teresa of Ávila. When the Emperor observed that Teresa had never married, she quickly changed the subject.*

When Ferdinand regained his throne, Don Eugenio was rewarded by being made Captain-General of the Realm. Don Cypriano
remained on in Paris, became a chamberlain in ex-King Joseph's
household, lived through the two abdications and the intervening
Hundred Days, and fled into hiding when the Second Bourbon Restoration was commenced. A year later he made his way home
across the Pyrenees, ever the dedicated Bonapartist.

He planned to join up with the liberal *afrancesados* who were
attempting to bring down Ferdinand, but was immediately put
under police surveillance; through his brother's intervention, he was
permitted to settle in Andalusia and adjured to abjure politics. He
set out on a Werther-like tour of the area, thereby hoping to as-
suage his sorrow-tinged dissatisfaction with the allegedly God-
ordained mess the Congress of Vienna had made of Europe.

During this period, the house of American Consul William
Kirkpatrick at Málaga was offering hospitality to those unable
to reconcile themselves to the returned—and now horribly
vindictive—Spanish Bourbons. Señora Kirkpatrick had by now
either gone to her grave or faded into the woodwork; her youngest
daughter, Doña Manuela, was presiding as hostess and resident
oracle, dispensing good food and wine and her considered opinion
that only "a tyrant of genius" (her words) like the martyred Emperor could save the civilized world.

Into this oasis of liberalism in a desert of Bourbon reaction came
the dashing one-eyed penniless aristocrat Doña Manuela had met in
Paris four years previously. The young lady from Paris whom Don
Cypriano decided to look up was now twenty-three, well past the
age of marriage. She had not been able to snare a man who could
give her what she and father William desired: entrée into Spain's
rigidly controlled aristocratic society. When Don Cypriano appeared at her doorstep, Doña Manuela took another look. His financial posture had hardly improved.

But there was hope. Don Cypriano informed her that his still-
childless brother Don Eugenio was not enjoying good health. Doña
Manuela murmured her regrets.

We have no way of knowing who proposed to whom. But we do
know that Don Cypriano, being a grandee first-class, could not marry
without King Ferdinand's approval, and for a Kirkpatrick to marry

a Montijo, proof of equal rank had to be produced. William Kirkpatrick produced a gussied-up genealogy proving his daughter's lineal descent from the legendary kings of Scotland and on down through the historically documentable ones. If that did not satisfy His Majesty, William was prepared to prove his daughter's lineal descent from the biblical Patriarchs of Israel. His Majesty was satisfied; not every Spaniard has the privilege of marrying a descendant of King Macbeth and Queen Gruoch.

The couple was married at Málaga on December 15, 1817 and, financed by Kirkpatrick, went off to reside in the Andalusian city of Granada. Ere long, the first signs appeared of the problem that would ultimately cause the marriage's collapse. Don Cypriano assumed his would be a quiet home, in keeping with his spartan tastes as a professional military man. Doña Manuela was not prepared to lead the simple life. She immediately made their home a magnet for foreigners, to whom most of the upper-class Spanish homes were closed. Since his father-in-law was footing the bills, Don Cypriano had little choice but to suffer the multilingual bedlam his house soon became.

It is worth noting that in those pre-pill times Doña Manuela, a practicing Catholic, did not become pregnant for seven years.

In 1820, Don Cypriano became involved in the revolution that saw the *liberales* seize power. When Ferdinand, with the help of Europe's reactionary monarchies, was restored to power, it was to absolutist power. So hideous was the King's program of suppression and revenge that even Don Eugenio withdrew his support of this unmitigated disaster he had originally helped bring to the throne. Now deprived of a friend at Court, Don Cypriano was banished to the northern city of Santiago de Compostella.

Eighteen months later, Ferdinand remembered that Don Cypriano was a grandee first-class and permitted him to rejoin his wife at Granada to serve out his life term of imprisonment. They were not permitted to travel; visitors were restricted; the small house at 12 Calle de Gracia was put under constant police surveillance.

Don Cypriano was manageable; with Doña Manuela, the police had their hands full. She managed to visit Málaga regularly; more, she refused to abandon her *salon*. That so many belletrists and ideologues of liberal persuasion, not to mention foreigners critical of the incumbent regime, succeeded in making their way lemming-like to her overcrowded drawing room bespeaks either true grit on the part of Doña Manuela or laxity (or perhaps exasperation) on the part of the secret police.

Early in 1825, Doña Manuela, then in an advanced state of pregnancy, returned to her father's mansion at Málaga, where Kirkpatrick could ease her confinement with the best medical care available. On January 20, she gave birth to her first child, Paca (Francesca), the future Duchess of Alba and Berwick. She returned to Granada shortly thereafter and was soon again receiving—and charming—visitors and demanding to know when that "tyrant of genius" was going to make himself known.

When next she found herself pregnant, Doña Manuela planned a return to Málaga. Unfortunately, by the time she broke off her hectic social activities to prepare for the journey, she was overtaken by nature.

In the spring of 1826, Granada was struck by a months-long series of tremors that led even the less devout to suspect divine punishment was imminent. Doña Manuela was unable to travel to the safety of Málaga, nor could even ordinary medical help be brought in. Early in the morning of May 5, she went into premature labor. As Granada literally rattled at the mercy of a mighty subterranean spasm that seemed to presage the end of the world, Doña Manuela was moved out into the garden lest the house collapse about her.

A few hours later, in a hastily erected tent, surrounded by a passel of clumsy and quite hysterical servants, she gave birth to the future Empress of the French. In hopes of conciliating the brother from whom he had been estranged by politics, Don Cypriano named the infant Eugenia. (The Gallicized form, Eugénie, she assumed as a child.)

Doña Manuela would never forget the ordeal she underwent in delivering her youngest daughter. That might explain why she always openly preferred her eldest daughter.

"We were children at a time when parents did not, as today, live for their children," the Empress would recall. "On the contrary, children at that time had to endure the principles and theories of their parents." More than having to endure their parents' principles and theories, Eugénie and Paca had to endure their parents' crotchets and eccentricities.

Doña Manuela was less concerned with playing mother to her two daughters than with playing hostess to her countless callers. Responsibility for the girls' upbringing was assumed by Don Cypriano. It was an extraordinary upbringing.

Great care was taken to protect his daughters from exposure to the inherent dangers of middle-class comfort. A program of fresh air and exercise was rigidly followed, weather notwithstanding. Compelled to wear the same excessively plain clothes in all seasons, the two often resembled unattached destitutes. While other little grandees traveled in carriages when visiting affluent kinfolk, Paca and Eugénie rode astride burros. Book-learning was eschewed, though respect for men of letters was encouraged; it was Don Cypriano's conviction that a man who wrote masterpieces merited more attention than the masterpieces he wrote.

Eugénie's and Paca's training was almost military in nature. There were nights spent in the surrounding countryside, sleeping by a fire under the stars. There were days spent astride a cannon, their father closely observing the girls' faces for signs of a forbidden flinch when the cannon was fired. There were visits to the gypsy encampments around Granada, with exposure to wild music, wild dance, wild superstition.

In those visits lay the genesis of a seemingly dichotomous personality that burst into full bloom when Eugénie became Empress. In public she moved about with an egregious piety that suggested she may well have been in a state of perpetual levitation. Out of the public eye, she often dressed, danced and otherwise whooped it up as if she were one among equals in some squalid *caverna española*.

Don Cypriano felt that little girls should know more about political science than about domestic science, should be more adept at riding a horse than at sewing on a button. Yet, if his ideas on child-rearing were not exactly consonant with the times, his attitude on the place of women in this world most definitely was. On the morning of her marriage, Eugénie wrote to Paca: "Papa said to me one day when we were talking politics: 'Women are for knitting stockings.' I know very well that *I* was *not* destined for *that!*" Everyone else knew it too.

Eugénie would long afterwards refer to hers as "a childhood without tears and almost without tenderness." Yet, she absolutely adored her father. Recalled her secretary, Filon: "The Empress had a sort of religious veneration for her father's memory and mentioned his eccentricities in the most tender and touching manner, even when she was obliged to smile at the recollection of them." She thrived on being Don Cypriano's surrogate son.

Unlike the complacent Paca, who was more their mother's daughter, Eugénie was flamboyantly wild, with a love of boys' games. She did not know fear. Children's parties bored her. Doña Manuela's reprimands that she was not being "ladylike" provoked spasms of willful defiance. Eugénie preferred the company of her father, especially on those occasions when he would recount his experiences as a volunteer in the service of the Emperor Napoleon.

For Don Cypriano, the martyred Emperor represented the ideals of his own youth. Until she married the Emperor's nephew, Eugénie's attitudes were in keeping with the nobler aspects of Napoleon Bonaparte's philosophy, as transmitted by Don Cypriano. When she became Empress, she forgot almost everything her father had taught her.

Her father's release from life imprisonment came in 1830. King Ferdinand, having failed to sire an heir by three consorts, realized that ambition by his fourth, the scandalous Maria-Cristina. Tragically for Spain, the heir was a girl: the future (and even more scandalous) Queen Isabella II. In order to secure the child's succession, and thereby finesse his brother Don Carlo, the moribund Ferdinand allied himself with the liberals he had spent the better part of his reign persecuting. The Inquisition was ended; political prisoners were amnestied; the universities were allowed to reopen.

Eugénie's family moved to a slightly less cramped house. There, while awaiting his brother Don Eugenio's death, Don Cypriano continued to raise his daughters in his image, while Doña Manuela continued to preside over her *salon*.

It was around this time that Doña Manuela bagged her biggest lion. While returning to Granada from Madrid, whither he had gone to visit his ailing brother, Don Cypriano made the acquaintance of Prosper Mérimée, to whom he took an instant liking and whom he insisted on bringing home. The twenty-seven-year-old Mérimée had come to Spain in order to fulfill some magazine assignments and recover from an unrequited love.

His friendship with Doña Manuela was immediate and enduring. From her, Mérimée gleaned a rich harvest of information on Spanish history, art and literature. Doña Manuela interested Spanish libraries in Mérimée's work, secured for him access to characteristically inaccessible Spanish archives, and advised him on what books to read so that he might sate his seemingly insatiable craving for Iberian folklore. (It was Doña Manuela who gave Mérimée the plot and local color for his most popular novel, *Carmen*.) The two became the closest of friends and mutual confidants; more than four hundred of Mérimée's letters to Doña Manuela survive—the last written barely two weeks before his death.

Mérimée would prove to be a loyal friend to Eugénie during her years as Empress, when she needed every loyal friend she could get. A mark of her high regard of Mérimée: Eugénie accepted with forbearance his contention that the pope was "nothing but an antiquated idol"; it was something this loyal Daughter of the Church would accept from no one else.*

"She is a wonderful friend," wrote Mérimée of Doña Manuela to his closest male friend, Stendhal, "but there has never been anything carnal between us." It was the truth. There was, however, probably something plenty carnal between Doña Manuela and the British statesman Lord Clarendon, when he served as British ambassador in Madrid. Mérimée alluded to the relationship in some of his letters; and while Mérimée enjoyed gossiping about his friends, he confined himself to logical gossip.

Admittedly, the evidence is circumstantial at best, though some would see it as being of Thoreau's trout-in-the-milk variety. But whether, as was charged, Clarendon was Eugénie's natural father is another matter. Clarendon did not join the British Embassy in Ma-

---

* *Many of her enemies claimed that the Empress was really Mérimée's illegitimate daughter. Since Mérimée did not come into her life until she was five years old, the charge is patently ridiculous. To be sure, many of her enemies claimed that Eugénie was actually a few years older than she allowed. But then, trying to prove the Empress's bastardy—and the Emperor's too—became among their critics a fad usually associated with parlor games of a more energetic nature.*

drid until 1833. He had visited Madrid often prior to then in a private capacity, though.

When questioned about this by her intended son-in-law, Napoleon III, Doña Manuela replied, in a provocative admixture of high indignation and low equivocation: "Sire, it cannot be true. The dates do not correspond." Whether Clarendon was her only lover is highly speculative; Doña Manuela was as discreet when it came to her private life as she was indiscreet when it came to everyone else's.

The Count de Montijo died in July 1834. Along with a string of names and titles, Don Cypriano inherited a considerable fortune, a magnificent mansion in the center of Madrid, and a country estate, Carabanchel.

The new Count de Montijo refused to compromise his convictions with his wealth, much to the new Countess de Montijo's extreme (and extremely vocal) perturbation. Taking easily to her new position in society, Doña Manuela felt the time had come to raise her daughters along lines more in keeping with that position. She found it embarrassing to have visitors to her *salon* suspect that she had spawned and was raising a pair of ragamuffins.

That their father still frowned upon their wearing silk stockings, riding out in carriages, and changing their wardrobes with the seasons was of little consequence to the girls. The two, but especially the more hoydenish Eugénie, preferred escaping out to Carabanchel, where one could ride horses and play with the children of the local indigents, to the social activities imposed upon them in the Plazuela del Angel by their mother.

The Montijos' rise to prosperity coincided with the collapse of their marriage. To their basic difference—Doña Manuela's determination to lead Madrilene society, Don Cypriano's determination to avoid it—was now added their diametrically opposed views as regarded the Carlist wars then raging. With the death of Ferdinand VII in the previous year, the dynastic struggle he had sought to avert had not only broken out, it had quickly become a struggle over ideologies (a struggle that obtains to this day among Spanish royalists).

Don Cypriano stood with those who rallied around the infant-queen Isabella; Doña Manuela favored the *apostolicos*, who sought to depose the Queen in favor of her uncle Carlo, the Church-supported champion of traditionalism and absolutism. Doña Manuela was one of those childhood liberals who, the older and wealthier they become, the more conservative they become.

Paca and Eugénie were now on the brink of pubescence. About the only thing their parents could agree on was to give the girls a formal education in Paris, a city they both loved. The move was made early in 1835.

The Paris that both Don Cypriano and Doña Manuela had known had changed. The old order had not so much passed as fled. The ultraconservatives among the aristocracy, the social props of the deposed Bourbon regime, had locked the doors of their *hôtels* in the Faubourg Saint-Germain and exiled themselves to their country estates with the coming of the Orléanist monarchy. In doing so, they had given way to the new order: a mélange comprised of a small band of "traitor aristocrats," rich financiers, industrialists, parliamentarians, and authors and artists.

"*Enrichissez-vous par le travail et par l'épargne,*" urged François Guizot, who was bringing aggressive capitalism to a foredoomed bourgeois government; "Get rich by work and saving." His enemies seized upon the two words "*Enrichissez-vous.*" It became the motto of the times.

Paris under the Orléanists was for the Countess de Montijo the ideal. Back in Madrid she was still, despite her pretentions and aggressions, no more than a Scottish tradesman's beautiful but brassy daughter, whose passport into the Spanish aristocracy was, metaphorically speaking, stamped "by marriage" instead of "by birth." Here in Paris, other standards prevailed. "To belong to good society," noted one contemporaneous observer of the times, "one has to have only two characteristics: one must be a foreigner and one must have money!"

The Countess de Montijo had money, though hardly as much as she thought she should have; the Count still pursued a fiscal policy of spartan conservatism. But Doña Manuela had waited out the death of the first Count de Montijo; she could wait out the death of his heir.

"We were not very well off at the time," the Empress Eugénie would recall. They were far from paupers, though. Their rented house in the Rue d' Angoulême (now the Rue de la Bactrie) was well staffed; the Countess made do on 5,000 francs a year—which was not bad, considering that the average workman earned two francs for a twelve-hour day.

The Montijos arrived in Paris in the spring of the year and immediately went their separate ways. Eugénie and Paca were packed off to a convent school; Don Cypriano spent most of his time seeking out old cronies from the Hundred Days; Doña Manuela went off to visit old school friends who had left Paris in the wake of Charles X and were living out their self-imposed exile in the south of France.

When Doña Manuela returned to Paris, Don Cypriano returned to Madrid. He was anxious to do his part in the Carlist wars. Doña Manuela accepted her husband's return to Madrid sanguinely; she did not write him one letter throughout the two years of this, their initial separation.

The girls were faithful correspondents, however. On the basis of surviving letters, it seems that Eugénie was hardest hit by the separation. "Write to me at once if you are ill," she pleaded in her first letter to Don Cypriano. This was followed by a steady stream of "My dear Papa" letters: ". . . how I long to press you in my arms . . ." ". . . you can not imagine how much I love you . . ." ". . . I am suffering so much from not having seen you . . ." ". . . when shall I see you, my heart aches for you . . ."

When Don Cypriano sent her a miniature of himself, Eugénie wrote: "Every time I look at it I think of the face I have not kissed for so long."[*] And: "What is the arm that keeps us apart?" And: "Time hurries forward and we remain behind, and we have less time to kiss each other." And: "I am longing to kiss you, Papa, and when I see the other side of the Pyrenees, my heart will not have enough room for its joy!"

In the light of present-day psychology, a good case could be made for the deleterious effect Don Cypriano may have had on Eugénie, however unintentionally, most notably in her frigidity and in the

---

[*] *According to Filon, "Count Cypriano de Montijo's miniature never left the Empress's possession, and from the first day of our exile I found it on her night table, exactly as I had seen it so often at the Tuileries."*

barely concealed contempt for men that she developed as she grew
older. That she spent an incredible fortune to adorn herself as Empress was not so much to satisfy the woman as to complement the
role that woman was playing.

Eugénie's was basically a masculine psyche in a woman's body.
She preferred the company of women to men, only because it was
among women that she found favor and received the compliments
her vanity thrived on; but intellectually and temperamentally she
sought out men, because it was only among men that she was accepted as a person as well as an Empress.

And not to be overlooked is the improbability that Eugénie would
ever have married, had Napoleon III not married her.

It should not be inferred, however, that Eugénie was a sexual
invert, even subliminally so; in fact, that is about the only charge
never leveled against her by her enemies, and rightly so. The point
is that, despite marriage, motherhood and, above all, Imperial glory
and all that *that* implies—and there is little doubt that she preferred
Imperial glory to marriage and motherhood—Eugénie was never
fulfilled as a woman. One wonders if it might have been different,
had hers not been "a childhood without tears and almost without
tenderness"; one wonders if it might have been different, had Don
Cypriano not made her his surrogate son.

Mérimée took the Montijo mother and daughters in tow. He
launched Doña Manuela into the new Parisian society, of which he
was one of the shining lights; rather, he made a few introductions
and the Countess launched herself. The aristocratic Molé, Cantel-
lane, Laborde and Viel-Castel families; the great bankers Lafitte
and Rothschild; the artists Delacroix and Viollet-le-Duc—the Countess de Montijo overwhelmed them all; they reciprocated in kind.
"When Mama is in Paris," wrote Eugénie, "she cannot stay at home;
you know how it is!"

Mérimée, who could never have children of his own, doted on the
Montijo girls. He inundated them with frocks and toys, stuffed them
with bonbons and sweetmeats; he paraded them up and down the
Rue de la Paix or sat with them at a table outside Tortoni's, demanding that everyone pay court to his two little charmers from beyond

the Pyrenees. Eugénie's wildness he found particularly amusing; he encouraged her little boyish pranks, such as shooting a pistol with real powder. He reveled in Eugénie's loquaciousness, which was about the only thing she inherited from her mother.

Mérimée established the lifelong friendship between the Montijo girls and Edouard and Cécile Delessert, whose father was Prefect of Police and whose mother was Mérimée's mistress.* One November day in 1836, while playing with her friends in the Hôtel de Jerusalem, the Prefect's official residence on the Ile de la Cité, Eugénie chanced to look out the window as the prison van entered the courtyard of the Prefecture below. Out stepped a spindly-legged prisoner who had been brought from Strasbourg, where he had attempted to overthrow the government.

Thus did Eugénie look down for the first time on the man who sixteen years later would raise her up to a throne.

Four years in three schools was the total extent of Eugénie's and Paca's formal education. It began in the Convent of the Sacré-Coeur, the most fashionable girls' school in France. At the Sacré-Coeur, whose curriculum was steeped in the centuries-old tradition of the Roman Church, the nuns were able to awaken in the Montijo girls a strong adherence to Church dogma and an even stronger love for everything that dogma encompassed.

To the end of her life the Empress "considered it very fortunate to be able to believe . . . to be definitely convinced of Christian truths!"; she "never had a doubt" that the pope was more than Christ's vicar on earth—he was Christ's surrogate.

Students at the Sacré-Coeur were given little more than a nodding acquaintance with the natural sciences, history, art and literature—four areas in which the Empress Eugénie proved to be so spectacularly deficient. One former classmate recalled that there were only two girls who could even spell correctly (neither Eugénie nor Paca was one of them); there was "no science, no good music, no Mozart, no Beethoven . . . only exceedingly vapid music"; artists

---

*A coincidence worth noting: Edouard's and Cécile's maternal grandfather, Count Alexandre de Laborde, wrote the words to Hortense's En Partant pour la Syrie and was the legal guardian to her abandoned bastard by Charles de Flahaut.

the likes of Raphael and Titian were ignored completely. Preparing the girls for marriage and motherhood was completely eschewed. Rather than making sure their students were mentally and emotionally equipped to take their place in the outside world, the nuns of Sacré-Coeur stressed the inherent dangers of that world. Life in a convent was to them the earthly ideal.

In July 1836, at Don Cypriano's insistence, Eugénie and Paca were withdrawn from Sacré-Coeur and enrolled in the Gymnase Normal, Civil et Orthosomatique. There the curriculum was laid down along the lines evolved by the Swiss educational reformer Johann Heinrich Pestalozzi. The best the director could say of Eugénie—other than to praise her natural aptitude and strong liking for physical exercise—was that her character was "good, generous, active, firm." Her academic achievements he found to be regretted, if not deplored. Her temperament he found "sanguine and nervous." Young Eugénie's mercurial moods, the way in which she could—and often would—switch from humor to hysteria in the bat of an eyelash, were congenital. Even as Empress, she was "sanguine and nervous."

She was, in fact, a clinical hysteric.

In April 1837, the Countess took her daughters to England and placed them in a boarding school at Clifton to perfect their English. They lasted two months and found the entire experience quite miserable. Those two months left Eugénie with a lifelong distaste for the English climate; as a young girl she decided she could never marry an Englishman because "the idea of living in fog was dreadful." That she spent the last fifty years of her life in England instead of back in her beloved sunny Spain was yet another aspect of Eugénie's paradoxicality.

When the girls were brought back to Paris (and the Pestalozzi school) in July, again at Don Cypriano's insistence, they were accompanied by an English governess, Miss Flowers; Doña Manuela was doing everything by the book. For Eugénie and Paca, returning to Paris meant a reunion with their beloved Monsieur Mérimée and that other avuncular idol, Monsieur Henri Beyle.

Stendhal—to the Montijo girls he would always be "Monsieur Beyle"—had been brought to the Countess's drawing room by Mérimée in the previous year. "We know a gentleman called

Monsieur Beyle who is very kind and very good to us," enthused Paca in a letter to her father. "In Napoleon's time, he was employed at Court and carried out all kinds of jobs for him, and now he is able to tell us everything that went on in the days of the Empire!"

In letter after letter, Don Cypriano had urged his daughters to study the Emperor's life; to read everything that was flooding the market: the memoirs of those who had accompanied him to St. Helena, the glorifying novels (of which Stendhal's would be the most glorifying), and, of course, the Word of the Martyr himself.

It was inevitable that Stendhal should increase the girls' enthusiasm for the Emperor. He had known him personally; had even been along on the Russian campaign. With his novelist's gift for detail and his celebrated affinity for children, Stendhal was able to re-create the life and greatness of Napoleon Bonaparte for the two enchanted Montijo girls. Thursday evenings became for them the most important night of the week: Monsieur Beyle called regularly, and they were permitted to stay up late. They hung on his every word and could never be told enough. (Recalled the Empress: "We wept, we laughed, we groaned, we went raving mad!")

To his two little friends Stendhal dedicated the Waterloo chapter of his immortal *La Chartreuse de Parme*. He literally illustrated those Thursday evenings with maps and miniatures. One of the Empress's prize mementos till the day she died was a painting Stendhal had given her, "Battle of Austerlitz." She would recall at the end of her long life, "Monsieur Beyle made us, my sister and me, intoxicated with his enthusiasm for the Napoleonic epoch."

What the Empress would not recall, though, was that she sobered up from that intoxication shortly after her return to Madrid. In all of Eugénie's letters that survive, there is a long hiatus in which her enthusiasm for the Napoleonic epoch is not even alluded to. In fact, she seemed to have all but forgotten about Napoleon I until she entered the life of Napoleon III.

Her subsequent asseverations notwithstanding, the Napoleonic legend meant precious little to Eugénie until she became an active part of that legend.

Early in 1837, Don Cypriano returned to Paris but did not stay at the Rue d'Angoulême; his and Doña Manuela's estrangement was complete. He spent all his time with Eugénie and Paca, taking them to the circus, boating on the Seine, and to the theater. Two months later, the Count returned to Madrid.

In February 1839, the Countess received word that her husband's health was deteriorating. She left at once for Madrid, arranging for the girls to follow with Miss Flowers during their school break. They left Paris on March 20. By the time they arrived in Madrid, Don Cypriano was dead. For the two girls, it was the end of their childhood as well as the end of their formal education. Paca was fourteen, Eugénie thirteen.

As she stared down at the grave of the father she not only adored but idolized, Eugénie could not have suspected he was the only man for whom she would ever feel such an attachment during a lifetime that would not end until eighty-one years later.

Chapter 3
Louis-Napoleon:
1831–1840

On arriving in London following her and Louis's second expulsion
from France, Hortense went off to secure passports for their return
home, and Louis went down with jaundice. The Prince's illness was
not as serious as were his mother's difficulties with the French
ambassador, Talleyrand. Talleyrand was in no hurry to see Hortense leave England until he could ascertain whether her and
Louis's professed desire to return to Switzerland was not in fact a
cover for some anti-Orléans *coup*. The Prince's reputation had preceded him.

While awaiting the passports, mother and son lived quietly. On
evenings when he could slip away from his mother, the Prince scur-
ried off to Vauxhall and Almack's for a bit of gambling and fornicating. He also considered a proposal from one Signor Mirandoli, who
proposed that Prince Louis join him and his merry band of dedicated
incompetents in a plot to overthrow the Orléanist regime and restore France to total anarchy.

Hortense got wind of Louis's involvement and dragged him off to
Tunbridge Wells. There he began an affair with one of the more
prominent local belles, a Miss Godfrey. Hortense relaxed when, a
few weeks later, Talleyrand decided it was safe to issue those
passports. She was anxious to get her son back to Arenenberg—and
away from the likes of Miss Godfrey and Signor Mirandoli.

Hortense used the homeward journey across France to complete
her son's Bonapartist education, pointing out—and expatiating on
volubly—those sites so closely associated with the Emperor. Nota-

ble among these were the camp behind Boulogne where he drew up plans for the aborted invasion of England, and the little house at Pont-des-Briques where he dictated the order that sent the *Grande Armée* reeling toward Austerlitz.

And then there were the family shrines: Josephine's burial place in the little church at Reuil, and Malmaison. A wealthy entrepreneur had purchased the estate and was charging tickets for admission. Heavily veiled—for she had promised Talleyrand she would detour around Paris—Hortense endured the indignity of watching a troupe of tourists shuffle through the rooms and gardens where she had played hostess to the crowned heads of Europe.

Every kilometer they traveled along the dusty roads of France, Louis saw more than Napoleonic encampments and family shrines. He saw old survivors of the *Grande Armée* rehashing the days of Imperial *gloire* for the edification of obviously enraptured young auditors. He saw on the walls of village huts and post stops prominently displayed reminders of the *gloire*—paintings and etchings of the great battles, idealized portraits of the Martyr who had given France that *gloire*. He heard more than his mother's Bonapartist catechism; he heard the voices of France.

If there had been any doubts in the Prince's mind that the past Empire had a future—he had no doubts but that the present regime would soon be having a past—those doubts were banished by the time he and Hortense arrived back at Arenenberg in late August.

Louis-Napoleon Bonaparte had left "Fool's Hill" a revolutionist in quest of a revolutionary movement. He returned to "Fool's Hill" a rebel with a cause.

Prince Louis was still only fourth in the line of succession to the phantom Napoleonic throne. Two, of course, could be overlooked; neither his father nor his uncle Joseph was interested in raising the standard. The heir-apparent was the Duke of Reichstadt; to Napoleonic diehards he was "Emperor Napoleon II." Those diehards—they made up in volume what they lacked in numbers—were waiting for "Napoleon II" to lead them into Paris. "Napoleon II" could not even lead himself out of Vienna.

His cousin at Arenenberg could lead them. But who were "they"? A small band of *Grande Armée* veterans well past their prime.

Besides, Louis felt that the path to empire lay not in the expenditure of arms and men but in the expenditure of words. Also, he truly hated war; he hoped to propagandize his way to the Imperial dignity.

He realized that hope by pioneering a technique that would a century later spawn a multi-billion-dollar industry and make "Madison Avenue" a household term: He proved it is possible—and prodigiously profitable—to create out of thin air a public demand for a product nobody really wants.

Louis's first pamphlet, *Rêveries politiques* (published May 1832), dealt with the most efficacious way to regenerate an already degenerating France. Though Orléanist rule was only in its second year, discontent among the French was deep, especially in Paris. Correlative with that discontent was a fear that to overthrow the government would be to pave the way for either a Bourbon Restoration (feared by the masses though not by the Church), a Communist "Red Republic" (feared by the aristocracy and bourgeoisie as well as the Church), or total anarchy.

Louis's "own belief" was that France could be saved only by "combining those two popular causes," Empire and Republic. Should the proposed Emperor be unfit to rule or in default of legitimate heirs, the succession—like everything else—would be settled by plebiscite. The nation was to be safeguarded by a constitution.

Here we have two basic concepts upon which Napoleon III would base his rule: a constitution—which he would dictate, to his own advantage—and the insistence that every move he made be voted on by a plebiscite—which his henchmen would rig.

Most critical of the pamphlet was its author's father. Wrote the elder Bonaparte, "You have a frenzied desire for fame. Let me tell you that, without realizing it, you are working against your own interests!"

Louis wanted fame, but "frenzied" was the last adjective one could use to describe him. (The lack of such a quality would often drive the Empress Eugénie into a frenzy of her own.) Actually, Louis was comparatively patient, cool—and calculating.

He was also, as events were to prove, imperceptive. The overwhelming majority of the French people were not necessarily eager for a return of Bonapartism. It would take more than the

Napoleonic legend to win Louis the throne of France. And it would take him ten years—and much humiliation—to realize this.

Prince Louis assumed the role of Pretender on July 22, 1832, with the death at the Schönbrunn of "Napoleon II." Hortense led the household in recognizing her son's altered status. Arenenberg became in fact what it had been in theory: the Napoleonic Court-in-exile. The Pretender assumed a solemnity more in keeping with his elevated position.

Having purchased Swiss citizenship, he acquitted himself admirably, both as a gentleman and, in summers, as an artillery officer with the Swiss army. He wrote a quite comprehensive *Swiss Manual on Artillery*, which, after being distributed clandestinely to the military profession in France, served notice that the Emperor's interest in and talent at gunnery had been quite successfully passed on to the second generation. He worked on his various political writings, all geared at gaining for himself a name and a following.

His first major propaganda piece, *Considerations politiques et militaires sur la Suisse*, purports to celebrate the virtues of the Swiss Republic, replete with a knowing discussion of cantonal constitutions and Swiss army organization. But, like Tolstoy's *War and Peace*, it is in the digressions that the main thrust of the book stands out in bold relief.

"The government of Napoleon, the People's Emperor," Louis informs us, "offered the world perhaps the first example of a regime in which all classes were welcome, none rejected, and in which institutions were set up equally favorable to all." What, asks the Prince rhetorically, would *"l'Empereur plébéien"* have gone on to do, but for Waterloo? He would have transformed his dictatorship into a constitutional regime. Its author truly believed what he was writing.

Louis was now over twenty-five, an age by which Bonapartes were usually married; Hortense urged him to find "a good little wifie," properly raised and adaptable to his genius. "All I ask," she told Louis, "is you—and a little sunshine!" (This was Hortense's euphemism for grandchildren.) But Louis had vowed he would never marry while in exile. He was determined to wait until he was Emperor, at which time he would marry into one of Europe's more respectable royal houses.

Then, in 1836, he became engaged to his cousin Princess Mathilde Bonaparte.

Whether the two were really in love with each other is questionable. The only person Louis ever genuinely loved was his mother; the only person Mathilde ever genuinely loved was herself. She, her brother Prince Napoleon ("Plon-Plon"), and their father Jerome, ex-King of Westphalia, played major roles during the Second Empire, and thus merit our attention at this point.

Jerome was the youngest of the first-generation Bonapartes, as well as the most ridiculous. In his six years as King of Westphalia, he built up a national deficit that exceeded by seven times the national revenues; made his pimp—a drunken illiterate he had met in a West Indies waterfront saloon—his Minister of Foreign Affairs; ran a thriving brothel; burned down a few palaces; and managed to get arrested for drunkenness and public lewdness by his own police— among other accomplishments. Jerome saw his life as a divinely ordained mission to ascertain how many fortunes—other people's—he could go through. By the time he was fifty, "Fifi" (his *nom de plaisir*) had gone through one kingdom, two wives, and enough of countless creditors' money to reduce Europe's national debts by half.

In November 1835, Jerome's second wife, Catherine of Württemberg, died after twenty-nine years of faithfulness to a man who had spent twenty-nine years being unfaithful to her. Catherine's death profoundly affected Jerome; the pensions granted her by her father the King of Württemberg and her maternal uncle the Tsar of Russia were promptly canceled.

Mathilde, aged fifteen, was less affected: "I knew little of her, and she, nothing of me." Mathilde's talents as a diarist—hers would be one of the sharpest pens (and sharpest mouths) of the Second Empire—became manifest around this time. As Catherine's health declined, Mathilde noted in her journal every detail of physical decay: the face was "wrinkling up," the breasts were "falling down," the body was becoming "increasingly deformed," cardiac arrest was "inevitable," the stench was "horrific," etc., etc. On the night of Catherine's death, Mathilde recorded dutifully: "face the color of wax, plumpness fallen in . . ."

As for thirteen-year-old Plon-Plon—the nickname derived from the manner in which as an infant he pronounced his given name, Napoleon—chances are, he was not affected very much. Plon-Plon was rather like Gilbert's bad Baronet of Ruddigore—compelled to commit a sin a day.

Out of the goodness of her heart, Hortense invited the widower and his two younger children to visit Arenenberg.* Jerome and Mathilde made it a brief visit; to both, the idea of living in anything less than a palace staffed by a regiment of servants was tantamount to subsisting well below the poverty level. They moved on to Rome, where Jerome resumed one of his quainter means of coping with life's tribulations: hitting Madame Mère for yet another loan and, behind her back, borrowing from creditors on the strength of what he expected to inherit from the clan's matriarch.

Plon-Plon, however, decided to remain on at Arenenberg. He stayed for quite a few months, and spent the better part of every day antagonizing everyone but his cousin Louis and aunt Hortense. Constantly, Valérie Masuyer, Hortense's loyal lady-in-waiting, complained of "that filthy little beast's" insolence, nastiness, and downright despotism. Hortense allowed as how "that young man is charming; he will do us honor—I hope!" Hortense hoped in vain.

Louis's fondness for his nasty little cousin—in time it would degenerate into painful forbearance—is not inexplicable. Like the Emperor, Louis was inordinately fond of children; like the Emperor, he was inordinately fond of anyone bearing the name Bonaparte; like the Emperor, he was inordinately fond of anyone who was inordinately fond of him.

And Plon-Plon took pains to demonstrate just how inordinately fond he was of cousin Louis. Cousin Louis was attentive to him,

---

* Jerome's and Catherine's eldest child, Jerome-Napoleon, played no role in the Second Empire, dying in 1847 at the age of thirty-three; nor did a son "Bo" by Jerome's first wife, the American heiress Elizabeth Patterson. Both were rather responsible young men, and in the Bonaparte scheme of things anyone who was responsible was perforce dull.

whereas father Jerome often had to be reminded of his existence; cousin Louis (and aunt Hortense) represented a sense of stability, whereas life with father Jerome represented drifting about in a parental lunatic asylum; cousin Louis was going to wind up on the French throne, whereas father Jerome was going to wind up in debtors' prison, or worse, if his incredible luck did not hold out.

Louis shared with Plon-Plon his veneration of their famous uncle, excused the little monster's ghastly behavior to the rest of the Arenenberg Court, and sought to fill the boy's distressingly broad educational gap by tutoring him in Latin and mathematics. Given Louis's weakness for the latter, here was a case of the lame leading the halt.

(When the Empress Eugénie complained about Plon-Plon's execrable behavior, the Emperor said: "He was so nice when I taught him mathematics at Arenenberg!" To which the Empress sniffed, in words that would have brought joy to the hearts of those nuns at the Sacré-Coeur, "Heaven defend us from teaching mathematics to anyone! It's worse than the plague!"

(The Emperor was always ready to give yet another chance to this cousin whose penchant for working against his interests should have earned him the guillotine at the very least. But let it not be thought that Napoleon III was any more guileless than Napoleon I, who established the precedent for tolerating in a relative what he would never tolerate in even a close friend. When the Prince Imperial, having been told by his tutor that the French language has no synonyms, asked his father to explain the difference between *un accident* and *un malheur*, an accident and a misfortune, the Emperor responded: "My child, here is an example that you will understand better than a definition. Suppose your cousin Plon-Plon falls into a well—that is *un accident;* but if he gets out, it is *un malheur!*")

In February 1836, Jerome's luck ran out again—temporarily. Madame Mère died, and his portion from her estate, far from covering his most recently incurred debts, did not even cover the interest on those debts. With Mathilde in tow, he headed back to Arenenberg. The ex-King of Holland, who rarely saw his brother but knew him well, fired off a letter condemning Hortense for giving hospitality to the "shifty" Jerome and his "brats." He suspected Jerome hoped to marry off Mathilde to Louis, who was now sole heir to the elder Louis's considerable estate. "Marry," the elder Louis urged his son, "but with a young woman rich, moral, and well born." He could discern none of these qualifications in his niece.

When the Prince had last seen Mathilde, she was a mere child; when he saw her enter Hortense's drawing room on the evening of her return to Arenenberg, she was a mature, self-assured young lady whose décolleté was so daring, her pendulous *poitrine* almost wound up on the floor.

If Mathilde set out to entrap Louis in marriage, as has been claimed, she is probably to be excused. She was spirited, more intelligent than any of the surviving Bonapartes (Hortense excepted), and anxious to escape the way of life her father offered.* With Louis, she felt secure. She found a few faults; his constant good humor tended to unnerve her. (To the end of his life, Louis's strongest expression was *"Absurde!"*) But at least he was kind, though a bit unrealistic. Mathilde dismissed Hortense's avowal that Louis would one day be Emperor of the French as little more than the unintended whimsy of an overly protective mother.

Louis was quite smitten with his beautiful cousin. As the days stretched into weeks, the two began to take their forthcoming engagement for granted. They spent idyllic evenings wandering in the Arenenberg gardens and kissing behind the Arenenberg trees, spied upon by the obnoxiously omnipresent Plon-Plon. Louis gave Mathilde a ring. To celebrate her sixteenth birthday, he arranged a night regatta on the Boden See, followed by a ball at which Mathilde wore the same gown she had practically spilled out of that first evening at Arenenberg.

A few days later it was ended. Jerome learned that the King of Württemberg would not give his granddaughter a dowry and pension if she persisted in marrying a Bonaparte. Jerome rushed off to Florence to consult with his brother Louis. When asked what he was prepared to do for the prospective bridal couple, brother Louis snarled that he was prepared to do precious little except maybe send along congratulations. Jerome rushed back to Arenenberg to collect Mathilde and Plon-Plon and drop them off at their maternal

---

* *She was also the most realistic of the Bonapartes: "Had my uncle not been Emperor, I should probably be selling oranges on the quay at Ajaccio!"*

grandfather's Court. As Mathilde rode off to Württemberg, Louis rode off to Baden.

Hortense did not really care for all those trips Louis had been making to that spa of late; conniving women frequented the casino there. ("Louis is not so seductive that all the women in the world should be running after him," she told Valérie Masuyer.) But she suspected her son must be depressed over the broken engagement; she did not object to his making this trip.

When he returned to Arenenberg a week later, the Prince was in so somber and withdrawn a mood, Hortense feared he might be pining away emotionally, whereas Valérie Masuyer feared he might be wasting away physically.

The Prince was neither emotionally nor physically indisposed. He was preparing to invade France.

It was to be another "Return from Elba." His uncle had landed at Cannes with a handful of loyalists and marched on Paris. Louis planned to duplicate that incredible feat by presenting himself at the frontier garrison of Strasbourg with a spurious nobleman and a nymphomaniacal contralto.

Admittedly, the entire conspiracy—hatched in Hortense's drawing room completely unbeknownst to Hortense—had about it the flavor of the Madwoman of Chaillot's celebrated tea party in the sewers of Paris; but the Pretender of Arenenberg was in truth no madder than the wily Madwoman of Chaillot. To dismiss his attempt at Strasbourg as abject lunacy is to ignore the political situation in France at the time.

Louis-Philippe had shrewdly avoided disaster in his six years to date on the throne; however, there was little doubt in anyone's mind that disaster was inevitable. Though enthroned by the Paris mobs (the French had an absolute genius for bringing reaction out of revolution), he ignored their interests. The franchise was restricted to a mere 250,000 out of a population of 34 million. The Industrial Revolution was increasing the wealth of the comparatively small financial and commercial class at the expense of everyone else.

Prince Louis-Napoleon did not err in believing that the majority of the French were prepared to see the Orléanist deposed.

Where he erred was in believing that the majority of the French were prepared to see the Orléanist replaced by a Bonaparte.

The masses cheered themselves hoarse when Napoleon Bonaparte's statue was returned to the Vendôme Column; publishers made small fortunes printing hagiographies of the Emperor; any actor, no matter how untalented, could sell out a house by portraying Napoleon. A veritable floodgate of adulation had been opened, thanks to the poems of Hugo and Béranger and the novels of Stendhal and Vigny and Musset. And with the publication of the great man's memoirs, here was testamentary evidence that the touchstone of Bonapartism had been liberalism, pacificism, nationalism, class equality and religious toleration.

But Bonapartism in the year 1836 was an enthusiasm for the memory of a man dead fifteen years.

It was a *historical sentiment as opposed to a political cause.*

Except among a handful of the faithful, the only political "causes" were Republicanism, Bourbonism, Communism, Socialism, Anarchism—and, of course, Orléanism.

Louis-Philippe's inherent weakness lay in his dismal kingship; his inherent strength lay in the various factions opposing him, each of which opposed all the others.

Louis-Napoleon's inherent weakness as he set out to depose the King lay in his failure to read the mood of France correctly; his inherent strength lay in attracting to himself the fanatical Viscount de Persigny.

The part played by this totally unscrupulous agitator's agitator in bringing Prince Louis to the throne should in no way be minimized. The entire fiasco—he all but pushed Louis into undertaking it—was, of course, foredoomed; France's turmoil notwithstanding, it takes more than the assistance of a hack journalist and a run-of-the-mill diva plus the purchased loyalties of a few disgruntled military officers to bring down a government.

But the fiasco gave Prince Louis the international notoriety he needed if he were ever to translate his vision into reality. The world would laugh at him after Strasbourg—but the world would at least *know* him.

Viscount de Persigny. No one knows where he found the name. The title he pulled out of a hat. Born Jean-Gilbert-Victor Fialin, he was initially an ardent and outspoken republican journalist. If we can believe Persigny's own words—and believing anything he wrote entails a monumental act of faith—his conversion to Bonapartism was a religious experience on the order of that suffered by Saint Paul while en route to Damascus.

It seems that Persigny was driving through Germany one night, when suddenly his coachman jumped up on beholding a passing coach that contained the Prince, flung his hat into the air, and cried aloud: *"Vive Napoleon!"* After suffering the raptures of revelation, Persigny began an intensive study of the First Empire period. "I want to be the Second Empire's Loyola!" he announced. He was.*

Persigny saw the French Revolution as having failed because it created class struggle; he saw it as having succeeded because its progenitor united all classes into a single entity; and he saw Waterloo as a resumption of the social war that would have to continue in France until the Second Coming of the Bonapartes. Since there was no Bonapartist party in France at the time, and since in Bonapartism lay France's only hope for salvation, argued Persigny, it was only logical that all political parties should support Bonapartism.

His was the sort of simple syllogistic reasoning that tends to put Aristotelian philosophy in bad odor among the less recondite of this world.

Louis and Persigny, who were only three months apart in age, became instant allies. The persuasive journalist had little difficulty convincing the susceptible Pretender that the moment for an attempt on the Orléanist throne was upon them. Both realized that enthusiasm among the civilians for a change of dynasty at this particular time was practically nonexistent. The year 1836 was a prosperous one in France, and revolutions are always bad for business. But both were too impatient to wait for a recession. *Ipso facto,* they reasoned that their appeal must be directed toward the nation's military caste.

It was not bad reasoning. The army still contained officers who

---

* *"How can I expect my government to get on?"* moaned Napoleon III when his government was not getting on very well; *"The Empress is a Legitimist! Prince Napoleon [Plon-Plon] is a Republican! Morny is an Orléanist! I am a Socialist! The only real Bonapartist among the lot of us is Persigny—and he is mad!"*

had served under the Emperor. The Orléans government was essentially civilian. The grievances of the military were hardly to be appreciated by a regime whose foreign policy precluded much chance of going to war. Professional soldiers are never satisfied when all they can look forward to is a seasonal change of uniform.

The game plan called for the Prince to present himself to the troops of the Strasbourg garrison, receive a tumultuous *"Vive l'Empereur!"* and march at their head to Paris, there to present the government—and the civilian populace—with a *fait accompli.* Just as the Emperor had done after escaping from Elba.

The choice of Strasbourg was an inspired one. Not only was it the most important city and fortress on the upper Rhine frontier, it had been a seedbed of Republican opposition to whatever government was ruling France at any given time. Its inhabitants were still half German in language, religion and thought; their loyalty to Paris was in direct ratio to their distance from Paris.

Throughout the summer of 1836, Louis made a number of trips to Baden—not, as Hortense suspected, to waste his money on conniving women, but to cultivate the officers who flocked there from Strasbourg to relieve the tedium and frustration of barracks life. What with his ability to exude as well as evoke sympathy, Louis had little difficulty enlisting a dozen or so young officers with whose grievances he, bearer of that charismatic name Bonaparte, was empathetic and whose ambitions he was prepared to foster. Now all that was needed was a senior officer.

Fitting the bill was Colonel Vaudrey, Commander of the Fourth Artillery. The Fourth Artillery was the Emperor's old regiment from his days as a subaltern in the armies of Louis XVI; to the superstitious Prince, the presence of this outfit at Strasbourg was a good omen. Vaudrey, a veteran of Waterloo, had recently been denied a request for change of assignment and promotion.

Unfortunately, even malcontented field officers are not usually susceptible to the promises of pretenders. They are usually susceptible to seductresses, though. Adding a touch of Gallic spice to the enterprise, Persigny dispatched his current mistress to Baden.

Enter Madame Eléonore Brault-Gordon, French widow of an eccentric Englishman; she was a part-time singer, part-time whore, and full-time devotée of the Napoleonic legend. Prince Louis dangled her tantalizingly in Colonel Vaudrey's direction. Vaudrey solicited an introduction. Louis complied, following this up with a dissertation on his own political principles. Colonel Vaudrey was less impressed with the Prince's principles than with the contralto's configuration.

He suffered a change of heart when Madame Gordon announced she would not submit to his advances until he succumbed to involvement in the conspiracy.

The colonel succumbed, the contralto submitted, the two went off on an idyllic holiday, and Louis and Persigny continued conspiring; they even attempted to win over General Voirol, the garrison's commander. Voirol reported the entire plot to Paris. Louis-Philippe's government dismissed the matter as too absurd to take note of.

A few evenings later, Louis stole into Strasbourg and addressed twenty-five of Vaudrey's malcontented fellow-officers. All were impressed with the grief he expressed as an exile, the sanctity he felt for his cause. Some were older men who had served under the Emperor and regretted the First Empire's demise; others were younger men who were made to see the chance of quick promotion and better pay under a Bonapartist regime.

No attempt was made to court the rank-and-file. These could be taken for granted; they would either follow their officers or be won over by the magic name Napoleon—or by the cash Louis planned to spread around. Or so he and Persigny presumed.

In the early evening of October 28, accompanied by his old comrade Colonel Parquin, who was in on the conspiracy from the beginning (and whom Louis grandiloquently promoted to the rank of general), Louis stole into Strasbourg and rendezvoused with his co-conspirators. He had brought with him a regimental standard surmounted by the Napoleonic eagle. Each of the conspirators "pressed the standard to his heart with deep emotion."

Then he explained that the imminent *putsch* should in no way be construed as a military revolt; it was an appeal to democracy. The officers took due note of this exercise in semantics.

Louis next read aloud three painfully periphrastic proclamations he intended to have distributed on the morrow: to the people of France, informing them that they had been betrayed by the Orléanist regime; to the military, informing them that the Emperor's shade was shining down from on high; and to the citizens of Strasbourg, informing them that their trade had been ruined by the Congress of Vienna.

H hour was six A.M. the following morning, a Sunday, when few people would be abroad to get in anyone's way.

At five A.M., as prearranged, Colonel Vaudrey called out his troops for a review. At the appointed moment, Louis, Persigny, Parquin and two of the suborned officers snuck into the encampment. (Louis wore a colonel's uniform of the French artillery and a replica of his uncle's cocked hat; Parquin wore his *Grande Armée* uniform that had lain so many years in mothballs; Persigny's uniform came from a fancy-dress costumer.) One of the officers, Lieutenant Laity, carried the standard surmounted by the Imperial eagle.

On beholding them, Vaudrey dramatically drew his sword and informed his regiment: "You see before you the nephew of the Emperor Napoleon! He comes to concern himself with the rights of the people! Let all who love the glory and liberty of France rally round him! Can the nephew of the Emperor Napoleon count on you?"

A roar of *"Vive l'Empereur!"* gave the Emperor's nephew the solicited assurance.

"Gentlemen," he cried, "the hour has struck! Now we shall see whether France remembers twenty years of glory! March with me against the traitors and oppressors of the fatherland with the cry *'Vive la France! Vive la Liberté!'* "

A thousand voices cried in unison, "We will!" The regimental band struck up. The Fourth Artillery marched out of barracks behind the Emperor's nephew and set out to win the allegiance of the infantry regiment in garrison, the Forty-sixth of the Line.

En route, Louis and Parquin broke into the quarters of General Voirol, who, on being awakened from a deep sleep, declined to recognize the Pretender.

"They had deceived you, Prince," said the garrison commander from the depths of his trundle bed. "The army will do its duty, and I am going to prove it here and now!"

Louis ordered Parquin to keep the general from doing his duty, rushed from the general's quarters, and ordered an artillery picket to surround the house and keep Voirol under arrest.

While Louis proceeded to the Finkmatt Barracks, garrison of the Forty-sixth of the Line, General Voirol proceeded to get out of his trundle bed. Parquin gave chase. Momentarily the scene took on the baser aspects of a French bedroom farce, with Parquin chasing Voirol about the house through a multiplicity of doorways. With the aid of his wife and mother-in-law, who had been awakened by all the ruckus and came running with brooms, Voirol subdued Parquin. Concurrently, troops loyal to the government overpowered that sentry picket Louis had standing in front of the house.

At the Finkmatt Barracks, the infantry declined to follow the artillery, the sergeant of the guard declined to recognize the Prince, and a subaltern declined Louis's demand that he "parade the battalion for me!"

As infantrymen and artillerymen stood about arguing amongst themselves, one of the loyalist officers had the presence of mind to shout aloud: "Soldiers! You are deceived! The man they are presenting to you as the heir to the Emperor is nothing but a dressed-up actor! He is only Colonel Vaudrey's nephew!"

Roused by their colonel, the officers of the Forty-sixth of the Line drove the conspirators back against the wall. The men of the Fourth Artillery quietly slunk from the scene and back to barracks. There was a brief scuffle. One of Louis's cronies scraped his knuckles. "You are wounded!" cried the Prince, eyeing those bleeding knuckles; "You have shed blood for me! We will be shot! But we will die a good death!"

No one was shot. A few were winged, though, by some stones lobbed in by a few workmen who had climbed atop the wall.

Less than an hour after the *putsch* began, the Prince and his confederates were in the town jail. Only Persigny managed to escape; he fled to London.

Queen Hortense snuck into France, and from a hideaway outside Paris appealed to Louis-Philippe to spare her son's life. She need not have bothered. The King was not about to allow the affair to be exploited by the political opposition. Louis was brought to Paris and informed that he was to be given a full and free pardon. So much for the good news. The bad news: he was to be deported to America.

On November 21, Louis was put aboard the destroyer *Andromède,* whose captain was given sealed orders not to let him off the ship until it arrived in America—after a slow voyage by way of Rio de Janeiro. As Louis boarded ship, he was handed a packet containing 15,000 francs, a gift from the King with which to start a new life in the New World.

The miserly King could afford to be magnanimous; that *viaticum* came out of the 200,000 francs taken from the Pretender's pockets in the Strasbourg jail.

"If the Emperor looks down from heaven, he will be satisfied with me," wrote Louis to his uncle Joseph Bonaparte.

The Emperor might have been satisfied, but his brothers were livid. The ex-King of Holland stopped the Prince's allowance and took to his bed in a dark chamber. Uncle Lucien sent word asking that Louis no longer consider himself his nephew. Uncle Jerome announced publicly that Louis was not a Bonaparte but a bastard. Uncle Joseph fumed that the Prince had "ignored his father and uncles as though they were already in their graves!" (In a manner of speaking, they were.)

As for Louis-Philippe, having shown uncharacteristic wisdom in turning the entire episode into a knee-slapping farce, he now played right into Louis's hands by putting all the little fish on trial after letting the big fish get away.

The trial lasted twelve days—in part because all the defendants availed themselves of the opportunity to make grandiose orations outlining their political aims (and, into the bargain, pointing up the failings of the Orléanist regime), in part because the proceedings had to be translated for most of the Alsatian jurymen, who did not understand French.

What started as a trial quickly degenerated into a prolonged pro-Bonapartist political rally. And, as they say in the theater, the defendants had the audience with them all the way.

The prosecution began to find the going rough when Lieutenant Laity's counsel delivered an impassioned speech proving beyond the shadow of a doubt that his client had a mother. When another of the defense counsel proved that *his* client *also* had a mother and, what is more, a mother who had attained the age of *eighty-two*, jury and spectators dissolved in tears.

Apparently bearing in mind that none of the defendants had ever been motherless, the jury took twenty minutes to bring in a verdict of Not Guilty.

Everyone agreed that Madame Gordon provided the verbal high point of the trial. When the prosecution asked her, "Is it not true

that you are in love with Prince Louis?" the diva dramatically
jumped to her feet (some claim she almost leaped out of the witness
box) and declaimed defiantly, *"Politically!"*—and then added, in
modulated tones, just to set the record straight: "To tell the truth,
he has the effect on me of a woman."

After the prisoners had embraced their counsel and each other,
all were embraced by the jury and spectators. The acquitted were
tendered a riotous public banquet, and the evening ended on a note
of conviviality, with Madame Gordon and her cohorts being accorded a public serenade outside their hotel.

The French government decided not to appeal the verdict or
penalize the troops who had taken part in the whole ridiculous affair.

Louis was convinced his dream was ended. A letter to Hortense
indicates that he intended to become a farmer in the New World.
His imprisonment aboard the *Andromède* lasted four months. On
March 30, 1837, he stepped ashore at Norfolk, Virginia, gave a
dinner party for the ship's officers, and made his way to New York
City, where he ensconced himself in the Old City Hotel on lower
Broadway.

Any thoughts of settling in America were abandoned when Louis
read newspaper accounts of the Strasbourg trial. He felt that the
cause of Bonapartism was strong enough to survive one fiasco.

Awaiting the Prince were an old Italian friend, Count Arese, and
the Prince's valet, Charles Thélin. Hortense had sent them out,
along with cash, personal gear and letters of maternal encouragement for her son. Hortense also sent a sketch of Mathilde; apparently she hoped Louis would marry his cousin. These hopes were
dashed when Jerome Bonaparte wrote to his brother Joseph after
Strasbourg: "I would rather have given my daughter to a peasant
than to a man so ambitious and egotistical as to play with the destiny
of a poor child who was almost confided to his care!"

(Jerome did worse than give Mathilde to a peasant; he sold the
poor child to a degenerate Russian millionaire. Mathilde did not
regret her failure to marry Louis—until he became Emperor. Then
she regretted it very much.)

Louis was shown hospitality by New York society—the Hamiltons, the Livingstons, the Schuylers and other of the New World's Old Families. American aristocrats have always suffered a curious fondness for European royalties, especially of the exiled and spurious variety. Wherever he went, Louis impressed people with his affection for his mother and his determination to save France. Recorded the poet Fitz-Greene Halleck: "He would sometimes say, 'When I shall be at the head of affairs in France' or 'When I become Emperor,' and I then looked upon him as being mad as a March hare. . . . He was rather a dull man, on the order of [George] Washington."

The King had never said Louis's exile to America was permanent, and no attempt was made to control his movements. Louis decided to remain on for a year, traveling the length and breadth of the country; he had already begun "to assess the many problems facing the young United States."

But in early June he received a letter from Hortense advising him that she was suffering from cancer of the uterus. Four days later came another letter: Hortense was delighted that she need not face surgery (the doctors apparently had not told her that her condition was inoperable). The letter was upbeat in tone; but unbeknownst to Hortense, the loyal Valérie Masuyer had added a postscript: "*Venez! Venez!*"—come quickly.

Louis booked passage on the next Europe-bound packet. While waiting to sail, he sent a letter to President Van Buren apologizing, as one head of state to another, for failing to call at the White House. President Van Buren was probably rather mystified; he had not invited the Prince to call in the first place.

Arriving at Liverpool in early July, Louis hastened up to London and applied at the French Embassy for a passport to return home through France, the most direct route. Unfortunately, Persigny had been running about London assuring one and all how fortunate the French were that soon they would have Prince Louis-Napoleon Bonaparte to reign over them. In addition to refusing Louis a passport, the French ambassador had him placed under police surveillance.

In desperation, in disguise, and now in possession of an English friend's passport franked by the Swiss Consul in New York, Louis took advantage of the celebrations attendant upon Queen Victoria's accession to slip out of London. He made his way to Rotterdam, sailed up the Rhine to Mannheim, and then traveled overland, reaching Arenenberg on August 4.

The death watch lasted two months. For Louis, the thought that this adored mother, who had so imbued him with his destiny, would not live to see him triumph was more than he could bear. For Hortense, the physical pain she suffered was as nothing compared to the emotional pain she felt in having to leave Louis alone in the world, now rejected by his family, an exile from his native land.

"The French have treated us so very badly," she told him. "They have such little minds. . . . Be very careful. Think of your personal safety. They are very much afraid of us; they would hurt you if they could!"

She died early in the morning of October 5. A funeral service was held a few days later at nearby Ermatingen. The Mozart *Requiem* was sung; mass was celebrated by a mitred bishop; people of all stations, peasants and aristocrats, flocked from far and wide. Hortense was lauded and eulogized; she had been the most popular of all the Bonapartes—except among the Bonapartes.

A week later, as requested in her will, Hortense's body was returned to France and interred next to that of her mother at Reuil. Louis, of course, could not attend. Hortense's only "family" at the last rites was her ex-lover, Charles de Flahaut, who had thrown in his lot with the Orléanists and was now a peer of France, and their son, the Duke de Morny, whom Hortense had not seen since the day of his birth.

In her will, Hortense spoke once more of Louis's mission in life: "I have no political advice to give my son. I know that he realizes his position and the duties imposed by his name." Louis was, of course, her chief legatee. There was, in addition to Arenenberg, a château at nearby Gottlieben, plus some shares in a Vienna bank and some investments in Spain and Portugal; a total capital of 3 million francs and an income of 120,000 per annum. (There were numerous bequests to servants, old retainers, even childhood friends. Plon-Plon was left 20,000 francs and some wholesome advice; he accepted the money but not the advice.)

Hortense's death precipitated a reconciliation between her husband and son; to Louis, whose letters he had returned unopened after Strasbourg, the elder Bonaparte sent a letter of condolence. In

the prologue to her will, Hortense hoped her husband would remember her "with indulgence." He did so to the tune of paying the
cost of *one mass* for the repose of her soul. (He also paid half the
cost of a statue to be erected over her grave, but he could not have
paid very much: the statue fell apart soon after it was erected.)

Unable to face Arenenberg after Hortense's death, Louis sold
it—with the precondition that he could buy it back at some future
date, which he did*—and moved to the château at Gottlieben. There
he was joined by Lieutenant Laity and a few of the other Strasbourg co-conspirators. The proceeds from the Arenenberg sale
Louis put into two journals, *Le Capital* and *Le Journal du commerce*, both of which were devoted to the propagandistic ideas that
would culminate in his *Les Idées Napoléoniennes*.

Early in 1838, the French ambassador asked that Prince Louis be
expelled from Switzerland. Graciously failing to remind the French
that the Prince was not only a Swiss resident of more than fifteen
years but a citizen as well, the Berne authorities contemptuously
passed on the request to the Canton of Thurgau, where Louis resided. The Canton of Thurgau reacted by electing Louis to the local
council and making him president of its shooting club.

In retaliation for France's request for his expulsion, Louis
encouraged Laity to publish *Relation historique des événements
d'octobre 1836*. This official version of the Strasbourg affair (which
may well have been written by Louis himself) proved that the fiasco
had in fact been a serious insurrection and served notice that the
Orléanist throne was now in jeopardy. Thanks to the efforts of
Madame Gordon, the entire press run of 5,000 copies sold out in
Paris.

Laity was hauled back to France and tried on the charge of *atten-
tat contre la sûreté de l'état* (attempt upon the security of the state),
sentenced to five years' imprisonment and a stiff fine, and condemned to police surveillance for the rest of his life.

This for the historian of an unsuccessful conspiracy whose actual
participants had been acquitted!

---

* *The estate was eventually willed by Eugénie to the Thurgau government to be used as a Catholic girls' school.*

Having martyred Laity, it was now time to martyr Laity's
leader. In a characteristic act of utter obtuseness, King Louis-
Philippe jumped into the trap he had thus far avoided merely by
requesting that the Swiss expel Louis. He *demanded* Louis's expulsion. Newspapers heralded Louis's and Hortense's many charities
to the Swiss people. The Prince became a symbol of Swiss resistance. The French—now backed up in their demand by Prussia,
Austria, Baden and Württemberg—moved an army corps into position along the Swiss border.

By the summer, with war fever at a high pitch, Louis—whose
talents with the bow and arrow had yet to be demonstrated—found
himself the greatest Swiss hero since William Tell. Wishing to spare
the Swiss the horrors of invasion, he departed for England, fairly
confident the French would never mobilize its armies along the
English Channel.

A year after creeping up the Rhine and into Switzerland, the
Bonaparte Pretender rode out of Switzerland amidst wildly cheering mobs, having progressed from an obscure failure to a figure of
international importance.

The French government had transformed a laughingstock into a
hero.

The hero would, of course, once again become a laughingstock;
indeed, his invasion of France two years later would hand Europe a
laugh that still has historians clutching their ribs.

Nevertheless, he would prove that Prince Metternich certainly
knew whereof he was speaking when, following the Strasbourg
trial, that Austrian statesman warned the Orléanist government:

> Be on your guard! This young fool acquires importance by your mis-
> take in making more than one need of everything which has to do with
> the Emperor Napoleon. You will end by making everyone believe in the
> future of the Napoleon dynasty!

On his previous visits to London, the Prince had been no more
than a transient refugee, an impecunious adventurer; now he was no
less than an established exile, a wealthy dandy. His precise financial
posture at this time is purely speculative; Louis's appearances always tended to belie the truth. Income from Hortense's estate,

after settlement of all debts and pensionary obligations, was barely enough to finance his lifestyle and propagandizing, and pleas to his father for an advance on his future inheritance went ignored. Creditors willingly carried the Prince, though. He was known to repay every cent he ever borrowed.

After sampling a few of the quieter hotels in St. James's and Waterloo Place, Louis came to roost in a magnificent townhouse he took on lease in Carlton Gardens. During those first migratory months, he established himself as one of the regulars at Lady Blessington's in Kensington. Lady Blessington was beautiful, witty, of a literary bent, and delightfully scandalous (her longtime resident lover, the epicene Count d'Orsay, was her dead husband's son-in-law as well as her dead husband's ex-lover); the *salon* presided over by this Irish shebeen-keeper's-daughter-turned-Countess was the favorite watering hole for the practitioners of *bon ton*.

Here the Prince met Disraeli, then on the threshold of his own spectacular career. He was the "Prince Florestan" of Disraeli's *Endymion:* "Prince Florestan encouraged conversation, though himself inclined to taciturnity. When he did speak, his terse remarks and condensed views were striking, and were remembered."

Among those who "remembered"—outside the pages of *Endymion*—were two members of the British peerage: an earl, who recorded that "nothing can persuade him he is not to be Emperor of France; the Strasbourg affair has not in the least shaken him; he is constantly thinking of what he is to do on the throne"; and a duke, who recollected that Louis was "always discoursing on what he would do when he was Emperor of France. . . . The idea that he would eventually be the Emperor of the French never for a moment left the mind of Louis Napoleon."

Sharing Carlton Gardens with the Prince was his suite of devoted adherents, among them General Montholon, who had shared the Emperor's St. Helena exile until the end (and whose published contribution to the Napoleonic hagiography was the most recent as well as the least reliable); Dr. Conneau, who had attended the Emperor to the very end, had gone on to preside over Hortense's fatal illness, and was now doubling as Louis's physician and chief aide; Colonel Vaudrey, cashiered from the French army and temporarily estranged from Madame Gordon (she was making the rounds of the Parisian concert halls and bedrooms proselytizing on the Prince's behalf); Charles Thélin, whose loyalty as Louis's valet would earn him the title Count and the position Keeper of the Privy Purse; and, of course, Persigny.

Persigny complained that the Prince was devoting too much valuable time to foppery and not enough time to plotting. Louis spent many a day (and night) in the company of the young aristocrats who lived parasitically on the hospitality of the wealthy, eccentric Lord Eglinton. He spent many a borrowed quid on a battery of servants, a stable of horses, a coach emblazoned with the Imperial eagle, and a box at the opera. He spent many an hour riding through London on his prized Arab steed, or along Rotten Row in a cabriolet. Occasionally there would be a breakfast party at Bulwer-Lytton's and boating on the Thames. (One day, Louis rowed Disraeli and his new bride onto a mud bank and elicited from the furious Mrs. Disraeli: "You should not undertake things which you cannot accomplish! You are always, sir, too adventurous!")

Prince Louis was proving there was method to his madness in leading the life of a dandy (just as, at Boulogne, he would prove that there was madness to his method). Louis-Philippe had dispatched agents to watch and report on the Prince's every move. The poor agents became so confused with all of the Prince's gadding about and sent back such conflicting reports, it was decided at the Tuileries that his declamations of intent were mere posturing, that his plotting days were at an end.

Now that Louis-Philippe was off the scent, mysterious gentlemen began flitting in and out of Carlton Gardens, money began flowing toward Paris for the formation of Bonapartist clubs. On a summer night in 1839, the Prince put the finishing touches to his *chef d'oeuvre, Les Idées Napoléoniennes.* (Disraeli accommodatingly arranged for his publishers to bring out the London edition.)

In this 50,000-word manifesto, Louis proclaimed that "the Napoleonic idea consists in a reconstruction of French society overturned by fifty years of revolution, and in a reconciliation of Order and Liberty, the rights of the people and the principles of authority." The first Napoleon was "the testamentary executor" of the French Revolution. "Strong in the support of the people, he proceeded at once to abolish every unjust law, to heal every wound, to reward every merit, to exploit every achievement, and to secure the collaboration of all Frenchmen for a single end, the prosperity of France."

But, what of the charge that Napoleon Bonaparte was a militarist? Argued the Prince: those wars were forced on the Emperor by the Allied powers; if at times he seemed to be the aggressor, it was simply because he wished to enjoy the advantage of the initiative. Besides, the aim of all Napoleon's wars was "to substitute for *l'état de nature* amongst the nations *l'état social*—a solid *association européenne.*"

If Napoleon failed in his divine mission—and here the Prince concedes that the great man erred, especially in his anti-British policies—the fault lay in the grandioseness of his noble project, commingled with the pace he set for himself: "He tried to do the work of several centuries in ten years of Empire." And, adds the Prince in peroration, for the edification of those who might seek a moral: Napoleon's system will be resurrected simply because Europe *needs* it.

The Prince then asks rhetorically, "Where today can be found that amazing man who impressed his personality upon the world through its respect for the superiority of his ideas?"—and goes on to hint rather obliquely that the Emperor's true heir is alive and well at Carlton Gardens.

Having thus appealed to the politicians (the previously published *Manuel d'artillerie* had been Louis's appeal to the military), what was now needed was an appeal to the common people. Persigny obliged with his *Lettres de Londres*, in which the common people of France were assured that, gossip to the contrary, their next Emperor was laboring conscientiously on their behalf:

> The Prince is an active working man, severe toward himself, indulgent toward others. At six A.M. he is in his study, where he works till noon—his lunch hour. After this repast, which never lasts longer than ten minutes, he reads the newspapers and takes note of the more important events and opinions of the day. At two he receives visits; at four he goes out on his private business; he rides at five and dines at seven; then, generally, he finds time to work again for some hours in the course of the evening.

Here was one of those rare instances when Persigny was not overdoing it. Louis spent many hours in the British Museum Reading

Room, visiting the Woolwich Arsenal, and inspecting, notebook in hand, the factories of Birmingham and the workshops of Manchester. This in order to bone up on history, acquaint himself with the latest innovations in artillery, and ascertain how the Industrial Revolution could be exploited when he came to the throne. Also, there was correspondence with two Bonapartist clubs in Paris: a woman's Club des Cotillons (supervised by Madame Gordon) and the military Club des Culottes de Peau (Vaudrey was sent over to take charge). Too, there were numerous editorial and financial matters attendant upon the two Bonapartist underground newspapers being published in Paris.

The Prince was indeed "an active working man."

Also in the *Lettres*, Persigny let the multitudes of France in on "the Prince's incredible likeness" to the Emperor:

> One is not long in perceiving that the Napoleonic type is reproduced with an astonishing fidelity. . . . There are . . . the same lines and the same inclination of the head, so marked with the Napoleonic character that when the Prince turns, it is enough to startle a soldier of the Old Guard; . . . and it is impossible not to be struck . . . by the imposing pride of the Roman profile, the pure and severe—I even say solemn—lines of which are like the sole of a great destiny.

Persigny was on fairly safe ground here. All but a piddling handful of the future Emperor's 34 million subjects lacked a clue as to what he actually looked like. And what he did *not* look like was his uncle.

By the time the nation got a good look at him, though, it did not make any difference.

On May 26, 1840, the French government decided to bring home the mortal remains of Napoleon Bonaparte and thus end, in the words of the moderate-liberal Adolphe Thiers, "the sublime agony of St. Helena, as resigned though more prolonged than that of Christ." In acquiescing to the return, King Louis-Philippe's attitude was that of an elderly, incapable kindergarten teacher who feels that the best way to restore order among his unruly moppets is to trot out their favorite fairy tale.

France's favorite fairy tale was the Napoleonic legend. The nation had its Arc de Triomphe and its statue of the Emperor atop the Vendôme Column; toy- and book-sellers were doing a thriving business in Napoleonianna; the restored Versailles was practically one continous gallery of art devolving upon the man and the legend that man had created.

The fairy tale had to be completed.

Louis-Philippe was astute enough to realize that Bonapartism was one of the expressions of opposition to his regime; with the completion of the fairy tale, the opposition would lessen.

But he was not astute enough to realize that Bonapartism was in fact the weakest of all those factions opposing him. There is a vast difference between a fairy tale and a legend.

Louis-Philippe did the right thing in completing the fairy tale. Where he erred was in taking the legend far too seriously.

So, too, did the Pretender to that legend.

Early in July, the French frigate *Belle Poule* ("Beautiful Hen"), commanded by the King's third son, the Prince d'Joinville, set sail from Le Havre for St. Helena.

Since the Emperor's ashes were being returned to France, the Pretender felt it only right that he be there to receive them.

At first a piratical attack was planned on the *Belle Poule* as it was steaming the long voyage back from St. Helena, but Louis decided that a military attack on the mainland held greater promise of success than hoisting the Jolly Roger of Bonapartism in the middle of the South Atlantic.

Thus the decision to mount a cross-Channel invasion. After landing at Wimereux in the Pas de Calais area, the invaders would win over the Calais and Boulogne garrisons and then march on Paris. The plan was, of course, Strasbourgian in concept.

This time, though, the outlook seemed brighter. General Magnan, commander of the area, gave the impression that he could be relied on. He refused the crude bribe of 400,000 francs by the Prince's agents—but, significantly, he neither arrested the agent nor informed Paris of the offer. Garrisoned at Calais and Boulogne were detachments of the Forty-second of the Line, an infantry regiment steeped in Napoleonic legend. A popular subaltern named Aladenize had been easily suborned.

Beginning in the early summer, bales of secondhand French uniforms began to arrive at Carlton Gardens, along with an order of insigniae and buttons representing the Forty-second of the Line and a shipment of muskets purchased illicitly in Birmingham. Dr. Conneau got busy sewing on the insigniae and cranking out Imperial proclamations on a hand press behind locked doors. As at Strasbourg, there were to be three appeals: to the people of the Pas de Calais, to the French military, and to the French nation.

The first was a sober summary of the economic advantages the locals would derive under the new Emperor's rule. The military was warned that "the great shade of the Emperor Napoleon speaks to you by my voice" and was urged to "get rid of the traitors and oppressors!" (As an added inducement, all ranks were promised promotion.) The proclamation to the French nation avowed that "the Ashes of the Emperor shall not return except to a France regenerated," commanded that "Glory and Liberty must stand by the side of Napoleon's coffin," advised that "I feel the Emperor's shadow urging me on," and assured that "I shall not halt until I have . . . replaced the eagle on our banners and restored the people to their rights!"

Interspersed among all those references to the Emperor's shade and the Emperor's ashes was a contemptuous dismissal of the Orléans monarchy as "ten years of falsehood, of usurpation, and of shame." Europe was reassured that Prince Louis's intentions were peaceful.

So confident was the Pretender of success that, when he dined at Lady Blessington's for the last time—sporting "a large spread eagle in diamonds clutching a thunderbolt of rubies"—he grandiloquently invited everyone at the table to dine with him a year to the day at the Tuileries.

Arrangements were put into the hands of Count Joseph Orsi, the Bonaparte family's Florentine banker.* Early in July, Orsi chartered the paddlewheel excursion steamer *Edinburgh Castle* "to take some friends for a pleasure cruise off the coast of France"; the captain would be given his orders at sailing time.

---

* Orsi later claimed that it was he who financed the entire invasion, to the tune of £20,000. "A fortnight of difficult negotiations enabled me to

So much for the invasion armada.

The invading army was to consist of, in addition to the Prince, a rather mixed bag. There were, of course, Persigny, General Montholon, "General" Parquin, Dr. Conneau, the valet Thélin, and a few other veterans of the Strasbourg venture. Also recruited from within Carlton Gardens were the Prince's chef, butler, tailor and fencing master. This was less an affectation on the Prince's part than a need to increase his numbers.

The remaining Argonauts were recruited, at a hundred francs a head, in the pubs of Leicester Square, at the time a veritable dung heap of foreign revolutionists and professional adventurers.

In the early hours of August 4, the *Edinburgh Castle* hoved to alongside the Customs House Wharf near London Bridge and, under Count Orsi's supervision, began to load on a rather extraordinary cargo—extraordinary for an invasion force, that is. In addition to two trunks of fancy dress, a pile of proclamations and those Birmingham muskets, went twenty-four dozen bottles of wines and spirits, two large carriages, and nine horses. (The Prince planned to "march" on Paris in Imperial style—as had the Emperor, by the way.)

After a delay in loading—two of the horses almost fell out of their nets while being hoisted aboard; Dr. Conneau's proclamations were momentarily misplaced on the dock—the *Edinburgh Castle* passed down river toward Gravesend, stopping at various wharves along the way to pick up detachment after detachment of the Leicester Square mercenaries (a number of whom complicated matters by reporting to the wrong wharf).

The Prince had specifically insisted that the ship arrive at Gravesend, its last port of call before heading westward, precisely at 3 P.M., "because we must land at precisely four A.M. of the fifth." It was known that Captain Col-Puygélier, Lieutenant Aladenize's superior—a staunch Orléanist—had been "invited to a shooting party on that day some distance from Boulogne, and probably he will not return until late. If we miss our landing tomorrow morning, we are doomed to utter failure."

---

comply with the Prince's wishes. On June 21 I handed him £10,000 in gold and notes. The second payment of £10,000 took place on August 3, the day before the start."

The ship arrived at Gravesend two hours behind schedule. While awaiting the Prince's arrival, Parquin went ashore to purchase some decent cigars; those on board were "detestable." En route to the tobacconist's, Parquin noticed a large bird chained to a pole, being fed shreds of raw meat by a street urchin. Determined that the next Emperor enter France with the Caesarian symbol of the Bonapartes, Parquin purchased the bird for a pound, took it aboard ship, and had it tethered to the mainmast.

When someone acquainted with the rudiments of ornithology pointed out that the "eagle" was in fact a rather weatherworn vulture, little concern was expressed. All were concerned with the Prince's nonappearance.

For some unknown reason, Captain Crow, the *Edinburgh Castle*'s skipper, had not been told to call at Ramsgate, where, someone remembered, the Prince had planned to board ship. Parquin gave the order, and Crow took the vessel down river. It docked at between one and two in the morning of the fifth—which was about three hours before the scheduled landing in France. The Prince came aboard a half hour later. Apparently he had gone to Ramsgate, had not found the ship there, and had then gone on to Gravesend— arriving there after it had left for Ramsgate.

Which is to say, the ship had been moving up and down the Thames looking for the Prince while he had been cabbing up and down London looking for the ship!

A council of war was held. Three of the Prince's twelve closest aides urged him to abort the mission. The other nine, led by Persigny, argued that it proceed. Persigny won the day.

Then it dawned on the invaders that Lieutenant Aladenize was probably standing on the beach at Wimereux at that very moment, looking for the incoming armada. Forestier, a cousin of Persigny, was promptly dispatched across the Channel—by rowboat!—to inform Aladenize that the invasion had been postponed by exactly twenty-four hours. Prayers were offered that Captain Col-Puygélier might meet with an accident while out on that shooting party.

The Prince was reminded of yet another problem: to remain on at Ramsgate might arouse suspicion; people who charter ships rarely do so for the purpose of sitting tied up at a wharf. The Prince gave

orders that the ship put out to sea and tack about until nightfall of
the fifth.

Out in the Channel, Captain Crow cruised about as ordered, a
storm came up, the Argonauts broke out the wine and spirits, and
everyone had a high old time. Late in the afternoon, when the storm
subsided, the uniforms were distributed (none fit properly) and the
Leicester Square regulars given their battle orders. Then the
Pretender—like all Bonapartes, a poor sailor—made his way to the
deck, collected his army about him, and addressed them as follows:

> Companions of my destiny, it is for France that we are bound. The
> only obstacle is Boulogne; that point once gained, our success is certain.
> Support me bravely and in a few days we shall be in Paris; our history
> will relate that it was with a mere handful of gallant fellows such as you
> are that I shall have accomplished this great and glorious enterprise.

The companions of Prince Louis's destiny cheered lustily (a few took
potshots at the vulture with empty wine bottles); the still ignorant
Captain Crow—neither he nor his crew understood French—
continued on to Wimereux, where the ship dropped anchor a mile off
shore in the early morning hours of the sixth.

From that point on, it was downhill all the way.

The ship's boat landed the entire invasionary force in four successive trips between two and three A.M. Lieutenant Aladenize was
waiting on the beach with Forestier (Persigny's cousin the rower).

So was a Customs officer who had become suspicious of the com-
ings and goings of the ship's boat.

When the *douanier* demanded an explanation, he received one
from out of the darkness: "We are soldiers of the Fortieth Regiment
on a voyage from Dunkirk to Cherbourg; but one of the paddles of
our steamer is broken, and that is why we are debarking." The
douanier found the tale difficult to swallow.

So, too, did his superior officer, who happened on the scene. The
latter was told that now was no time for talking.

This from Colonel Parquin, who materialized out of the darkness,
musket in hand, and advised the superior *douanier* that, either
willingly or forcibly, he would have to act as guide to the body of
men who had just landed. The *douanier* replied that he would lose
his job if he started acting as a tour guide. A bribe was offered. The

bribe was refused. Parquin cocked his musket. The *douanier* pleaded fatigue and collapsed.

Louis materialized out of the darkness and ordered Parquin to pack his weapon; he wanted no bloodshed.

Lieutenant Aladenize then stepped forward and politely reminded Parquin that *he* was capable of guiding the troops into town; he had just come from there; as a matter of fact, he was stationed there. The expedition started the march to Boulogne—apparently forgetting that the game plan had called for a march on the Calais garrison first—and the two *douaniers* rowed out to impound the *Edinburgh Castle*.

The invaders stumbled into Boulogne about 5 A.M. At the Place d'Alton a sentry became suspicious and demanded the password. Aladenize told him: "Behold the Prince!" The sentry replied that this was not the password. Again Parquin whipped out his musket; again the Prince forbade bloodshed. The jolly band resumed their march along the main street, and the sentry went off to sound the alarm.

Moments later, the column ran into a Sub-Lieutenant Maussion, who demanded to know what was happening. The Prince begged Maussion to join the enterprise. Maussion refused. As the conspirators fell to discussing this latest rebuff, Maussion managed to slip away. He rushed to Captain Col-Puygélier's quarters (the latter had returned from his shooting party) with the news that a detachment of men of the Forty-second of the Line, sloppily dressed and comporting themselves in a most unmilitary manner, had suddenly materialized in the town square at the ungodly hour of 5:35 A.M.

When the invaders arrived at the barracks, Aladenize cried out to the sentry: "To arms! Don't you see the Prince?" The sentry did not know the Prince; but he *did* know he had better obey an officer's command. The sentry promptly presented arms. Parquin posted two of his own sentries at the gate, with orders to prevent anyone from entering or leaving the area.

Concurrently, a crowd of townspeople en route to their morning labors gathered, drawn by the commotion. Persigny flung money in their direction and called for shouts of *"Vive l'Empereur!"* The crowd obliged. Money was not that easily come by in Boulogne. Dr. Conneau moved through the crowd, handing out proclamations.

Meanwhile, inside the barracks yard a pair of inquisitive

sergeants demanded to know what was happening. Lieutenant Aladenize grabbed each by the arm and presented them to the Prince, who promptly promoted them on the spot to Captains of Grenadiers.

At that moment, Captain Col-Puygélier came running into the yard and was urged by the Prince's sentries to "join us; here is the Prince! Your fortune is made!" Col-Puygélier drew his sword and ordered the sentries to "clear the way—let me get to my soldiers!"

The Prince came toward Col-Puygélier and said: "Captain, I am Prince Louis-Napoleon. Join us, and there is nothing which you may not have." As Louis prepared to promote him to the rank of colonel, the Captain replied: "Prince or no Prince—get the hell out of my barracks! And take your idiot friends with you!"

When the Prince refused to move, Col-Puygélier rallied his troops, who came tumbling out of their barracks half-asleep and in a state of semi-dress. Carried away by the heat of the moment, the Prince fired his pistol; the bullet went through the cheek of one of his newly created Captains of Grenadiers.

Mass confusion. The invaders found themselves surrounded and outnumbered; the dregs of Leicester Square became disoriented. Captain Col-Puygélier ordered them all from his barracks, and out they stumbled; it was all very embarrassing, especially when Col-Puygélier slammed the gates shut behind them. (Col-Puygélier deemed it beneath his professional dignity "to have my troops chase those idiots about town!")

As the town clock struck six, the civil authorities went on the alert, having been informed that a band of drunks in fancy dress was running up and down the streets spreading proclamations and scattering coins. Within ten minutes, the invaders, having broken ranks and fled in all directions, were being pursued by the militia. One group, led by the Prince, hurried a half mile out of town to the Column of the *Grande Armée*, built to commemorate the immense preparations made by Napoleon Bonaparte in 1805 for his aborted invasion of England.

The Prince dramatically ascended the column and planted atop it the Imperial flag Persigny had been toting. When his adherents noted that the local militia was approaching, the Prince had to be dissuaded from committing suicide on the spot.

His mortification is understandable.

Galvanized by Persigny, a small party surrounded the Prince and all made a dash down to the seashore. The pursuers followed. The majority of those surrounding the Prince surrendered. Persigny, Dr. Conneau and a few others followed the Prince into the water in hopes of reaching a small boat that was fortuitously floundering about in the surf. They got into the boat. So did some bullets from the heavy fire on the beach. The boat capsized.

Their ignominy was complete when the invaders of France had to be saved from drowning.

By eight o'clock, all were lodged in the town jail.

In the meantime, the "Imperial eagle" was dispatched by the *douaniers* to the local slaughterhouse. Finding the surroundings comparatively dull, it escaped after a few hours. Next day, apparently suffering a change of mind, it returned to the slaughterhouse. Since the authorities doubted there was much of a market for vulture meat, the bird was auctioned off to the highest bidder.

It ended its days as the pet of a harelipped charcoal merchant from Arras.

The invasion was such an unmitigated, not to say laughable, disaster, many suspected the French government of having colluded in it so as to entrap the Pretender and thus end his Imperial pretensions once and for all time.

Louis-Philippe was not that clever.

But he *was* clever in his disposition of the invaders. There would be a trial; not before a local jury of Boulogne peasants who, like their Strasbourg counterparts, might vote for acquittal, but before the supreme Court of Peers, who could be relied on to deal with the Prince severely.*

Any illusions that the Napoleonic legend posed a threat for the Orléanist government were laid to rest when the *Débats* of August 13 editorialized:

> We will acknowledge that, if there be a popular reminiscence in France, it is that of the Great Captain whose name is associated with our immortal victories; but if there is a forgotten family, it is the Imperial

---

* *Not all, however. Count Charles de Flahaut and Admiral Verhuell were two peers who abstained "for personal reasons."*

family. The son of Napoleon, in dying, carried with him to the tomb the remnant of interest which was attached to the blood of the Emperor. France has pardoned in the Emperor the unsupportable harshness of his domestic government, the unheard-of rigors of conscription, the disasters of 1812 and 1813, and the evils caused by his unbounded ambition; and in the popular mind the hero has been almost deified. The image of Napoleon is everywhere, from the humble cottage to the public monument; but Bonapartism is extinct; even the *éclat* of the glory of the Emperor crushes those who ridiculously attempt to cover themselves with it. Where was Monsieur Louis Bonaparte arrested? At the foot of the Column of Boulogne—the column raised by the Grand Army in honor of its chief! *It was reserved for Bonapartism to expire on that spot!*

Fifty hours after landing in France, "Monsieur Louis Bonaparte" was driven out of Boulogne. Security was heavy; orders were given to shoot the prisoner if he attempted to escape. He was brought into Paris at midnight on August 12 and taken to the Conciergerie.

The trial, which opened on September 28, followed the French tradition of a debate between defendant and prosecutor. The King realized that by putting the Pretender on trial the government ran the risk of giving him an ideal forum for self-advertisement. But it was no secret that Louis-Napoleon Bonaparte was more effective on the printed page than on his feet.

He was, in fact, one of the worst public speakers among all nineteenth-century monarchs.

Now, though, after hearing the indictment read, Louis rose to his feet—and to the occasion. It was an impassioned, masterful performance. Far from standing accused as an agitator, argued Louis, he was standing condemned for a principle—that touchstone of democracy: government by consent of the governed. The plebiscites (1800, 1802, 1804, 1815) that had conferred power on the Emperor and his heirs, he argued, had never been revoked; the Emperor had been deposed only by foreign armies; consequently, the restoration of the Bourbons and the successive enthronement of Louis-Philippe was illegal.

As for himself, the Prince avowed, he had no personal ambition, no Imperial goal. Rather, he had come to demand that the people of France be consulted—through plebiscite—as to who their monarch should be.

"I stand before you as the representative of a principle, a cause, and a defeat," he perorated. "The principle is the sovereignty of the people; the cause is that of the Empire; the defeat is Waterloo. You have acknowledged the principle; you have served the cause; as for the defeat, it is for you to avenge it."

Sentences were passed on October 6: transportation for life for Lieutenant Aladenize; twenty years for Parquin, Montholon, Persigny and Dr. Conneau; fifteen years for some of the other conspirators; ten years for the remaining conspirators; two years for those recruits from Leicester Square. (All were subsequently commuted.)

For the Prince: perpetual imprisonment in a fortress within the borders of France. Louis-Philippe had made a grievous mistake in exiling the Pretender after the Strasbourg caper. This time he was taking no chances.

As Prince Louis-Napoleon Bonaparte was being led away, he uttered with a hooded smile what has come down as one of the most titillating questions posed in nineteenth-century Europe: "How long does perpetuity last in France?"

Chapter 4
Eugénie:
1839-1848

Doña Manuela de Montijo was now one of Madrid's wealthiest *señoras grandes*. She was also one of the most talked-about. As soon as the prescribed year-long period of mourning for Don Cypriano was ended, she threw open her drawing room. (Many claim she threw open her bedroom as well.) Her townhouse in the Plazuela del Angel was given over nightly to congenial dinner parties for the chosen many, cozy tête-à-têtes for the chosen few; there were weekly At Homes, when anyone newly arrived in town merely dropped by uninvited. For ambassadors posted to Madrid, it was *de rigueur* to call on the Countess de Montijo immediately upon presenting accreditation to the girl-queen Isabella's scandal-ridden, politically besieged, socially dull court.

Out at Carabanchel, there were grandiose garden parties, magnificent fancy-dress balls, even concerts; music was one of Doña Manuela's great joys. That Eugénie did not emulate her in this respect, among others, was to the Countess a tribulation. There were also amateur theatricals and opera productions.*

---

* *In after years, the Empress recalled: "As I could neither sing nor play, I was told to walk on in* Norma, *carrying the little child whose presence is necessary in the scene. I entered with the baby, who at once commenced to cry loudly, perhaps because I was so nervous that I did not notice that I was holding its head downwards. I hurriedly put the baby on a chair and rushed off the stage. I was never asked to do anything again. So now you know all about my career as an actress!"*

Contact with Paris was maintained through correspondence with Mérimée, who held an important cultural post in the Orléans government. His steady stream of letters, well larded with Parisian gossip, laced with amusing asides, kept the Countess abreast of the fate of mutual friends and public curiosities.

Until Paca and Eugénie had passed through puberty, their existence was all but overlooked by the Countess. Their upbringing was seen to by Miss Flowers. The English governess did the best she could, but it was rough on her; poor Miss Flowers was like something out of a Jane Austen novel, and thus out of her element in the Montijo ménage. Paca was manageable, but Eugénie was a chatterbox, refused to be a demure little grandee, threw monumental fits whenever her will was contravened, and—to Miss Flowers the ultimate crime—was incapable of mastering the aspirate "aitch" in English.

Though far from an affectionate mother, the Countess was a dutiful one. (Recalled the Empress: "My mother wished to make everybody happy, but in her own way, not theirs!") Her daughters were fed and clothed and trotted about in keeping with their station in life. Unlike the complacent Paca, who was ever eager to please, Eugénie patronized and antagonized her coevals.

"The young girls of Madrid are so stupid that they speak only of their clothes, unless they talk about scandal to each other," she wrote to Stendhal in late-1840. "I don't talk to them, and when I visit, *adieu* is the only word they hear from me!"

Between Eugénie and her mother there raged a battle of wills that would endure as long as they lived under the same roof. ("You know my character is not in agreement with Mama's temperament." This in a letter to Paca after the latter's marriage.) While the Countess found Eugénie's tin ear deplorable, her antisocial behavior inexcusable, and her unwillingness to read a book inconceivable, she found the girl's penchant for riding bareback around the streets of Madrid quite beyond the pale. Horseback riding was one of Eugénie's great passions. (Many suspected it was her only passion.) There were occasional scenes, but it was impossible to best Eugénie in an argument; if push came to shove, she eschewed logic for hysteria. (Even when she was Empress, Eugénie's tantrums were marvels to behold.)

Relations between mother and daughter climaxed when a new

law was passed granting equal inheritance rights to all children. The Countess demanded of Eugénie that she surrender her rights in favor of Paca. Eugénie refused. Bitter scenes followed. Eugénie stood her ground. And that was that.

Over the long haul, it was a pyrrhic victory. The Countess managed to go through Eugénie's inheritance as well as her own.

Had Eugénie not wound up in the Tuileries, both she and her mother would have wound up in the poorhouse.

Other than willfulness toward her mother and impatience with her contemporaries (Paca excepted), what did Eugénie feel as she passed out of adolescence? We have no way of knowing. The Empress refused all offers to write her memoirs.

In her last years, though, she consented to being interviewed by the French diplomat Maurice Paléologue. Unfortunately, Paléologue was more concerned with flattering an old woman's vanity than provoking it. He did not press. Perhaps Paléologue knew that probing would be futile; the Empress's obstinacy was as legendary as the Empress herself. She did, of course, touch on her adolescent years. But it was touching, no more.

Following is a description of Eugénie by a contemporary who knew her in Madrid as she approached her seventeenth birthday:

> Her slender figure is well defined by a costly bodice, which enhances her beauty and elegance. . . . Her little feet are encased in red satin boots. Her head is crowned with broad golden plaits, interwoven with pearls and fresh flowers. Her clear brow shines with youth and beauty, and her gentle blue eyes sparkle from beneath the long lashes which almost conceal them. Her exquisitely formed nose, her mouth, fresher than a rosebud, the perfect oval of her face, the loveliness of which is only equaled by her graceful bearing, arouse the admiration of all. She is the recognized queen of beauty.

Among those whose admiration was aroused was the youngest son of ex-King Jerome Bonaparte of Westphalia.

By the time the once hoydenish Eugénie had blossomed into a seventeen-year-old unmitigated beauty, the once nasty thirteen-year-old Plon-Plon had blossomed into a twenty-one-year-old unmitigated horror. After gambling, wenching and intriguing his way through Württemberg and Tuscany (intrigue was to Plon-Plon what redemption was to Peter the Hermit), he decided on a sojourn in

Spain. Since he bore the magic name Bonaparte—he was, in fact, the only one of the entire clan who was a dead ringer for the dead Emperor—Plon-Plon was soon a regular at the Countess de Montijo's.

The Countess seems to have been enchanted with Plon-Plon, though he was "not the *right* Bonaparte." In February 1843, Mérimée wrote her: "Tell me what kind of a man is this Bonaparte who has come to play Don Juan among you?"* And in March: "Your little Napoleon seems to be a budding genius, according to what you tell me. But what is he after? That is the question."

He was after Eugénie.

Whether Plon-Plon wanted to marry her or merely seduce her is unascertainable and immaterial; Eugénie wanted no part of him. He moved on to greener, more oat-filled pastures. A decade later, Eugénie was to learn that hell hath no fury like a Plon-Plon scorned.

Eugénie fell in love only twice in her entire life, both times with men who did not love her. The first of her unrequited loves, when she was sixteen years old, was the twenty-year-old Don Jaime, eighth Duke of Berwick and fifteenth Duke of Alba, a distant cousin. The shy, taciturn Don Jaime, heir to Spain's greatest fortune, came calling at the Plazuela del Angel with regularity; presumably he meant to marry one of the two beautiful Montijo sisters but could not decide which one.

The Countess made the decision for him. Though she knew Eugénie was in love with Don Jaime, the Countess advised him that it was Paca who loved him and who was awaiting a proposal. Don Jaime proposed and was accepted.

As Paca prepared to become a bride of Alba, her heartbroken sister prepared to become a bride of Christ. Eleven days after her seventeenth birthday, Eugénie wrote Don Jaime:

> My very dear cousin,
>   You will find it strange that I write such a letter to you. But as all things on earth come to an end and my end is very near, I will tell you

---

* *Mérimée eventually got to know what kind of a man this Bonaparte was: "When I have an enemy, I send him to see Prince Napoleon when he is in a bad mood. Afterwards, I am avenged forever!"*

everything my heart contains. My character is wild, that is true, and I do not want to make any excuses for my actions, but, if anyone likes me, then I do everything for that person. But when I am treated like an ass that is beaten in public, then I cannot endure it. My blood boils, and then I no longer know what I am doing.

Many people think I am happy, but they are wrong. I am unhappy and am to blame. I should have lived centuries earlier. The ideas that are dearest to me are ridiculous. And I fear ridicule more than death. I love and I hate to excess. I do not know which is better, my love or my hate. I have a mixture of dreadful passions in me; all are strong. I fight against them, but I lose the struggle, and in the end my life will end miserably, lost in passion, virtue, and foolishness.

You will say that I am romantic and stupid. But you are good. You will excuse a poor girl who has lost everything that she loved and who was confronted with indifference everywhere, from her mother, from her sister, and I dare say it, even from the man she loved most, for whom she would have begged—you know this man!

Do not tell me I am mad. I ask you to have mercy upon me. You do not know what it means to love someone and to be disdained because of that love. God will give me courage. He gives it when it is needed, and He will give me courage to end my life in a convent. No one will ever know whether I have lived or not.

There are people who are born to be happy. You are one of them. May God allow it to be so always! My sister is good; she loves you. You will soon marry: your happiness will not lack anything. If you have children, then love them; remember they are your children, and never let one feel that you love the other more. Take my advice and be happy. Your unhappy sister Eugénie wishes it.

Do not attempt to change my plans. That is unnecessary. I will live outside this world. With God's help nothing is impossible. My decision is made; my heart is broken.

Your sister,
Eugénie

The letter is, of course, a rather embarrassing study in teenage pathos and bathos with, here and there, suggestions of Eugénie's religious orientation ("God will give me courage") and self-awareness ("I have a mixture of dreadful passions in me"), along with the hope that others may be spared what she suffered ("Never let one [child] feel that you love the other more"). Yet, reading it is like reading a Chekhov play: what is said is less trenchant, less thought-provoking than what is unsaid.

There is no evidence that her "very dear cousin" led Eugénie to believe he preferred her to Paca. Eugénie would have to have been aware that if anyone treated her like an ass that is beaten in public,

it was her mother; and no evidence exists that she condemned the
Countess for so shabbily, but so characteristically, interposing herself.

What, then, was the point of Eugénie's sending such a letter?
Was it the novelty of falling in love for the first time? Envy that her
more favored sister had gotten Spain's prize catch for a husband?
We have no way of knowing.

We do know, however, that Eugénie not only "forgave" Don
Jaime (the idea of having to "forgive" Paca probably never entered
her mind), she became almost an extension of his marriage. She
spent more time at the Palacio de Liria than in her mother's house
on the Plazuela del Angel. Her love for Paca, strong to begin with,
became almost obsessively possessive. When the sisters were separated by the Pyrenees, Eugénie bombarded Paca weekly with the
sort of solicitude usually found emanating from an overly protective
mother who never knows when to let go. When Paca died tragically
at an early age, the Empress transferred that love to Paca's children
and grandchildren (many of whom she outlived).

Becoming a nun was about the only avenue open at the time to
good Catholic maidens who felt incapable of surviving such secular
tragedies as unrequited love. (Bad Catholic maidens had the added
option of suicide.) If Eugénie believed she might take vows when
she threatened to, she was simply reacting out of a momentary
passion, in keeping with the attitudes of the times. Eugénie did not
know she was destined to sit on a throne, but she did know she was
not destined to sit in a cloister.

There is a legend that as Eugénie was about to take her vows, an
antediluvian nun stared at her vacantly a long moment, rattled
about convulsively, and then shrieked: "My daughter! Do not seek
for rest within our walls! You are destined to adorn a throne!"

The legend is as apocryphal as the words of a gypsy to the effect
that Eugénie's happiness would bloom with violets—the Bonaparte
family emblem—and that ever after she wore violets. (Actually, she
preferred jasmine and orange blossoms.)

Another of the more fanciful Eugénie legends: One day, when she
was about thirteen years old, Eugénie was sliding down the bannis-
ters of her mother's townhouse when the most extraordinary thing
happened. Miss Flowers opened the door, and Eugénie went flying
out of the house, landing unconscious in the gutter at the feet of still

another gypsy hag, who examined the child's hand and then pronounced gravely: "There is a fairy tale here! She will be a queen!"

The business about her sliding down the bannister is acceptable
(as is Miss Flowers's opening the door and letting her fly out into the
gutter). Eugénie was the champion bannister-slider-downer in all
Madrid; the habit—if that is what it can be called—stayed with her
until she married. But as for her having landed at the feet of an
omniscient gypsy, let it be noted that this and other Eugénie
legends originated in the fertile minds of a number of obliging courtiers.

Obliging to the Emperor Napoleon III, that is. Having concluded
he had no choice but to marry Eugénie and that his subjects had no
choice but to accept her as their Empress, Napoleon thought it
might make things a bit more palatable for those subjects if they
learned that it was Destiny that had raised her to the throne, and
not, as everybody believed—and rightly so—an admixture of lust
and spite on his part.

That the Empress did nothing to discourage the retailing of such
tales suggests that, given her superstitious nature, with time she
came to believe them herself.

Having decided not to become a nun, Eugénie decided to become
a young Phalansterian; which is to say, she leaped from unrequited
love into Utopian Socialism. It was the period when far-from-
practical solutions to the social problems of the day were enjoying a
great vogue.

None enjoyed greater vogue than the philosophy of François
Fourier, last of the great pre–Industrial Age Socialists, who
presumed society could better itself through supplanting government by the state with government by the individual. Instead of the
family household, society was to be subdivided into working and
living communes called *phalanstères*—large households composed
of people from all walks of life prepared to live in sylvan surroundings and mutual congeniality.

As a means of removing society's growing dependence on
machine and factory, handiwork was stressed. ("Each one of us
decided to learn a trade," recalled the Empress. "I chose wood
carving.") Also called for was an emphasis on the coeducation of
children, with a scrupulous denial of differentiating curricula. Girls

were taught to build houses; boys were taught to run them. ("Being youthful enthusiasts, we were blind to his ridiculous ideas.")

Eugénie's involvement with Fourierism was less than total. Instead of living on a *phalanstère*, she opted for the comforts of her mother's mansion; instead of sitting out in some sylvan glen carving wood, she threw herself with abandon into swimming, fencing, and turning up at bullfights decked out as an Andalusian gypsy. Still, delving into Fourierism touched in Eugénie an admirable chord: her concern for the rights of all peoples.

This was a time when, as heretofore indicated, many suppressed minorities were striving to achieve national integrity—the Poles and the Italians, for example; while others were striving to achieve dignity—many of Eugénie's own practically starving co-nationals, for example. The Countess de Montijo now had something else with which to find fault. Her congenitally loquacious, argumentative and highly opinionated daughter was turning her *salon* into a one-woman debating society, holding forth, at length, on the problems of the day and the progressive theories then abounding—many of them absurdly unrealistic—for the resolution of those problems.

Compounding the Countess's irritation was Eugénie's lack of haste in finding a husband. The most eligible bachelors in all of Spain were summoned to the Plazuela del Angel for Eugénie's consideration. She preferred to talk about "poor Poland" and "poor Italy" rather than about the advantages of connubial bliss. The suitors—and they were legion—found it all perplexing.

Mérimée expressed the hope that "Eugénie will let herself be influenced by her sister's example." Alluding to her bareback rides through the streets of Madrid (which always sent the Countess in search of her smelling salts), Mérimée allowed: "What I fear for Eugénie are penniless lieutenants in the hussars with fine moustaches and brilliant uniforms. I hope to see her settling down, before she has begun the first chapter of a romance of that sort!" He added, with a touch of his characteristic whimsy: "Too bad Eugénie is not a boy!" And when no word was forthcoming of any marriage, Mérimée sarcastically wrote of "the caprices of the señorita."

Those "caprices" were causing the señorita's mother untold agonies of embarrassment. Eugénie had by now become the scandal of Madrid. Having decided that she was an emancipated woman, Eugénie wanted to be sure everyone else knew it. She rode at night, at high gallop, in the mountains; so far as the Countess was concerned, only God knew what her virginal daughter was doing amongst those filthy gypsies. (Actually, nothing that could cause undue alarm; Eugénie enjoyed listening to their music, watching them dance, and having her palm read.) She did not particularly care whom she hurt with her many impertinent, sometimes downright insulting remarks.

The mothers of Eugénie's rejected suitors were scandalized; ere long, everyone was openly conjecturing as to why the beautiful young Señorita de Montijo was turning down one marriage offer after another. Had she resolved to become, God forbid, one of those *lionnes*—those outrageous women with whom George Sand, the leading *lionne* of the century, was peopling her outrageous novels? Was Eugénie de Montijo bent on emulating those scandalous creatures from the uppermost strata of society who openly disdained social conventions, cared not a fig for their personal appearance, and indulged in such unwomanly pursuits as hunting, swearing, fornicating, affecting men's clothes, smoking cigars, and otherwise making sure everyone knew how contemptuous they were of their backgrounds?

She was.

The Countess decided the time had come to take drastic action. She dragged Eugénie off to Pau in the Pyrenees, in hopes that Eugénie would find at least *one* man who might interest her among the many eligible suitors who frequented that fashionable spa.

Eugénie did not find a prospective suitor to her taste.

She found, instead, a *plutôt souffréteuse* charmer named Madame Gordon, who sang contralto.

The dedicated diva had been spending the five years since Prince Louis Bonaparte's Boulogne fiasco making the rounds of Europe's watering holes soliciting support for "the cause that is to me so noble, so great and holy that it is my religion, a religion of which I shall always be a faithful and devout disciple!" The pickings were slim. Not only was the Napoleonic "cause" a forgotten one, save among the few diehards like Madame Gordon who were not behind lock and key, so was the man she always referred to as "my Prince."

Eugénie was intrigued. Was the Prince *really* no more than the buffoon everyone made him out to be? Or was he in fact a man willing to suffer ignominy, not to mention perpetual immurement, for the ideals of Bonapartism, the ideals with which her beloved father and dear "Monsieur Beyle" had sought to imbue her as a child?

No, Madame Gordon assured her, the return of the Emperor's ashes was not the end of the legend; it was the beginning of the resurrection. Yes, Madame Gordon assured her, when the Prince ascended the throne of France—and make no mistake about it, he would do just that—the ideal world those dreadful Allies had kept the first Napoleon from creating would be realized.

As a matter of fact, Madame Gordon informed her new friend, she was heading north in a few days to visit the imprisoned Prince. Would Mademoiselle de Montijo care to come along?

Eugénie was curious. Could it be arranged?

Of course; the Prince entertained visitors regularly.

Well, why not, thought Eugénie; it was worth the journey to satisfy her curiosity.

Doña Manuela had reservations, not the least of which was an understandable unwillingness to let her quite (in fact *too*) liberated daughter go off with the likes of Madame Gordon. Eugénie persevered. The Countess agreed. She would go along and have a look for herself. If nothing else, the trip would be worth an evening's conversation back in her Madrid drawing room.

Madame Gordon rushed off to make the necessary arrangements—

—and the Countess rushed her daughter back to Madrid. General Ramon Narvaéz was now in firm command as Teniente-General of the Realm (a euphemism for dictator), and Narvaéz was one of the Countess's intimates. (Just how intimate must be left to speculation.) A number of her whimsical friends had suggested the Countess should be playing a major role in the running of the Spanish government. The Countess saw the wisdom of such a suggestion.

While the Countess maneuvered for a political appointment from the depths of her drawing room, Eugénie resumed an active life. She attended the balls and hunts organized by Paca and Don Jaime, worried about "poor Poland" and "poor Italy," told people exactly what was on her mind, persisted in upstaging her mother in the latter's *salon*, rode bareback about Madrid and up into the mountains, and appeared at bullfights turned out as a high-class *puta*. (One contemporary has recorded that "her dainty hand [was] armed with a riding whip instead of a fan, for she generally [arrived] at the bullring on a wild Andalusian horse, and in her belt she [carried] a sharp-pointed dagger.")

The Countess progressed from wanting Eugénie to marry to demanding that she marry. Eugénie was now past twenty, the age at which most of her female contemporaries were already commencing their second pregnancies—as the Countess never failed to remind her.

The question now obtrudes: Did Eugénie *want* to marry? Who knows? Marriage offered escape from her mother; Eugénie was not so liberated a woman that she was prepared to go off and live by herself; indeed, her ideas about being a true *lionne* seemed to be abating, along with her fascination with Fourierism.

Eugénie had plenty of opportunities to marry. Eligible, qualified prospective suitors abounded. Eugénie did not discourage such attention; in fact, she thrived on it. She flirted, she beguiled; she brazenly flaunted her sexuality. She enjoyed playing the siren. But, she always backed off whenever any man showed signs of taking her as seriously as she took herself.

Eugénie was, as they say in today's more fashionable gutters, a "C-T." Did she behave this way only as a means of buying time till the right man came along? Or did she in fact hope to avoid marriage? Or fear marriage?

Mérimée wrote the frantic Countess that perhaps an Englishman might be the answer. After all, the Countess was an Anglophile; British diplomats and business agents at Madrid were *ex officio* members of her inner circle; her drawing room was practically an extension of the British Embassy (much to the irritation of the Spanish government).*

The Countess thought Mérimée's advice had merit. When Ferdinand Huddleston arrived in Madrid on a business trip, the Countess invited him into her home for the duration of his visit. Huddleston was very wealthy, very Roman Catholic, and very single. He

---

* *From the* London Times: *"To be invited to the Countess de Montijo's* tertulias, *in which, it is noticed, the English are made especially welcome, is considered a sort of passport to the best society in Madrid."*

was also very shy. He fell in love with Eugénie. But instead of declaring his intentions to the object of his infatuation, he discussed them with—Madame Gordon.

The diva had come to report on her recent visit with "my Prince." Eugénie asked her to stay on as a houseguest, less to discuss the Prince than to discuss Madame Gordon. (Eugénie was one of those inherently prudish women who are fascinated with their less prudish sisters; even as Empress, she would admit to her inner circle a few of the Second Empire ladies who were in a position to keep her well tuned in on the latest scandal simply because they were helping to create that scandal.) Madame Gordon did not have to be asked twice. Her voice was practically gone, along with what was left of her reputation; she was, to put it mercifully, "between engagements."

She led Huddleston to believe that of all Eugénie's suitors, he was far and away the frontrunner. A few weeks after arriving in Madrid, Huddleston departed on business. Whereupon—from a safe distance—he sent Eugénie an impassioned declaration of love and a proposal of marriage. Eugénie discussed the proposal with Madame Gordon, who then wrote Huddleston:

> She has told me that she would rather be hanged than marry an Englishman. She did not bind me to secrecy when she told me this. You are frankly in love—*eh bien!* frankly I tell you that you have not one single chance of success, and you had better realize that I am right and that my advice is good. If you want to bury yourself, that is your affair, there are forms of suffering which are not without their charms and yours is no doubt of that kind. *Adieu, monsieur.* I wish you luck!

Eugénie, on the other hand, wrote more delicately:

> As a *friend* [italics in the original] I shall always be happy to see you. You tell me that I am undecided, and you would wait for me to make up my mind. But I feel too much friendship for you to raise your hopes which I could never fulfill. At the risk of losing your friendship I prefer to act loyally towards you. I hope nevertheless to see you here again, if not at present, then later on. You know that you will always find in me a friend.

Was Madame Gordon's brutal interjection part and parcel of some cruel game on Eugénie's part? Or had poor Huddleston turned down some commitment to the contralto's "cause," thus causing her to involve herself out of pique, with Eugénie none the wiser? (Or had he, in fact, turned down Madame Gordon?) We have no way of knowing. We do know, though, that the Countess threw the contralto out of her house bodily when Miss Flowers, who had been pushing for Eugénie's marriage to a compatriot, informed her of the letter. Too, we know that Eugénie had not seen the last of Huddleston. He was shy, but he was also persevering.

Shortly thereafter, the Countess received what she had been angling for from Narvaéz. In October 1847, she was named *Camarera Mayor* to Queen Isabella. It was the highest political appointment in the royal household. The Countess felt she deserved nothing less. With her into that bastion of intrigue, delation and perversity went Eugénie, whom Narvaéz had named one of the Queen's maids-of-honor.

"So you have already become *Camarera Mayor*, and you are happy!" wrote Mérimée by way of congratulations. "That is sufficient to satisfy me. You can make the post profitable—that is enough! But you may say what you like, Countess, you were created for a restless life; and it would be ridiculous to wish Caesar a peaceful existence as second citizen in Rome!"

There is no doubt the Countess hoped to make the post profitable, nor is there much doubt she would have succeeded.

Unfortunately, she did not last long enough in the post to exploit the possibilities. She became the innocent victim of a wily young Italian adventurer who stole first her heart and then her jewels. Narvaéz withdrew his influence, and the two Montijos were thrown out of Court.

And then came Eugénie's disastrous love affair with Don Pepe Alcañisez.

Whether she really loved him or merely imagined herself to be in love with him, the fact remains that the affair was the emotional climacteric of Eugénie's adult life. The irony of it all is that she was an innocent victim. Don Pepe was the only suitor Eugénie never coquetted or "teased." Moralists might say Eugénie got only what she deserved.

Certainly all the Madrilene aristocrats whose sons had thrown themselves at Eugénie were saying it.

Pepe—the Marquis de Alcañisez and Duke de Sesto—was titled, wealthy, socially connected, handsome, witty, politically ambitious, Roman Catholic, and single. In sum, he possessed every quality the Countess sought in a son-in-law; one can well imagine her ecstasy when Eugénie reciprocated this bargain's advances. Ere long, following a twice-daily exchange of love letters and many morning serenades beneath her window, Eugénie prepared her trousseau while the Countess prepared to post the banns.

Then it was learned that Don Pepe was merely using Eugénie as an entrée into the Palacio de Liria. It was Paca he really loved. Don Pepe subscribed to the tried-and-true gambit practiced by cavalry officers of yore: When billeted in a house where there are two sisters and you want one, start courting the other!

Eugénie swallowed poison.

For hours she hovered between this world and the next, refusing the agonized request of her mother and sister that she swallow the antidote. In desperation, the Countess had Don Pepe brought into the bedchamber. That gallant bent over and whispered into the dying girl's ear, his voice fairly breaking with understandable emotion: "Eugénie! Where are my [love] letters?"

Whereupon Eugénie, her face contorting into a mask of abject contempt, grabbed the antidote, bolted it down, and screamed at Don Pepe: "You are like the spear of Achilles! You heal the wounds you make!"

A few weeks later, she and the Countess left for Paris.

Eugénie's attitude toward men is worth noting here; it may have derived from her experience with Don Pepe. Toward the end of her life, when a friend sought to explain away the collapse of a marriage between mutual friends with the femininely chauvinistic excuse: "After all, Your Majesty, men are worth very little," the Empress retorted with vigor: "Since we are alone, I will tell you: they are worth *nothing!*"

The Countess and Eugénie embarked on a years-long journey along what Mérimée called facetiously "the grand route": Paris, the fashionable German resorts along the Rhine, London "for the season," back to Spain, on again to Paris, etc., etc., all interspersed with stops in the Pyrenees "to take the waters."

Wherever they went, the two aroused comment: the vulgar mother carting her beautiful unmarried daughter around Europe in hopes of nabbing for her a proper, and properly wealthy, husband; the haughty daughter enjoying the sight of men fairly groveling at her feet. To many, they were a pair of out-and-out adventurers; to many, they were a pair of well-upholstered grotesques. To many, they were a bit of both.

Base of operations, as it were, was a rented apartment at 12 Place Vendôme in Paris, whither they headed directly upon leaving Madrid. Their arrival came on the heels of the "February Revolution" that brought down the Orléans monarchy. Mérimée was not on hand to greet his Spanish friends, having decided to exile himself until the dust settled ("we now have a republic without any enthusiasm").

The Countess renewed her acquaintance with the few old friends who had remained on in Paris in anticipation of an Orléanist restoration. Wrote Eugénie sarcastically to Paca: "Mama loves witty conversation with ladies of the *ancien régime*, which is so chic!"

To one of those ladies of the *ancien régime*, Mérimée wrote: "I do not know if Madame de Montijo is still pretty; she was so in my time. She was virtuous as well. It is possible that she has lost these two qualities."

Mérimée's correspondent wrote back that Madame de Montijo had indeed lost those two qualities.

In her letters to Paca dating from this period, Eugénie makes no mention whatsoever of the great events that were occurring in France, other than to complain that "the revolution left nothing more for Palmyre." Madame Palmyre was Paris's most fashionable dressmaker.

A sense of fatalism begins to sneak into Eugénie's letters to Paca dating from this period: "I shall always think back longingly to the times we spent in Paris with each other. But we must forget the past. What is certain is that it all really is past." And: "You will have a son. A fortuneteller told me so. . . . Probably my ability to have faith is so strong that I must express it in these things, for so much that I once believed has not come true." (Within the year, Paca had a son.)

As they moved along "the grand route," the Countess pushed prospective suitors toward Eugénie. Strangers found it all rather distressing: that aggressive woman—who looked as if she applied her makeup with a trowel instead of a brush—being much too sociable with male strangers; that beautiful daughter of hers—well past the marrying age—allowing young men to chase after her like bees after honey.

There was a reunion with Huddleston in London. Eugénie agreed to ride to hounds with him, but she would not ride to the altar with him. The Countess was furious. Huddleston was "willing to wait."

When Eugénie and the Countess returned to Paris late in 1848, a new social circus was in town, its impresario the aforementioned Princess Mathilde Bonaparte. Mérimée led his Spanish friends into the center ring.

Mathilde had been married off by her father to Prince Anatole Demidoff, a Russian millionaire whose idea of amusement was to have one of his mistresses dragged by wild horses through the streets of St. Petersburg. "I am happy beyond belief," confided Mathilde at the time to her diary; "I cannot tell you with what confidence I regard the future."* That confidence was shattered on her honeymoon. Recalled by Tsar Nicholas for assaulting the Russian ambassador to Rome, Demidoff broke the monotony of the six-week journey to St. Petersburg by forcing Mathilde to drive through raging blizzards with the top of the carriage down; he was anxious to observe the effects of sub-zero weather on a beautiful woman.

---

* *Her father Jerome was even happier: he did not have to fork over Mathilde's 290,000-franc dowry, which was nonexistent; Demidoff agreed to settle 200,000 francs per annum on Mathilde, twenty-five percent of which was set aside for her father; and Demidoff paid not only for the bride's trousseau but for her father's trousseau as well. When Demidoff wondered what to give Mathilde as a wedding gift, Jerome sold him a magnificent pearl collar which his brother the Emperor had given to Catherine of Württemberg and which Jerome had sold to, and stolen back from, his current wife, a wealthy Italian widow whose fortune he was now in the throes of plowing through.*

After a few years of public humiliation and private weekly whippings by Demidoff, Mathilde ran off to Russia and begged her autocratic kinsman to intercede. Nicholas decreed a formal separation and a settlement for Mathilde that was identical to her marriage settlement. Mathilde returned to Paris—where she was permitted to reside, as were Jerome and Plon-Plon, despite the proscription on Bonapartes that was still in force—took as her lover the handsome young sculptor Count Nieuwerkerque, and was soon presiding over the most glittering *salon* in Western Europe.

"I am much upset today," wrote Eugénie to Paca. "I have to go with Mama to see Princess Mathilde, and I do not know anyone there. . . . I have just come back from the party. My premonition was correct. No one spoke to me. There were two reasons: first I am not married, and I am a stranger."

If no one spoke to Eugénie at Princess Mathilde's, it was hardly for those two reasons. Being unmarried was practically a ticket of admission to Princess Mathilde's ever-widening circle; she loved to arrange matches between her unmarried friends almost as much as she loved to arrange assignations between her married ones. As for being "a stranger": Parisian aristocrats have never cultivated the charming penchant their fellow-Frenchmen have for wishing that all foreigners would stay home and send their money.

One attended Princess Mathilde's Thursday Evenings to be witty, to partake of the festivities; the Princess, like all other great hostesses, expected her guests to pull their own weight. Those guests who merely stood against the wall were allowed to fade into it. Eugénie could harangue a drawing room full of people she knew, but could not function in a drawing room full of strangers.

Even as Empress, she was comfortable in large crowds only when she was the center of attraction.

The Countess was beginning to panic. She was spending a small fortune parading her daughter (and herself) along "the grand route." And a total ignorance of, or perhaps a total disinclination toward, fiscal conservatism was one trait—one of the very few—the two travelers had in common. In desperation, the Countess began to refer to, point out and otherwise exhibit Eugénie as if the poor girl were a prize filly at a stock auction. There is no evidence that the poor girl rebelled at this; nowhere in her letters to Paca does she complain about their mother's rather vulgar routine.

"Paris talks of nothing but Eugénie's beauty," the Countess wrote to Paca. "We went to the opera the other evening. . . . All eyes were turned toward our box, and everybody wanted to know who the pretty lady was. Next day, they talked about her more than the opera, and she has become the fashion of the day."

The Countess got carried away with herself here. Eugénie was not the only beauty in Paris. And if "they" talked about anything the next day, it was the same thing "they" talked about every other day: In what direction was Prince-President Bonaparte taking himself and the rest of the country?

There were, of course, quite a few who were talking about Eugénie, but these already knew who the pretty lady was. According to Madame de la Ferronnays, one of the leading dragons of the day: "Mademoiselle de Montijo's position in Paris is distinctly doubtful. Her free manners, which one often finds in women of the South [i.e., south of the Pyrenees], coupled with a certain lack of social support, are the cause of her not being admitted into the best society. She falls into that category of foreigners who are entertained by men, but who are avoided by the women of the *grand monde*."

When, during their courtship, Napoleon III would mention some of the tales in circulation about her—one of her constant escorts about town was the heir of the Rothschild fortune—Eugénie was able to reply in all honesty: "I have been in love with others, but I have always remained Mademoiselle de Montijo!" Regardless of what people were implying, and in some cases saying outright, Eugénie's conduct with some of the gayer Parisian blades was nothing more than extravagance at best, imprudence at worst.

It was also baffling.

In letters to Paca dating from the period directly prior to her marriage, Eugénie took to comparing herself disadvantageously, and rather self-pityingly, with girls her own age (she was now past her mid-twenties) who were already married. She was even beginning to feel embarrassed about the whole thing in the eyes of society.

Chapter 5
Louis-Napoleon:
1840–1851

The Pretender was sent to Ham, a decrepit thirteenth-century fortress that stood on low ground, surrounded by marshes, and was eternally at the mercy of overhanging cold mists. Ever afterward he referred to it as the "University of Ham," claiming to have been "graduated from there with honors."

He was virile and healthy when he began his confinement. When he ended it, he was physically broken; weak, wan, emaciated, rheumatic, he walked with the stoop of a man twice his age. Imprisonment also had a deleterious effect on his character: he became more inward, more withdrawn.

Though watched constantly by his jailers, he was allowed great freedom within the limits of the fortress proper. The loyal valet Thélin, after serving his own two-year sentence, was permitted to come and go; he brought in clothes, bed linens (embossed with the Imperial "N" and golden bees that were the Bonaparte logo), delicacies to ease the monotony of prison fare, and memorabilia with which Louis lined the walls of his two-room suite (miniatures of the Emperor, Hortense and Josephine).

He was permitted to correspond with and receive friends, given a small plot in which to grow flowers and a small laboratory in which to conduct experiments, allowed to ride occasionally around the compound on horseback, and permitted to practice his marksmanship in a long gallery.

He was even allowed the companionship of Alexandrine-Eléonore Vergeot, known as *La Belle Sabotierre* ("the Beautiful Clog-

Dancer"), whose father had had her appointed "bedmaker to State Prisoner No. 1." Shortly after she started making the Prince's bed, she started sharing it. The Prince gave her "lessons in orthography and grammar." She gave the Prince two sons.*

Still, it all added up to enforced stagnation—in the most stagnant of places—for a hyperactive thirty-two-year-old whose political ambition was both monumental and obsessive. Having gone through so much tribulation and humiliation to bring his name before the public, Louis now stood in danger of being completely forgotten by the public. He spent his first few months at Ham in an understandable state of severe depression. This peaked on December 15, when the Emperor's ashes were received by King Louis-Philippe amidst the most impressive ceremonies in French history since the wedding of Henri IV to Marie de Medici.

Louis published a rhetorical address to the dead Emperor that castigated those who honored him with words while thanking God he was dead—and thanking God that the living heir was safely immured in perpetuity. It had no impact on public opinion. The year then ending had seen the Napoleonic legend reach its zenith—and Bonapartism as a political reality reach its nadir. Depression soon gave way to resignation on Louis's part.

With the coming of spring, his spirits rose, thanks to such loyal friends as Hortense Cornu, who wrote regularly and visited whenever possible. Louis knew how fickle the French were. They had accepted three dynasties and four sovereigns since they rose in 1789 to abolish monarchy. Who—and in what guise—would follow the inevitable fall of the Orléans Bourbons? France must be made to realize that the Napoleonic heir was merely in his prison, not in his

---

* *Louis recognized and ennobled both boys when he became Emperor. Alexandre-Louis-Eugène (1843–1910), Count d'Orx, served in the diplomatic corps; Alexandre-Louis-Ernest (1845–82), Count de Labenne, was an official in the Inland Revenue Service. Their mother eventually married Pierre Buré, Treasurer-General to the Crown, at which time she legitimized her bastards by Louis-Napoleon along with one by Pierre. Apparently the future Emperor was a better student at the "University of Ham" than a pedagogue. When the beautiful Alexandrine-Eléonore danced her last clog in 1886, she was still deficient in grammar and deplorable at spelling.*

grave. Bonapartism may have reached its nadir as a political reality, but nadir is a far cry from nullity.

Louis now plunged into, in his own words, "thirty-six thousand things at a time." He planted flowers, entertained visitors, corresponded with friends, conducted experiments under the guidance of a friendly local chemist, drew up plans for a minor improvement in French musketry, sketched maps for a trans-isthmian canal across Nicaragua, and churned out a series of published articles on a curious variety of subjects: the sugar-beet industry, production of electric currents, artillery, constitutionalism, economics, etc.

And, of course, there was the propaganda.

After a few forgettable efforts at glorifying the dead Emperor and cashing in on his charisma, Louis concluded that it would take more than the Napoleonic legend to put him on the throne of France. No more must he try to tell the public what Napoleon Bonaparte had hoped to accomplish. Now he must let the public in on what *he* hoped to accomplish.

Instead of trying to sell the French on their late Emperor, he must try to sell the French on their *next* Emperor.

By far his most effective piece was *Extinction du paupérisme*, a neither subtle nor profound (nor really well thought out) exercise in economics, but a superb exercise in self-promotion. In it he advocated the abolition of unemployment—one of France's most pressing chronic conditions—by the transfer of the surplus labor force in the textile industry to semimilitary agricultural colonies, which would be formed to develop the nation's underdeveloped areas. The plan was simplistic to a fault, and when it appeared in the Paris press it was shot full of holes by more seasoned economists.

But the masses—themselves simplistic when it came to solving their own complex problems—thought they saw a champion in the until-now-forgotten prisoner at Ham. This new interest led to the publication of the Pretender's previous works. Members of the political opposition began to correspond with him. A few even came by for chocolate and cookies.

Louis had assumed amnesty would be forthcoming following the death or deposition of King Louis-Philippe. But the old monarch was still hanging on, and Louis's patience was running out; more so in light of the fact that people were now beginning to remember he was still alive. There was just so far he could go, sitting in a prison for life churning out pamphlets.

In April 1845, Louis prevailed upon his old friend Lord Malmesbury to seek the British government's intervention in his behalf. A month later, the French government suggested a release might be considered—provided Louis formally pledged to renounce all claims to the throne and, furthermore, abstain from any anti-government activities forevermore. Louis refused. It is a mark of the man that he did not simply sign the pledge and then renege on it. In January 1846, he appealed directly to the King, who replied that amnesty might be considered, provided the Prince would sign a renunciation of his claim to the throne and request official pardon for his "offenses" at Strasbourg and Boulogne. Louis refused: "I consider such a course unworthy of me." He found it not "consistent with my honor."

He did manage to find escape consistent with his honor, though.

The escape plan, which took four months to work out, had about it the *opéra-bouffe* quality of his Strasbourg and Boulogne escapades. Its financing alone was worthy of the best of Offenbach. The Duke of Cumberland, a rather lovable lunatic who had been running about Europe for years amassing a tidy fortune and trying to establish his untenable claim to the nonexistent throne of Lithuania, was approached by intermediaries. In return for a sum of money, the Prince would recognize the Duke's claim when he himself gained the throne of France.

Repairs were being made at Ham; soon laborers were passing in and out. They all looked alike, as French laborers will. The valet Thélin easily smuggled in a workman's outfit and made the getaway arrangements (forged passports, a hired carriage, and the like). On the morning of May 25, Louis shaved his moustache, dyed his naturally pale face to give it a ruddy complexion, donned a black wig and his workman's disguise (coarse shirt, blue blouse, blue trousers with an apron, and a pair of sabots over his boots), stuck a pipe in his mouth, picked up a large plank of wood, and calmly walked out of Ham. Twenty-four hours later, following a train journey to Ostend, whence he and Thélin crossed over to England, the "Count d'Arenenberg and valet" checked into the Brunswick Hotel on Jermyn Street just off Piccadilly Circus.

For Prince Louis-Napoleon Bonaparte, perpetuity had lasted just five months short of six years.

He dined that first evening at Lady Blessington's, where all the regulars were appalled at the weight he had lost while in prison.

Louis had lost more than weight; he had lost—rather, shed—the illusion that his Imperial goal could ever be realized through a military *putsch*. He would not attempt to incite the people to follow him any more. He would wait for the people to invite him to lead them.

After reassuring the British and French governments that his intentions were peaceful, Louis sought permission to visit his ailing father in Florence. Permission was denied. On July 25, the ex-King of Holland died of a cerebral hemorrhage. (Fittingly, he was alone in a dark chamber when the end came.) By the terms of his will, Louis was left 1,200,000 francs in cash, the domain of Civitanova, valued at 642,000 francs, and the residue of the estate after other bequests had been settled.

The inheritance did nothing to relieve Louis's chronic financial embarrassment. There were loans to be paid off. There were those pensionary obligations he had inherited from Hortense. There was a magnificent new house he took on King Street, which meant furnishings, a liveried staff of servants, and such necessities as a team of horses to drag that magnificent cabriolet bearing the Imperial crest. There was the support of all those loyalists who joined him in London (Persigny, for one, liked to dress and dine well), the cost of publishing his underground newspapers in Paris, and the cost of maintaining contact with his agents there and otherwise keeping his name before the public. The people of France could hardly call on the Pretender to lead them if they had no idea where he was.

And then there were his mistresses—of whom the most costly was the great French tragedienne Rachel. Her lovers were predominantly royal, and Rachel was of the firm conviction that any woman who sleeps with a prince deserves to be treated like a queen. The two began their liaison shortly after Louis's return to England, when Rachel crossed the Channel with the Comédie-Française for a tour of London and the provinces.

The following summer, when Rachel returned to tour Scotland, Louis journeyed north to be with her. He took along Plon-Plon, whom he had named his heir and who was over on a visit. One night Louis fell asleep, only to awaken and spot, out of half-closed eyes, his mistress and his cousin in a calisthenic embrace. With consummate tact, Louis shut his eyes, pretended to sleep through the night (and through the racket), and took the next train back to London. He never mentioned what he had seen, but Plon-Plon got the message; he wisely waited a few years for Rachel and the Emperor to tire of each other before making her his mistress.*

Louis was not always on the giving end throughout his two-year wait in England. He had the good fortune to be on the receiving end of a relationship with a mistress whose bank account was as smashing as her figure. She was born Elizabeth Ann Haryett in England, she died the Countess de Beauregard in France, and she is known to history as Miss Howard (in France she took the more dignified "Madame").

Miss Howard merits our attention because it was she who bankrolled Louis's return to France and helped to finance the *coup d'état* that brought him to power. All told, she spent, in terms of today's purchasing power, upwards of five million dollars on the man whom she believed would make her an empress.

By the time she entered Prince Louis's life—a month after his escape from Ham—this daughter of an impecunious Brighton bootmaker had surrendered her virginity to, and taken her name from, a sleazy racehorse jockey, whose disappearance from her life coincided, more or less, with her thirteenth birthday; gone through a stage career (and a half-dozen fellow-thespians) by the age of fifteen; and worked her way in and out of some of the most illustrious beds south of the Humber.

She was at that time the mistress of an enormously wealthy major, by whom she had borne a son (her delicacy demanded that she pass it off as her baby brother). Unable to marry her—there

---

* *When, after Louis's death, Eugénie was told of the Scottish incident, she replied with a smirk: "Just like him, wasn't it!" It always irked the Empress that the Emperor avoided confrontations.*

was an invalid wife in the picture—the major established his fair Elizabeth in a magnificent mansion in St. John's Wood, with a magnificent bank account in her name at Baring's.

Miss Howard and Prince Louis met—where else?—in Lady Blessington's drawing room. It was lust at first sight. One night, Miss Howard confessed that she had been living with the major since she was eighteen. The Prince forgave her. Later that night—rather, early the next morning—Miss Howard awakened the Prince to make another confession. She admitted to having a bastard son. The Prince took her in his arms and admitted he also had a bastard son. Two, as a matter of fact. "The fruits of my captivity," he murmured into her ear. A day later, Miss Howard told the major she did not love him; she was in love with Prince Louis-Napoleon. The news came as no surprise to the major; he took it quite well.

London society was about equally divided on the question: What does the physically appealing Miss Howard see in the physically appalling Prince Louis? Half felt that Miss Howard was just out for marriage and respectability; the other half, that Miss Howard was just out of her mind. Whatever she was out for, Miss Howard bought herself a decade of expensive aggravation.

For the first—and last—time in his life, Louis began to lose faith in himself and his mission. It was now more than a year since he had decided to wait for the people of France to summon him. He began to wonder if perhaps he was not waiting in vain.

King Louis-Philippe could not last much longer, but four of his sons were still alive; the Orléanist succession was secure. Louis was in his fortieth year. He had suffered humiliation and exile. Too, his health was broken; frequent trips to Clifton and Bath had failed to alleviate his anemia, his rheumatism, his hyperesthesia.

"Nothing can be done at the moment," he wrote Plon-Plon. "The nation is asleep, and will remain asleep for a long time. Whatever may be said . . . I have failed hopelessly. I can't and won't try again. . . ."

He seriously entertained the idea of marriage; and he had always said he would never marry until he came to the throne. To Plon-Plon he wrote of the sadness he felt at the realization of how few

Bonapartes there were left to carry on the family name: "It is sad to think that neither you nor I have any [legitimate] children. There will be no Bonapartes left but the bad branch of Lucien. So I should be very glad to marry. But there hasn't been a word from Dresden; she must be an extraordinary woman!"

That "extraordinary woman" has never been identified. Others have, though. There was the beautiful Miss Seymour; but she lost her heart to another. There was Angela Burdett, recent inheritor of the Coutts banking fortune; but a precondition of that inheritance was that she marry an Englishman. There was the half-Spanish beauty, Miss Emily Rowles. Miss Rowles was fond of the Prince; she had sent him parcels while he was at Ham. The Prince began to envision a future with Miss Rowles.

Her father owned a lovely house called Camden Place, at Chislehurst in Kent, and when Louis first visited there he saw it as an ideal setting in which to play out the life he envisaged for himself as a gentleman farmer. But Miss Rowles lost her heart to an embezzler.

On top of the news that Miss Rowles would not have Prince Louis came news that the French people might.

Ironically, Louis would live at Camden Place, Chislehurst, Kent; in fact, he would die there—twenty-five years after he first visited it.

"In God's name," cried Tocqueville, "change the spirit of the [Orléans] government; for, I repeat, that spirit will lead you into an abyss!"

That spirit began its march to the abyss on a cloudy morning in February 1848, when a small crowd gathered outside the Madeleine and began to chant "Reform!" Their ranks inflated after a march to the Place de la Concorde, they continued on across the Seine and started to lob a few stones toward the Chamber of Deputies—which was not sitting at the time.

It started to rain, and the crowd was easily dispersed. Louis-Philippe was assured by his reactionary Prime Minister, Guizot, that the whole business was at an end; the rabble of Paris had returned to their hovels.

They had returned to their hovels to collect their hammers and nails. By the next morning the barricades were up.

Guizot called out the National Guard; nine of the twelve battalions refused to take orders from him. The King dismissed Guizot, and there the affair might have ended—but for an accidental clash in the Boulevard des Capucines between a few nervous National Guardsmen and a small band of agitators. The King called out the regular army—which, fearing wholesale bloodshed, backed off. Seeking his way out of this latest muddle, the King asked Thiers, his leading political antagonist, to form a government. Reform was promised.

It was too late for promises; it has always been easier to fill the streets of Paris than to empty them. As the mobs, now out for blood, began to storm the Tuileries, the King abdicated, removed his wig, picked up his umbrella, and led his Queen out through the garden, where they got into a taxi and headed for the Channel coast and exile in England.

"Worse, worse than Charles X," muttered the deposed Orléanist; "a hundred times worse than Charles X." It was. Charles X had had time to make a grand exit; and he had kept his wig to the end.

In the Chamber of Deputies, Alphonse Marie Lamartine proclaimed France a republic, promising that the new state would be "pure, holy, immortal, popular and peaceful." Beyond that, the poet-politician hadn't a clue what to do with it. Neither, for that matter, did the professional politicians who rallied to his side.

Prince Louis-Napoleon Bonaparte—who left London so fast on hearing the news of the revolution that he did not bother to pack a trunk—would know what to do with that republic.

By the time Louis reached Paris on February 25, the Provisional Government was being set up and the barricades were being dismantled.* His first act was to dispatch Persigny with a letter of reassurance to the Provisional Government: "I hurry from exile to place myself under the banner of the newly proclaimed Republic. Having no ambition but to serve my country, I hasten to report my

---

* When, as Emperor, he gave Baron Haussmann carte blanche to rebuild Paris, Louis's first order was that the city be crisscrossed with wide, wide boulevards through which militiamen might move with dispatch and which could not be barricaded in a hurry.

arrival . . . and to assure [the provos] of my devotion to the cause they represent."

The provos took due note of the Prince's arrival and ordered him out of France within twenty-four hours. They feared, with good cause, that he would be less an ally than a rival in their quest for popular support. Persigny, Lieutenant Laity, Colonel Vaudrey and Madame Gordon urged him to launch another *putsch*.

Sensibly, he returned to London—leaving behind a second letter to be delivered to the Hôtel de Ville: "You think that my presence in Paris at this moment is embarrassing; I therefore withdraw for the time being. You must take this sacrifice as a sign of the purity of my intentions, and of my patriotism."

With cunning and patience, Louis sat on the other side of the Channel for seven months, directing his Paris agents in a flood of Bonapartist propaganda, all aimed at cowing his political opposition by appealing directly to the people. He knew the time would come when disillusionment with the results of this latest revolution would register with the very masses who had brought it about.

Louis knew something else: His propagandistic efforts had to be keyed to the mood of the times. Revolution was sweeping Europe; some monarchies were falling, others were tottering. In France the Provisional Government was faced with an inflamed proletariat and an indifferent bourgeoisie. What was needed to bring order out of mounting chaos was someone who could restore "law and order" and thus head off the "Red Menace" of Communism.

Prince Louis openly became *"un homme d'ordre."*

When his agents insisted that he stand for the first elections, held that spring, Louis was adamant in his refusal: "Either the Republic will consolidate itself . . . or it will give rise to a period of disorder and bloodshed—and then I shall go and plant the standard of my name in a place where it will stand for a good cause, plain and clear for victory." He did, however, allow three Bonaparte cousins (including Plon-Plon) to enter the lists. They were elected to the Constituent Assembly.

In the last week of May, Louis allowed his agents to enter him as a candidate in the special supplementary elections scheduled for the following month in thirteen departments. His program of "law and order" could not but appeal to a nation whose new semi-Socialist regime was continuing the Orléanist philosophy of centralizing the economy in the hands of the few, and seemed unable to cope with (if not entirely oblivious to) the nation's most pressing problem, large-scale unemployment.

The people were now reminded by his agents of the man who had written *Extinction du paupérisme*. Workers, canvassers and billposters, all directed by Persigny (and financed, in large measure, by Princess Mathilde, ever the dedicated Bonapartist), covered France with reproductions of what the candidate who was going to make pauperism extinct looked like and believed, brass medals detailing his virtues, and handbills outlining his principles, his credentials and his eagerness to ameliorate the sufferings of the poor and "restore law and order."

By that rather weird pluralism that is a hallmark of French politics, the Prince was elected a Deputy for Paris, Corsica and three other provincial departments.

The Provisional Government ordered his immediate arrest if he returned to France.

Whipped up by the Prince's agents, crowds paraded the streets shouting *"Vive Napoleon!"* Bonapartists infiltrated the mobs in the Place de la Concorde and handed out tricolor flags inscribed *"Vive le Prince Louis!"* Madame Gordon emptied her lungs from the steps of the Madeleine. The National Guard was put on the alert.

The barricades were not up, but the passions of the people were; the man who had promised to solve their problems was being denied what was legally his.

When it seemed things might get out of hand, the Assembly ruled that Louis's election was valid and that he must be allowed to take his seat.

Whereupon Deputy Bonaparte showed he was a cleverer tactician than even his most sympathetic supporters had supposed.

After writing an open letter of thanks to the people of France for electing him, he wrote an open letter to the Provisional Government asking for a leave of absence and regretting with consummate dignity the recent disturbances—of which, he conceded, he might have been the indirect cause. The letter ended on an ominous note: "If the people were to trust me with duties, I should know how to carry them out."

Republican protest in the Assembly was immediate and violent—as Louis had anticipated. He then wrote another letter in which he emphasized his ardent republicanism—and resigned his seat.

Now having established himself in the eyes of the masses as a martyr to principle against the tyranny of the unpopular Constituent Assembly, Louis found the ideal pose: the Prince Across the Water.

The resignation was not only a shrewd move, it was a fortunate one. In hopes of meeting the problem of a large unemployed proletariat, the government established a series of National Workshops, which proved to be a national disaster. The foremen were afraid to discipline the workers, who themselves had little desire to maintain production. These *ateliers nationaux* were soon closed, dumping into the streets an army of 177,000 laborers who had come from all over France and who now, supported by the poor of Paris, rose up against a "republican government" which favored, and depended upon, a bourgeoisie that still maintained a monopoly on the nation's wealth while the masses were not only out of work but out of food. The Assembly commissioned General Louis Eugène Cavaignac, hero of France's recent bloody triumphs in Algeria, to put down the ill-armed mobs. When the so-called June Days ended, more than 3,000 civilians were dead, more than 6,000 rounded up for exile.

Had Louis taken his seat in the Chamber of Deputies, he would have been faced with a perhaps fatal dilemma. Supporting the uprising would have cost him the respect of the army and the politicians; supporting the government would have cost him the reputation he had sedulously cultivated as the only friend of the workless and foodless.

During the ensuing three months, as Cavaignac maintained military order and the Assembly began to draft a constitution, the Prince remained Across the Water. When supplementary elections were called for in September, Louis allowed his agents to put forth his candidacy. Pains were taken to disabuse anyone of the idea that Prince Louis's ultimate aim was to reestablish the Empire. Money (much of it Miss Howard's) flowed across the Channel to finance election addresses and posters, all of which devolved upon one theme:

There is but one name today which is the symbol of order, of glory, of patriotism; and it is borne today by one who has won the confidence and affection of the people. Let the choice of the people be also the choice of commerce, industry and property. Let his name be a first pledge of reconciliation. He will obtain an amnesty for the victims of June; and his knowledge of political and social questions will help to deliver you from unemployment, destitution and anarchy.

The campaign was geared to the temper of an electorate that hated its government, cared less for theoretical socialism than for the realization of material needs, and now saw Messianic hope in the name "Napoleon."

On September 17, Louis was elected—again—Deputy for Paris, Corsica and three other provincial constituencies. When the results were announced at the Hôtel de Ville, there was a torchlight victory procession.

One week later, the Prince returned from Across the Water. His thirty-three-year exile was at an end.

Two days later, Deputy Bonaparte took his seat and asked permission to address the house. He swore to labor "for the preservation of order, for that is the primary need of the country—and for the development of those democratic institutions which the people rightfully demand." The Deputies did not believe him.

But they did not fear him either. He spoke nervously; his foreign accent (he pronounced *République* "*Ripiblique*") was to them as amusing as the popinjay costume he wore; there was nothing of the great Emperor Napoleon about *this* insignificant little man.

The new Constitution included a President on the American model, elected to a four-year term but ineligible to succeed himself. Slowly it dawned on the professional pols that the erstwhile laughingstock of Europe was campaigning for that office. Still they did not fear him.

They should have.

Louis's appeal to the electorate was masterful. He promised reduction of taxation, protection of property, relief from unemployment, old-age relief, improvement of industrial conditions, free enterprise, freedom of the press. To the anticlerics he promised freedom of worship and education; to the ecclesiastics he promised educational control and protection of the papacy. To the businessmen he promised peace; to the army he promised—well, not exactly war, but to look out for their interests. There was something for everybody in those pamphlets Persigny ground out and with which he peppered the provinces.

The politicians began to come around. They were confident he was manipulable. They began to offer advice of a public relations nature. The Prince needed no advice. He knew what the people wanted. Was he not being seen constantly riding around Paris on a horse? The people loved it. (Which was a blessing for Louis, who cut a better figure astride a horse than sidling about crab-like on those bandy legs.)

Election day was December 10. There were six candidates, including Cavaignac, the government's nominee (in itself a rather obtuse maneuver on the government's part). Of the 7.3 million votes cast, Prince Louis-Napoleon Bonaparte received 5.4 million.

It was the nineteenth century's weirdest election. Each faction believed the President would be a tool in its hands. There had to come a time when disillusionment would set in. Louis had to move fast. But not precipitately so.

In the obligatory inaugural speech, he swore "to remain faithful to the democratic Republic and to defend the Constitution." Then he left for his official residence, the Elysée Palace, which was just down the road from the Tuileries. Persigny and the other loyalists urged him to go there directly. But Louis was not ready.

Not yet.

The Prince-President knew where his chief strength lay: "My true friends are in the cottages, not the palaces." He also knew it took more than provincials to bring down a government, especially when to those provincials he was less a person in his own right than bearer of a magic name. And what guarantee had Louis that the provincials would support a Parisian *coup d'état?* He could use his strength in the provinces to threaten the capital (which had barely supported his election); France was so centralized a state, it feared the provinces as a child fears the bogeyman.

"The government stands for order, authority, religion, the welfare of the people, and a national dignity," proclaimed President Bonaparte—adding pointedly: "particularly in the country districts."

But there was a limit to how often he could throw that at the Parisians without his bluff being called.

Before Louis could mount a *coup d'état*, he had to seduce the military and the aristocracy. A program was begun to court the army: parades, promotions, spanking new uniforms, even roast-fowl-and-champagne dinners. A program was begun to court the aristocrats and opinion-makers: there were glittering weekly receptions at the Elysée, *bals-masqués* out at Fontainebleau, banquets at Saint-Cloud, and the like. (Arrangements were handled by the Princess Mathilde, who moved with her lover Nieuwerkerque into the Elysée as the President's Official Hostess.) The government footed the bills gladly; each faction assumed it was a good investment—the President was *their* man.

To disquiet the antagonistic Chamber of Deputies, he picked a popular middle-of-the-road parliamentarian to be Chief Minister. The Prince-President sat in on all Cabinet meetings, but did not attempt to impose his will; rather, he sat silently, listening. Tocqueville concluded that "the words one addressed to him were like stones thrown down a well; their sound was heard, but one never knew what became of them."

Though silent in Cabinet meetings, Louis was quite voluble in the provinces. His first tour was in the summer of 1849; wherever he went, he took pains to study local interests and appeal to local patriotism. Unlike the first Napoleon, he resorted to the political harangue. So what if he spoke hesitantly and had that rather Teutonic tinge to his mother tongue? He was telling the people what they wanted to hear. And they loved it.

Everywhere he went, President Bonaparte carried the same message: "Don't forget to spread amongst the workers sound ideas of political economy. Give them a fair share of the dividends of their labor, and so prove to them that the interests of the rich are not opposed to those of the poor." The employers did not take too kindly to such advice, but the workers ate it up.

The politicians back in Paris watched that tour with apprehension. President Bonaparte ignored their apprehension. He had an apprehension of his own: guaranteeing that at the next election—rather, the next plebiscite; Louis was a firm believer in plebiscites—his "true friends in the cottages" would be voting for a man and his policies instead of merely for a name.

By the end of that first tour, President Bonaparte felt less apprehensive. He and the provincials had gotten to know each other—and to like each other. Very much. When ultimately he became Emperor, Louis was asked what his program was. To this he replied: "My name is a complete program in itself." It was.

Unfortunately, over the long haul of Empire, it was not enough.

Louis stood as the champion of order between the opposite poles of revolution and reaction. Nowhere did this fatal doublemindedness cause him more embarrassment than when the so-called Roman Question came to a boil early in his presidency. It would be best to examine that Question here, albeit superficially; for while the unification of Germany might not have come about but for the collapse of the Second Empire, the collapse of the Second Empire might not have come about but for the unification of Italy.

Once the Austrians had put down the *Carbonari*, there had been no serious uprising on the Italian peninsula during the fifteen-year pontifical reign of the archreactionary Gregory XVI. With the death of Gregory and the accession of Pius IX (June 1846), it looked as if things might change for the better.

But then, after Gregory XVI anything was a change for the better.

In 1849, the people of Rome rose successfully under Mazzini and established a republic. Pius fled to the Kingdom of Naples and called upon Catholic Europe to restore him to his sovereignty. In France, the Republicans and Leftists opposed the prospect of their Republic crushing a Roman one in order to restore an autocrat to power. Opposing this view were the strong Catholic sentiments of so many French, who felt that the pope must be returned to his capital and to his full Temporal Authority. The religious sentiment was reinforced by the political fear that Austria would intervene if France did not; and the idea of further extension of Austrian influence in Italy was insupportable.

Going along with the interventionists, Louis—himself an ardent anticleric—sent an expeditionary force to restore the pope. Twelve years later, he would admit it was the biggest political mistake of his career. He stood exposed as a betrayer in the eyes of all Frenchmen who had hitherto seen him as a champion of liberty and national determination.

Fortunately, the French expeditionary force suffered initial reverses at the hands of the Roman Republicans. Criticism of President Bonaparte was put aside as all Frenchmen rallied behind him in their anxiety to retrieve the national honor with a victory. The French were victorious; Mazzini fled; Pius returned to the Vatican. Louis's popularity with the army rose immediately. He won back the affection of the disaffected by openly demanding liberal reforms in Italy ("the French Republic did not send an army to stamp out Italian liberty in that city"). Louis assumed his problems in Italy were ended.

In fact, they were only beginning.

It was during this period, when his popularity was at its height, that Louis's open struggle with the politicians began. It had suddenly dawned on them that he was neither this, that, nor the other faction's man. President Bonaparte was his own man. His democratic leanings stuck in the craw of the largely conservative Assembly; and that body did not appreciate it when the Socialists, whom Louis had wooed, scored great success in the by-elections. The Chamber of Deputies, deciding it would no longer be complacent, twice refused Louis's proposal to amnesty all those convicted of having participated in the "June Days."

That refusal was not lost on the workers of Paris. Persigny spread the word to their provincial cousins.

Panicking at the President's almost mesmeric hold on the masses, the Assembly reduced the electorate from 9 million to 6 million. Louis began a shuffling of his ministers that would, over the next two years, see eighty men come in and out of the Cabinet (the average ministry numbered ten) in a futile attempt to stem the ever-mounting opposition.

In the autumn of 1850, he undertook a second tour of the country. Once he had passed through the large industrial cities, where republican sentiment was strongest, the tour evolved into a royal progress. Wherever he went, Louis told the people: "The Assembly supports me when I propose repressive measures, but never when I seek to do any good." The people got the message.

By the following summer, the executive and legislative branches were each going their own way. Political war was declared when Louis dismissed the popular General Changarnier as Minister of

War over a triviality and replaced him with the unpopular General Saint-Arnaud. It was said that Louis was acting out of pique; Changarnier was given to referring to him publicly as *le perroquet mélancolie*—"the depressed parrot."

Actually, Louis could not care less what people called him. He was anxious to have Saint-Arnaud in that critical ministry; Saint-Arnaud had given assurances that he was willing to stake his own future on Louis's future—even if that future saw the President emerge as dictator.

War with the Assembly came when it refused Louis's request for a further grant of 2 million francs. That refusal gained Louis widespread sympathy; there was even talk of raising a public subscription. Among the most sympathetic were the Parisian aristocrats, who enjoyed all those receptions in the Elysée, and the military, who feared that a reduction in the Privy Purse would mean a commensurate reduction in new uniforms and weekly roast-fowl-and-champagne dinners.

President Bonaparte now faced his greatest problem since assuming office: how to circumvent the constitutional limitation on that office's term.

Persigny drew up a petition praying that the Assembly revise the Constitution either to extend the term of office or to allow for reelection of an incumbent. The Assembly refused to be moved by that prayer.

Louis then laid a beautiful trap into which the Assembly obligingly leaped. He proposed the restoration of universal suffrage. The Assembly refused, for the same reason it had reduced the electorate in the first place: its fear that more votes would only redound to the advantage of so popular a chief executive.

That refusal redounded more than the Assembly dared fear. Louis now stood as the champion of the rights of the disenfranchised. He had outlined a bold program that ran the gamut from more railways to model farms to draining and improving the streets of Paris; there was something in the package for everyone in all walks of life.

He was now in a position to show how, but for a reactionary legislature, he could—and would—give the nation a prosperity it had never enjoyed even in the balmiest days of Louis-Philippe.

The Prince-President was also in a position to do what he had sworn never to do when he took his oath of office—break that oath.

Louis-Napoleon never let anyone push him in any direction he had not already anticipated; conversely, more often than not he needed someone to prod him in the execution of his own intentions. It was his intention to be an emperor. But first he had to become a dictator. Enter Auguste-Charles-Joseph, Duke de Morny, his illegitimate half-brother. "I believe I can affirm that there would have been no *coup d'état* without me," claimed Morny. It was an honest claim.

And without the *coup d'état*, there would have been no Second Empire.

His surname was Demorny, that of the man whom Queen Hortense had paid a nice sum to assume the child's paternity of record. He rearranged his name, ennobling himself in the process, when he became aware of his illustrious antecedents. Never the shy one, Morny prided himself—openly—on being illegitimately descended from Queen Hortense, the Empress Josephine, Talleyrand, and King Louis XV (whose bastard daughter was Morny's paternal grandmother).

Morny was a glib, handsome, pleasure-loving rake who made it a practice to know the right people at the right time. If his philosophy could be reduced to one line, it would be: "The only way to control your opposition is to get a jump on it."*

At the age of twenty-four, with a fairly respectable army career behind him, Morny began a decade of pleasure and foppery in Paris. To finance such a life, he took as mistress Countess Le Hon, wealthy wife of the Belgian ambassador. He mingled on terms of intimacy with all the entrepreneurs of the Orléanist regime and enjoyed a

---

* *Nowhere is this better illustrated than in Morny's attempt to prod Napoleon III into proclaiming the so-called Liberal Empire that had been the latter's ultimate aim all along. Unfortunately, Morny died before the eternally vacillating Emperor felt confident enough to accept that final, vital prod. Had Morny not died in 1865, the Second Empire might not have died in 1870.*

successful career in stock manipulation. (During the Second Empire's heyday, the knowledge that he was involved in a financial venture all but guaranteed success; investors would say, "*Morny est dans l'affaire*," and nod their heads knowingly.)

When the Orléanist regime, of which he was a part, collapsed, Morny considered throwing his weight for the Legitimists. But, with so many factions jockeying for position, he decided to let the dust settle before committing himself. Like Talleyrand, he always kept his options open and his hand concealed; also like that grandsire, Morny had a positive genius for leaping from high places and landing on his feet.

Hortense's two surviving sons each knew of the other's existence long before they met. Louis had been told immediately after her death, and had taken this news of his adored mother's indiscretion bitterly. For his part, Morny is believed—the evidence is sketchy—to have sent Hortense a written promise that he would never attempt to contact Louis. (One reason the evidence is sketchy: Hortense did not mention this son in her memoirs.)

Shortly after Louis's escape from Ham, Morny saw him on a London street but made no effort to speak with him; so far as Morny was concerned, his half-brother was "a dreamer awaked out of a sleep." When the dreamer awoke to find himself President of France, Morny began to see him as a comer.

Besides sharing a mother, the two shared a mutual friend: the pandering, disreputable Félix Bacciochi, Louis's *maître de plaisir*. At Morny's suggestion, a meeting was arranged early in 1849. That initial meeting was friendly but reserved; as if by tacit mutual agreement, Hortense's name was not mentioned. It was the first of many meetings. Each saw he needed the other in order to fulfill an ambition.

Morny determined that the *coup d'état* must not be another Strasbourg, another Boulogne. In addition to himself and the Prince, only four other men were included in the planning: the aforementioned Saint-Arnaud; Jean-Constant Mocquard, once Hortense's secretary and now Louis's; Charlemagne-Emile de Maupas, Prefect of Police, an ambitious young horror whom Morny rightfully detested but whom Louis rightfully insisted was the perfect man for that post; and, of course, Persigny. A few military men were brought in at the last minute: General Magnan, who had obligingly failed to report that bribe offered him prior to the Boulogne fiasco; and Colonel Vieyra of the National Guard—who, like all the others, felt he had nothing to lose and everything to gain.

The date chosen for the *coup* was one that had precious meaning for Louis: December 2. It was the anniversary of the Battle of Austerlitz as well as of Napoleon Bonaparte's coronation. "Machiavelli himself," exclaimed the Empress Eugénie more than fifty years after the event, "would have had nothing but praise for the Second of December!" She was not overstating the case.

It was like waiting for the second shoe to drop. All Paris felt that something was about to happen, but nobody knew what or when. Louis's opposition enemies felt instinctively that he might well attempt a *coup d'état*—but in the early spring, when his term of office was due to expire.

Fortunately, December 1 fell on a Monday, when the Prince-President usually gave a grand reception at the Elysée. Members of the aristocracy, foreign ambassadors, French diplomats and government officials, military officers and distinguished visitors danced and chatted and otherwise enjoyed their President's predictable hospitality. As was his wont on these occasions, Louis circulated unobtrusively amongst his guests, offering a compliment here, a vague smile there.

Nobody seemed to notice that he stepped into an adjoining private room from time to time to have a cigarette—and consult with Mocquard, who was seated at a table preparing orders.

After dinner, Morny announced he was off to the *Opéra-Comique* to hear the latest success, Limnander's *Seven Brides of Bluebeard*. No one was surprised. Morny's passion for musical comedy was well known.* A few of the wags suggested that if the performance was dull, Morny would at least enjoy one of the female performers in the privacy of some *chambre séparée*. Everyone laughed as Morny winked in exaggerated lasciviousness and skipped out to his waiting carriage. Someone suggested that if there was going to be a *coup*, it would certainly not occur on this of all nights, what with the

---

* *Under the* nom de plume *Monsieur de Saint-Rémy, he wrote a number of forgettable librettos, one of which was set to music by his protégé Offenbach. Sarah Bernhardt was one of his discoveries.*

Prince-President entertaining at the Elysée and his chief adviser cavorting at the Opéra. Everyone agreed.

As he entered the opera house, Morny was stopped by a woman of his acquaintance, who remarked: "It is said they are going to sweep out the Assembly one of these days. What will you be doing?"

Replied Morny with a smile: "I shall try to be on the same side as the broom." Then he kissed her hand gallantly and turned away to say hello to generals Changarnier and Lamoricière, who had just entered the auditorium—and who within hours would be on the other side of that broom.

At ten o'clock Morny slipped out during the performance and returned to the Elysée. As was customary, the reception was ended and the guests were gone. Everyone knew the President liked to retire early.

The six conspirators adjourned to a private study, where Louis seated himself under a portrait of Queen Hortense and took them through a final briefing. Then he picked up a packet of papers containing the draft of a decree and proclamation that were to be printed; on the packet he had written the word "Rubicon." He handed Saint-Arnaud "Rubicon" and a packet of money to be distributed to the troops, gave Maupas a list of those who were to be arrested, and wished everyone success.

It was not quite eleven o'clock when four carriages drove away from the Elysée. Maupas went off to the Prefecture of Police to arrange for the arrest of the opposition leaders. Saint-Arnaud went off to move his troops into position and to give Colonel Vieyra the decree and proclamation, which he and his National Guardsmen were to have printed and circulated. Mocquard rushed off to a party. Morny decided to drop in at the Jockey Club for a nightcap and a rubber of whist.

The Prince-President went to bed—alone, for a change. Persigny decided to sit up, in case there was any last-minute hitch.

He needn't have bothered.

Shortly after midnight, six army brigades moved into position around major buildings; 40,000 regulars stood by in barracks to lend support if needed. Vieyra's National Guardsmen had the decree and proclamation printed and by 3 A.M. were rushing around Paris plastering copies onto every tree and lamppost. Fifty parties of

Maupas's police fanned out through the capital to arrest the opposition leaders in their beds.

As dawn rose over Paris, early workers en route to their jobs saw, wherever they turned, a proclamation signed by President Bonaparte explaining that the National Assembly had become "a center of subversion" and, beneath that, notification that between the hours of midnight and six, the following had been effected: the National Assembly was dissolved, the Council of State was dismissed, universal suffrage was restored, martial law was in effect. It was decreed that all holding the franchise were to partake in a special plebiscite to be held two weeks hence.

The *coup d'état* ended on a rather melodramatic note. Morny entered the bedroom of the Minister of the Interior at seven-fifteen A.M. and informed him affably: "Monsieur, you have been dismissed. Do pardon me for informing you of it so suddenly. It is I who have the honor to succeed you." Morny then went home to get a few hours' rest.

It had been a long night.

At ten in the morning of what would be known evermore as "the Second of December," President Bonaparte rode out to test the temper of the public. With him were generals Saint-Arnaud and Magnan—and the ex-King of Westphalia, his uncle Jerome.* Jerome and Plon-Plon, who, true to form, had been touching base with opposition leaders within the government, did not share Princess Mathilde's joy at this latest turn of events. The two had met in hurried consultation and decided that Jerome should stand by Louis while Plon-Plon went off to strengthen his ties with the opposition Republicans; in that way, at least one of them would survive.

Jerome congratulated his nephew and vowed to support him; Plon-Plon told Victor Hugo: "Louis is a disgrace to the family—if he belongs to it, the dirty bastard!"

---

* *The nephew he had publicly disowned as a bastard had made Jerome Governor of Les Invalides, a purely ceremonial position that carried with it a handsome salary and perquisites. One of the stories circulating along the boulevards had the sixty-five-year-old Jerome, who made a small fortune selling Bonaparte family mementos, seeking a buyer for that most prized of all mementos: the Emperor's ashes.*

There were cheers of *"Vive l'Empereur!"* and *"Aux Tuileries!*
Aux Tuileries!" when Louis showed himself in the Place de la Concorde. (Most of those cries came from Magnan's troops, who had
been deployed around the area in case the public showed signs of
distemper.) There were also cries of *"Vive la République!"* Later
that day came a student demonstration in the Place de la Bastille;
that night, a well-dressed orderly crowd marched down the Rue
Saint-Martin singing the *Marseillaise*. Morny, who had been
through a few Parisian uprisings in his time, warned that the truly
dangerous moment would come on the third day.

Meanwhile it was business as usual. One of those distinguished
visitors who had attended the previous evening's reception at the
Elysée was Lady Clifford-Constable, wife of a wealthy Yorkshire-
man. To her friend the Countess de Montijo, at the time visiting
back in Madrid, Lady Clifford-Constable wrote:

> The *coup d'état* has interested us very much. We found it possible to
> take walks on the boulevards on all the days except Thursday [Morny's
> "third day"], and even on that day it was possible to go out as usual on
> the Champs Elysées. On Monday evening we were at the Elysée, and on
> Tuesday M. Drouyn de Lhuys gave a reception [at the Foreign Office],
> as did Princess Mathilde. But the whole thing happened like a thunder-
> bolt. I hear . . . that many balls and fêtes are being given at the Elysée
> and by the ministers, but that not many private soirées are being held.
> . . . I hope that you and Eugénie are well?

Another English visitor to Paris, Elizabeth Barrett Browning,
noted in a letter to a friend that along the boulevards the wits had
replaced the Napoleonic *"Liberty! Equality! Fraternity!"* with *"In-*
fantry! Cavalry! Artillery!" General Magnan's troops patrolling
the city found it all rather amusing.

There were, of course, some feeble gestures on the part of the
opposition politicians. A few of the Assembly members met in rump
session on the morning of the *coup* and decreed that the President
was deposed, the executive authority was now vested in the Assembly, and their incarcerated colleagues were to be released at
once. Colonel Vieyra and a few of his National Guardsmen broke up
the meeting and invited the members to join those incarcerated
colleagues in the Mazas prison.

A number of Republicans rushed off to seek Victor Hugo's advice. He advised that 150 Deputies of the Left should march in

solemn procession through the streets of Paris shouting *"Vive la République!"* and *"Vive la Constitution!"* on every street corner, thus rallying the people.

But there were not 150 Deputies of the Left left in circulation. Hugo went to bed for a good sulk, got up before dawn the next morning, and spent an agreeable hour or so running through the streets of Paris tearing down the presidential proclamations, before heading into exile across the Channel.

On the night of December 3, the reaction set in and the barricades went up. While Louis sat grieving in the Elysée—he had sincerely hoped bloodshed could be avoided—his cousin Plon-Plon rushed about the city calling upon the people to "put down the usurper!" *(whose heir he still was!)*. In the Boulevard des Italiens a few nervous soldiers fired on a crowd. The Leftists now had the martyrs they needed.

It is probable that those horror stories which have come down to us—a thirteen-year-old boy being slaughtered by soldiers who salivated gleefully as they enlarged his wounds with their sabers; a pedestrian being shot only because he was trying to reach his home; a pregnant woman being clubbed to death by musketeers after she slipped in the gutter—were figments of Hugo's fertile imagination.

Undeniably there were deaths. When the barricades came down and all resistance ended two days later, the total casualties stood at 215. (This was far fewer than in 1848, and a mere fraction of the more than 20,000 people who would be executed by the Third Republic after the Commune of 1871.) A total of 26,000 people, mostly Republicans, were arrested; many were transported for life.*

Resistance within the Bonaparte family ended a week later, when Plon-Plon, who swore he would not submit to the new regime, learned from Jerome that cousin Louis would exile them both if he remained obstinate. Plon-Plon sent a note: "My dear Louis, all my feelings of brotherly friendship revive as keenly as ever." He recognized the new regime. He would never support it, though.

---

* *Louis grieved ever after that the* coup d'état *had drawn blood. Recalled Eugénie: "One day, seeing him plunged in gloomy thoughts, and guessing the cause, I could not avoid saying, 'You wear the Second of December like a shirt of Nessus,' and he replied, 'Yes, it is always on my mind.'"*

In the plebiscite held on December 21, the nation voted on whether the presidential term of office was to be extended to ten years. Out of a little more than 8 million voters, 7.4 million answered "Yes." (As an indication of where Louis-Napoleon's real strength lay, only 113,000 out of 300,000 Parisians voted "Yes"; 80,000 voted "No," and the rest stayed home.)

Louis-Napoleon Bonaparte was not yet Emperor of the French. That would come within a year, after certain formalities—including another rigged plebiscite—had been dispensed with.

However, he had already met the woman he was to make his Empress.

Chapter 6
Imperial
Courtship

More versions abound on how the royal couple met than on who invented the wheel. These range from the utterly romantic—that they were introduced in Princess Mathilde's drawing room sometime in 1852—to the utterly scurrilous—that they cruised each other in Piccadilly Circus sometime in 1848. In fact, they met in the Elysée on April 12, 1849, at a reception to which Eugénie and her mother had been invited by Count Bacciochi.

The two had only recently returned to Paris, their first visit since Louis-Napoleon's election to the presidency. The Countess de Montijo told Mérimée she wanted to ascertain at close range whether Louis was her long-sought "tyrant of genius." Mérimée did not particularly care for the "ugly little man on squat legs" (his words), but accommodated the Countess by introducing her to the presidential ponce. Bacciochi took one look at Eugénie and decided his cousin Louis would rather meet *her*.

On being presented, Eugénie said, "Monseigneur, we have often talked about you with a lady who is very devoted to you."

"And who is that?" asked the President.

"Madame Gordon."

The President smiled sphinx-like (some observers claimed that he winked obscenely, but Louis was not a winker), gallantly raised Eugénie's hand to bestow a kiss, and moved on in his crab-crawl fashion to greet other guests. Eugénie was not aware that one did not mention Madame Gordon in society—unless one was a sister under the skin.*

A week later, Bacciochi invited the two Montijos to dine with the President out at Saint-Cloud. On the appointed night, the two donned their most elaborate gowns and set out for the château. There they were directed into another carriage and driven to a small lodge at nearby Villeneuve-l'Étang, where the Prince-President was waiting—at a table set à quatre.

Louis, who always wolfed down his meals as if they were medicinal dosages to be stoically endured, broke his own record that moonlit night. Eugénie and the Countess had barely begun to tackle their soup when Louis jumped up and suggested a little stroll through the park. Against all rules of etiquette, he offered his arm to Eugénie. By prearrangement, Bacciochi offered his arm to the Countess and suggested she might enjoy seeing the rest of the house. Eugénie got the message.

As she recalled decades later: "I said to the Prince, 'Monseigneur! My mother is here!' I stepped aside to show him that he must offer his arm to my mother. He did so without wasting another word, and I took Bacciochi's arm. . . . I do not believe [Louis] was very pleased about this evening. He certainly thought the evening would turn out differently!"

He certainly did! The stroll through the park lasted little longer than the meal that had preceded it. Normally reticent when it came to conversation, the Prince indulged himself in a few perfunctory grunts and then saw the ladies to their carriage. There were no further invitations. Two months later, Eugénie and the Countess left for Schwalbach-on-the-Rhine, their next way station on "the grand route."

In the early autumn of 1851, they stopped off in Paris en route to Madrid, where Paca had only recently given birth to her second child and eldest daughter. By now, President Bonaparte and his legislature were moving toward a showdown.

---

* *The diva had died only a month previously, abandoned and alone. One of Louis-Napoleon's less admirable habits was to cut adrift any loyalist whose questionable reputation might in any way reflect on his own questionable reputation, mistresses excepted. He did have a conscience, though. Madame Gordon was granted a small pension to ease her last poverty-stricken, disease-ridden days.*

Eugénie read—along with the rest of Paris—how the President, off on another tour of the provinces, was telling the people—rather, warning the people: "Should the day of danger arrive, I shall not act like the governments which preceded me and say to you: 'March, I shall follow,' but I shall say: 'I march, follow me!' "

Eugénie was impressed. This return to Paris seemed to have awakened "my lifelong taste for politics." She saw in the Prince-President a man through whom that Napoleonic legend on which she had been weaned might be fulfilled after all. (Or so she would later claim.) She decided that France had no future as a republic; that President Bonaparte should proceed as Napoleon Bonaparte had proceeded: directly from consulate to empire. (Or so she would later claim she had decided.)

It was at this time that Eugénie allegedly sent a letter to Bacciochi in which she offered to place her entire fortune (which by now did not amount to very much) at Louis-Napoleon's disposal, a letter which Bacciochi allegedly did not show Louis until after the *coup d'état*.

That offer is in no way verifiable and in every way doubtful. Responsible historians have concluded that the story was created from whole cloth by Eugénie's partisan biographers, who began to rush their wares into print shortly after she became Empress. At the beginning of her fifty-year exile, Eugénie was giving the story credence.

At the end of her life, she believed it herself.

Louis was determined to be a constitutional ruler. With his political enemies either safely in jail or out of the country, he turned his ideas over to the Assembly—now overpopulated by men who were either longstanding loyalists or opportunists with remarkable vision who could read the handwriting on the wall even in stygian darkness. The Assembly spent a few weeks debating fine points, the way medieval theologians debated just how many angels *can* dance on the head of a pin. Louis lost patience and thrust the matter into the hands of Eugène Rouher, one of Morny's political protégés. Within twenty-four hours, including time out for sleep, that clever conservative produced an eight-section, fifty-eight-article document that would make present-day Africa's constitutional despots collapse in lachrymose envy.

Combining an omnipotent electorate with an impotent parlia-ment, it vested all powers in the person of a President whose term of office was to run ten years. The Corps Législatif was to deliberate at the behest of—and subject to the irrevocable veto of—the President. To the President was arrogated the naming of (and right to dismiss) all ministers, a window-dressing Senate, a *pro forma* Council of State, and a High Court of Justice, which was convened only at the presidential will and whose authority was limited to adjudicating all crimes against the President "or the safety of the State."

The nation that Louis had so obligingly deigned to save from itself returned to the polls in March. Thanks to the efforts of Morny and Persigny, the prefects and subprefects—experts all at electoral management—made sure only the official candidates in each of the nation's single-member constituencies had much chance of winning. On March 30, the President announced in *Moniteur,* the official press organ: "The dictatorship with which the people have entrusted me ceases today."

The announcement was an exercise in semantic masturbation. It would be a long time before such post-*coup* fiats as press censorship, dissolution of trade unions, suspension of trial by jury, and the lot were revoked.

The rest of Europe did not quite know how to react to events in France.

Queen Victoria was reduced to girlish glee when she wrote to her favorite correspondent, uncle Leopold at Brussels, soliciting his opinion of "the *wonderful* proceedings at Paris, which REALLY seem like a *story* in a book or a play!"* Uncle Leopold felt that "as yet one cannot form an opinion, but I am inclined to think that Louis Bonaparte will succeed." Most of the European royals were inclined to agree. As to how they would handle President Bonaparte, the sovereigns more or less took the attitude inherent in Victoria's as-surance to uncle Leopold: "We shall try and keep on the best of terms with the President . . . for whom, I must say, I never had any *personal* hostility."

---

* *Victoria compensated for a rather limited vocabulary by overcapitaliz-ing, overitalicizing, and at times overunderlining her every written thought; some found it charming, others found it an eyesore.*

A few weeks later, Victoria discovered she had some *"personal hostility"* after all, when President Bonaparte confiscated the entire Orléanist fortune in France (conservative estimate of value: 35 million francs). Victoria, who was related by marriage to the Orléans family (her and Dearest Albert's mutual uncle Leopold was Louis-Philippe's son-in-law), called the move *"too dreadful and monstrous!"* Dearest Albert went her one better: it was to him "a crime that cries to the Heavens!"

Reaction among the other sovereigns—and among the Legitimists within France itself—followed in a like vein. Stealing a government might be acceptable, but stealing a king's fortune, no matter how ill-begotten, was hitting below the belt.

(The Duke de Morny resigned as Minister of the Interior in protest of the confiscation—though many charged the resignation was actually a coverup for some of his shady speculative enterprises then coming to light. That Louis allowed him to go reflected an inherent dislike of this half-brother simply because he was living proof of Hortense's indiscretion, which Louis feared might call his own legitimacy into question. After announcing publicly that Louis's would "become a government of nonentities," Morny rejoined the government, serving as president of the Corps Législatif until his death twelve years later. Louis constantly complained that Morny's corruption would disgrace the Empire. It did.)

It is nice to know—something Louis's critics conveniently overlooked—that every Orléanist franc went to the French people in the form of orphanages, hospitals, agricultural banks, free burial and mutual benefit societies, asylums, public baths and washhouses, workmen's dwellings, and the like. When the French trooped to the polls to put their seal of approval on that glorious Constitution, they did not forget that their Prince-President had returned the money stolen from them by the deposed "Citizen King."

Unarguably, it was a brilliant stunt on Louis's part—plus a brilliant way of settling old scores.

By the summer of 1852, the *Garde Impériale* had been revived, the Imperial eagle was reappearing atop regimental standards, the former Imperial palaces and châteaux were being spruced up, Imperialist petitions (drawn up by Persigny, now Minister of the Interior) were circulating in the provinces, *Altesse Impériale* had once again become a fashionable term of reference in certain quarters, and throne rooms in all the Imperial residences were being given a good dusting.

Perspicacious Frenchmen were beginning to suspect that Prince-President Bonaparte might be having delusions of Imperial grandeur.

In early September, he again took to the road to test the temper of the people. Preceding him as a sort of advance man, Persigny made sure the crowds were well up in their cues. Wherever Louis went, he was greeted with cries of *"Vive l'Empereur!"* and *"Vive Napoleon III!"* He professed to find it all terribly embarrassing.

At Lyons, he simply had to set the record straight: "If the modest title of President makes it easier for me to carry out the mission entrusted to me, then I am not the man to let personal interest exchange that title for the name of Emperor!" Die-hard Republicans in the crowd gagged on that one, but were drowned out by more *"Vive l'Empereur"*s and *"Vive Napoleon III"*s. The people of France simply would not be satisfied until Louis had shed the presidential cutaway and donned the Imperial toga.

At Bordeaux, on October 10, Louis addressed himself directly to the problem: "France seems to want the return of the Empire." Then, having reluctantly opened the cellophane bag to let the cat crawl out, he hastily reassured Europe: "But there are people who say, The Empire means war. I say, The Empire means peace. It means peace because France desires peace. And when France is satisfied, the world has repose."

A week later he returned to Paris. Horace Rumbold, a member of the British Embassy staff, watched the entry from the flat of a compatriot on the Boulevard des Capucines. Recalled Rumbold,

> The public excitement was at its highest pitch—the President distinguishing himself by boldly riding along, on a magnificent chestnut, several horses' lengths in front of his brilliant staff and escort. It would be extremely interesting to know with what feelings the sight was watched by a lovely girl, who, with her mother, was standing at one of the windows of this bachelor apartment. The occupier of the rooms was Huddleston of Sawston, a Roman Catholic squire of good estate and very ancient lineage, hopelessly in love with his guest, who was none other

than Mademoiselle de Montijo—a few months later to become Empress of the French.

Toward the end of her incredibly long life, the Empress spoke of a correspondence she carried on with Louis between their first meeting in the spring of 1849 and her return to Paris in late September of 1852. Through the course of this correspondence, they "discussed many political questions" (Eugénie's words) devolving upon France's future.

In her dotage, the Empress was known to retroject. Not that she occasionally lied; rather, she occasionally told the truth as she preferred to remember it. At any rate, none of that correspondence has ever come to light. Perhaps, like Shelley's blithe Spirit, it never wert.

We have no way of knowing what Eugénie's feelings were as she stood looking down from Huddleston's windows upon Louis-Napoleon's triumphant entry into Paris. But we do know, given the society in which she now moved, that another meeting was inevitable. We also know that she would not marry simply for money; had that been the case, there was Huddleston. And we know, on the basis of her letters to Paca, that Eugénie's spinsterhood—she was now in her twenty-seventh year—was a source of personal humiliation.

It may not be true, as many have claimed, that Eugénie decided at this time that she could do worse than marry France's next Emperor. But it is true that she arrived at that decision within the month. Too, she had little difficulty getting her mother to concur in that decision. These four years of traveling had been more than the Countess had bargained for. In a word, she was practically broke. Having by now gone through her and Eugénie's inheritances, the Countess was reduced to depending on discreet loans her son-in-law ("my deerest Jeemy") doled out.

Filon, an Eugénie loyalist to the core, has written: "Madame de Montijo [was] responsible for the whole matrimonial campaign, and . . . played her great game with a boldness which the rest of the family had stigmatized as dangerous, and which indeed was so in the highest degree."

In truth, both ladies played the "great game" in tandem.

A few days after his return to Paris, Louis announced in the *Moniteur* that "the striking manifestation all over France in favor of reestablishment of the Empire imposes on the President the duty of consulting the Senate." On November 9, after being consulted, all but one of the eighty-seven hand-picked Senators decreed that Louis-Napoleon was to be Emperor—subject, of course, to a plebiscite.*

On November 20, the people of France were given the option of "Yes" or "No" on whether they wanted "the reestablishment of the Imperial dignity in the person of Louis-Napoleon Bonaparte." Two million voters abstained (these were mostly in the big cities, where republican sentiment was still strong), 250,000 voted "No," and 7.8 million voted "Yes." Eleven days later, the new Emperor announced that he had assumed the regnal title Napoleon III; he was not starting a new dynasty—he was carrying on that of Napoleon I and the ill-fated "Napoleon II."

Next day, Napoleon III rode in procession to the Hôtel de Ville and officially proclaimed the commencement of the Second Empire. The date was carefully chosen: it was the first anniversary of his own *coup d'état*, the forty-seventh anniversary of Austerlitz, and the forty-eighth anniversary of Napoleon I's coronation.

There would be no coronation for Napoleon III. He insisted that only the pope could crown and anoint him. The pope insisted he would as soon turn Methodist as accept the honor. When Pius VII went to Paris to crown the first Bonaparte, he wound up as the Emperor's prisoner for four years and almost lost the Vatican. Pius IX was not about to take any chances with the second Bonaparte.

---

* *The lone dissenter was the Senate President—Jerome Bonaparte. Louis had decreed that Jerome and Plon-Plon were to succeed him if he died without legitimate issue, though he reserved the right to adopt an heir. The Senate absolutely refused to contemplate the possibility, however remote, of Jerome acceding to the throne. Jerome resigned in protest. That Louis did not make an issue of it suggests he only made the gesture to flatter the old man who, his catalogue of faults notwithstanding, was still Napoleon Bonaparte's lone surviving brother and thus France's link with its Imperial past.*

It may have been at this time that Jerome snarled to his nephew, "You have nothing of my brother the Emperor about you!" To which Louis replied with forbearance: "You are wrong, dear uncle. I have his family about me."

Louis's first official act as Emperor was to ennoble his uncle Jerome and cousins Plon-Plon and Mathilde with the title and dignity of Imperial Prince and Princess, with commensurate estates and incomes. Jerome was given the magnificent Palais-Royal (which he shared with Plon-Plon) for his townhouse, plus three country estates, plus 3 million francs a year to cover household expenses, 1 million francs a year from the Civil List, and an added lump sum of 3 million francs to be paid out at the rate of 55,000 a month. Yet when he died seven years later, Jerome was practically destitute. Plon-Plon was made a Senator, a Councillor of State, and a general in the army—all high-paying jobs—and had his own Civil List allowance of 200,000 francs a year.

He and his father showed their gratitude for such largesse by continuing to be a collective thorn in the Emperor's side.

The European Powers were appalled. Had not the Congress of Vienna vowed that never again would a Bonaparte sit on the throne of France? Still, there was one incontrovertible fact that could not be ignored: the sovereign people of France had made their decision.

After much passing of notes back and forth between chancellories, the monarchs decided to metaphorically shrug their shoulders and hope for the best. As Leopold of Belgium put it: "We are here in the awkward position of persons in hot climates who find themselves in company—for instance, in their beds—with a snake; they must not move because that irritates the creature, but they can hardly remain as they are without a fair chance of being bitten."

Britain was the first of the major Powers to give the new regime a seal of approval. On December 4, Victoria addressed a perfunctory letter to "My Good Brother the Emperor of the French," this in keeping with the formula reserved for legitimate sovereigns. Russia, Prussia and Austria absolutely refused to consider Napoleon III *their* good brother. While Austria and Prussia held back, Tsar Nicholas pointedly addressed a perfunctory letter to "Our very good friend, Napoleon."

All Europe held its breath. Would the Tsar's good friend mobilize his troops after such a rebuff? Nations had been known to go to war with less provocation.

Europe relaxed when Napoleon informed the Tsar's envoy, with diplomatic grace and tact: "We put up with our 'brothers' and we choose our 'friends.' " Austria and Prussia felt safe in following Nicholas's example. Napoleon III was accepted—albeit with great reluctance—into, in his words, "the pale of the old monarchies."

Barely had those old monarchies ceased speculating on the French Emperor's martial intentions when they found themselves speculating on his marital intentions: Would he take as his Empress "that Spanish woman"?

It was an extraordinary courtship. They were together on no more than six or eight occasions, and always surrounded by mobs of people. Even when they snuck off to be alone, ten minutes here, a half hour there, someone—in addition to the Countess de Montijo—was always listening behind a closed door, lurking behind a bush.

Had Louis been able to marry into one of Europe's royal houses, he never would have married Eugénie. And she knew it. Both went to the altar the way George Bernard Shaw and his Charlotte went to the Register Office: "cleared of all such illusions as love interest, happiness interest and all the rest of the vulgarities of marriage." Both were in love, but not with each other. They were in love with Louis's career.

That was enough.

Eugénie reentered Louis's life in the last week of October, when Bacciochi invited her and the Countess to a banquet out at Fontainebleau. There were a few more invitations over the next ten days: receptions at the Elysée, more banquets at Saint-Cloud. People began to talk. It was obvious that Louis hoped to install Mademoiselle de Montijo as his resident mistress. All those around Louis, especially the Princess Mathilde, hoped he would succeed.

They all found the current *maîtresse-en-titre*, Madame Howard, impossible.

The fair Elizabeth had followed Louis over from London, was installed in a townhouse conveniently close to the Elysée, and was maintaining a high visibility around Paris, on the assumption that the French should get to know the woman who was going to be their Empress. She made a habit of never being seen without an ostentatiously large bouquet of Parma violets, the Bonaparte flower.

As if that were not enough, Madame Howard had brought over from London a large sheaf of signed receipts and IOUs with which she would occasionally fan herself in mixed company.

All Paris was talking about the Emperor's difficulties with this pretentious and irritating strumpet, who annoyed him with her habits yet fascinated him with her body. Princess Mathilde, whom Madame Howard had had the audacity to upstage while promenading during intermission of a gala at the *Théâtre Français*, kept everyone up to date. Mathilde made it a point to know what went on behind everyone's closed doors except her own. (She was the last to learn that her resident lover, Nieuwerkerque—whom she prevailed upon the Emperor to name director of the Louvre—was carrying on with half her best friends.)

Everyone was on Princess Mathilde's side. They wanted Madame Howard replaced by Mademoiselle de Montijo. That Mademoiselle de Montijo was not submitting easily was a point in her favor: she obviously had more class than Madame Howard. By the second week in November, the talk along the boulevards was not *if* Mademoiselle de Montijo would become the Imperial mistress, but *when*. Everyone hoped it would be soon.

No one hoped so more than the Emperor.

On November 13, Louis inaugurated the opening of the hunting season with a house party out at Fontainebleau. When the entire group charged off into the Great Forest on *La Grande Chasse*, Eugénie—by far the most accomplished rider of the lot—was first in on the kill. Louis, who had not taken his eyes off Eugénie since her arrival at the château, presented her with a magnificent bouquet.

That night, some of the bachelors started a daily book on "when the walls will be breached and the fortress will surrender." (This choice bit of gossip—and subsequent, even choicer ones—wound up in dispatches to the British, Austrian and Prussian foreign offices.)

Eight days later, Louis gave a ball at Saint-Cloud to celebrate the anticipated outcome of that day's plebiscite on "the reestablishment of the Imperial dignity." To Enrique Galvé, Eugénie sent a note demanding that he escort her to the ball: "You have no idea what they are saying about me!" Don Enrique was the younger brother of Don Jaime, who had had him posted to the Spanish Embassy to chaperone the two Montijo ladies about Paris. He had a very good idea of what "they" were saying. Lord Cowley, the British ambassador, summed it all up in a dispatch to the Foreign Office:

> The Emperor's entourage is getting seriously alarmed at his admiration of a certain Spanish young lady, Mademoiselle de Montijo by name. Her mother is, with the young lady, playing a bold game, and, I cannot doubt, hopes that her daughter may wear the Imperial Crown. Some of the Emperor's friends are not without apprehension that she may succeed in her intrigue. . . .

That apprehension was premature on the part of the Emperor's entourage and friends. He was looking for a wife—but elsewhere. Outside France, in fact. Louis wanted an alliance with one of Europe's royal houses, which would thus add legitimacy to his own house. By the middle of November his agents had fanned out on the Continent to make discreet inquiries.

Louis's personal choice was Princess Carola Vasa of the deposed, legitimate house of Sweden. She was beautiful and was young enough to turn out a complete platoon of royal heirs. But Austria was paying the Vasa family a pension. The alliance was vetoed.

Other refusals came in from the Spanish, Portuguese, Russian and Bavarian courts. Napoleon III was a usurper and a Bonaparte; he was not to be considered as a son-in-law. Louis went back to the *Almanach de Gotha* and lowered his sights a notch. There was a Beauharnais cousin, Princess Stephanie, of the cadet branch of the Prussian house of Hohenzollern. Cousin Stephanie turned him down. Louis decided to look westward. He considered Princess Mary of Cambridge, granddaughter of King George III. Princess Mary was amenable to the idea, but her cousin Victoria vetoed it.*

In early December, Louis had Count Walewski, his ambassador to London, sound out Victoria on her niece, Princess Adelaide of Hohenlohe-Langenburg (daughter of Victoria's half-sister Feodora). The Hohenlohe-Langenburgs were hardly in the same league

---

* *Had Victoria consented to the marriage, Elizabeth II would not now be sitting on the British throne. Mary of Cambridge eventually married Francis of Teck; their daughter Mary was Elizabeth's paternal grandmother.*

as the Habsburgs, Hanovers, Hohenzollerns, Bourbons, Braganzas and Wittelsbachs; however, being a nephew-in-law to Queen Victoria certainly had its advantages—especially since Louis was determined to ally France with England.

Victoria was of two minds about the whole thing. Not only had the Emperor usurped the Orléans monarchy, there was no telling how long he would last on the throne; too, French queens had not enjoyed much luck over the past seventy years. But Victoria was a romantic at heart; and seventeen-year-old Adelaide, who happened to be visiting her royal aunt at Windsor when the idea was broached, was simply dying to be an empress. Victoria decided to let Adelaide's parents make the decision.

Walewski rushed back to Paris and told Louis he must stop seeing Mademoiselle de Montijo—their "entanglement" was the chief topic of conversation at Windsor—lest he jeopardize his chances with Princess Adelaide. Walewski also urged Louis to disencumber himself of Madame Howard, who had also found her way into Lord Cowley's dispatches. Louis made no attempt to communicate with Mademoiselle de Montijo.

As for Madame Howard: "His Majesty was here last night," she wrote to a confidant, "offering to pay me off; yes, an earldom in my own right, a castle, and a decent French husband into the bargain! Oh! the pity of it all! I could put up with a dose of laudanum to this! The Lord Almighty spent two hours arguing with me. Later he fell asleep on the crimson sofa and snored while I wept!"

If Eugénie was unaware of why the Emperor was maintaining a silence—and chances are she was not; her mother made it a point to know all the gossip at Court—she was enlightened by an old family friend residing in Paris, Sophie de Contades. A week or so after the Emperor fell into a heavy snore on Madame Howard's crimson sofa, Madame de Contades dropped in for tea at 12 Place Vendôme.

Admitting only that she had been sent by "parties vitally interested in your welfare and happiness," she asked Eugénie to be the Emperor's *maîtresse-en-titre*. The appeal was couched in rather philosophical terms: "Remorse is better than regret." What is worse, demanded Sophie rhetorically, transitory remorse for a moral lapse, or eternal regret at having missed the opportunity of a lifetime?

Eugénie coolly replied that she had no intention winding up with remorse *or* regret.

On December 17, the Emperor held the first Imperial house party of the reign at Compiègne. The gathering was planned for four days; Louis assumed he would accomplish his mission—to bed down Mademoiselle de Montijo—in that time. The gathering lasted eleven days; Louis failed in his mission. While more than 280 servants flitted about in livery, 101 guests—government officials, foreign envoys, the Imperial family—watched the Emperor watch Mademoiselle de Montijo's every move. They sat at table together; they rode together. Her every wish was his command. Actors from her favorite Parisian theater were brought out for a special performance; she sat beside the Emperor in the Imperial box.

One evening as the two were strolling in the garden, Eugénie admired a dew-covered clover leaf. Bacciochi was dispatched to Paris; he returned on the morrow with a clover leaf of diamonds glittering with emeralds.

One night there was a game of hide-and-seek. As Eugénie, whose turn it was to be "it," edged her way down a corridor, the Emperor jumped out from behind a curtain and thrust himself at her. A few of the eavesdropping guests heard Eugénie dampen the Emperor's ardor with a cold verbal douche: "Not until I am Empress!"

Two days later, as the two were strolling in the garden, the Emperor exposed his innermost desire. (According to a few of the guests hiding behind a nearby bush, he exposed even more of himself.) To this, Eugénie replied: "Yes—when I am Empress!"

Recalled the Empress sixty years later: "It was at Compiègne that he first spoke to me of love. I thought he was joking."

He was.

On New Year's Eve there was a grand dinner and ball at the Tuileries. The Emperor, along with the rest of his official entourage, appeared in britches and silk stockings. Princess Mathilde, along with the other official ladies, appeared in high dudgeon. The Emperor was making a fool of himself over "that foreigner," who, without diplomatic or official status, was taking too prominent a place at Court.

Highlight of the evening was the appearance of the foreigner in question, along with her brash mother. As grandees of Spain, they assumed that a foreigner of rank took precedence over the wives of French ministers. Those ministerial wives assumed otherwise.

As the guests were forming by pairs to enter the dining room, Eugénie stepped ahead of Madame Fortoul, wife of the Minister of Education. Madame Fortoul hissed indignantly: *"Aventurière!"* Eugénie froze, "pale as a lily in her white satin gown." Then she said coolly: "Lead on, Madame," marched into the dining room, and took her place at the Emperor's table. The ladies were scandalized; the Imperial family was livid.

Recalled the Empress: "The Emperor did not fail to notice my distress. He . . . asked me what was the matter. 'Do not ask me now, we are being watched,' I replied. After the supper he again asked me what was the matter. 'I must know the truth! What has happened?' 'I have been insulted—but no one shall have that opportunity again!' 'Tomorrow no one will dare hurt your feelings.' "

To Eugénie and the Countess this meant that a proposal of marriage was immediately forthcoming. They sat home all New Year's Day waiting for word from the Tuileries.

They had a long wait.

The Emperor had that day convened his ministers and family to sound them out on the idea of his marrying Mademoiselle de Montijo if Princess Adelaide's parents were to turn him down.

Admittedly, he could go back to the *Almanach de Gotha*, lower his sights once more, and probably find in one of the lesser royal houses "some scrofulous German with big feet."

On the other hand, as he took pains to point out, Mademoiselle de Montijo was young and beautiful; she would make an ideal mother for a future Emperor of the French.

Save for the odd one or two, the reaction ran the gamut from outrage to horror. Five ministers threatened to resign on the spot. The Princess Mathilde called for her smelling salts. Uncle Jerome threw a fit. Cousin Plon-Plon argued: "One does not *marry* women like Mademoiselle de Montijo: one makes love to them!"

Louis sighed in exasperation; he had already tried it Plon-Plon's way.

Among the family, only Morny favored the marriage. He felt that a remarkably beautiful woman would be "a pleasant novelty in a French consort; the masses have always tended to find their queens aesthetically wanting." Among the government officials, only Achille Fould, Minister of State (and the Second Empire's most brilliant financier), supported the idea.

While the Emperor floundered about in a state of characteristic indecision, Paris was flooded with a torrent of abusive pamphlets hostile to a match that had not yet been decided upon. Persigny and the Imperial family had a hand in the preparation and distribution of those pamphlets.

Even the press got into the act. Since censorship was strict in France, editorials inimical to the government were shipped across the border for publication in accommodating Belgian newspapers. The following, taken from the *Indépendence Belge*, typified the opinion of the French press:

> A union with a Spanish lady meets with no sympathy from the nation, and can only be the result of personal gratification. The head of a great State like France, anxious to found a new dynasty, should entertain more serious thoughts and higher aims than to satisfy a whim and succumb to a young woman's beauty.

Opposition to Mademoiselle de Montijo cut across social, economic and political lines. The French refused to accept another foreigner on their throne; Marie Antoinette and Marie Louise were only two among a bevy of imported royal consorts, dating back to the two Medici queens, who had brought out the xenophobia in them. Anonymous letters poured into the Tuileries "proving" that Eugénie was the daughter of, among others, the Queen-Mother of Spain; others, that she was in truth the Countess de Montijo's daughter but that *that* dissolute woman lacked the vaguest clue who the father was.

Concluding that she had no choice but to make a tactical retreat, Eugénie begged the Countess to take her immediately to Rome. The Countess felt that such a move would be not a tactical retreat but a rout.

An invitation was received to attend a court ball at the Tuileries on January 12. Mérimée, Lesseps and Don Enrique were called in for advice.

Lesseps did not know what Eugénie should do, though he supported her contention that a grandee of Spain did indeed take precedence over a French minister's wife. Mérimée was indecisive: to leave France would run for Eugénie the risk of seeming to give credence to all the slander, but to remain on would run for her the risk of becoming further involved with an Emperor whose morals were "deplorable" and whose Empire really did "not seem to have much of a future." Don Enrique Galvé insisted that Eugénie return to Spain immediately, and volunteered to challenge the Emperor to a duel over her honor. The Countess de Montijo argued that Eugénie must remain on in Paris and "see this through."

As Don Enrique and the Countess stood screaming at each other over the invitation, Eugénie decided she would go to the ball, she would outshine every damned minister's lady there, she would show the Emperor what he had lost—and then she would bid him a memorable farewell! She ordered the Countess to call in Madame Barenne, the Coco Chanel of her time, to fashion a ball gown to end all ball gowns.

The Countess wondered if Madame Barenne would extend any more credit. . . .

Lord Cowley reported that throughout the festivities the Emperor "seemed woefully out of sorts." As well he should have been. Princess Adelaide's parents had turned him down. He had not come to a definite decision in his own mind about marrying Eugénie; and just about everyone around him was demanding that he abandon the idea.

The guests were all seated, waiting for the Emperor to dance the first quadrille, when Eugénie—a genius at the art of timing— entered on the arm of Baron James de Rothschild. She was dressed in ivory brocade trimmed with silver tassels; in her hair, a wreath of orange blossoms. The onlookers had a collective fit; in France, orange blossoms were worn only by a bride on her wedding day.*

In accordance with protocol, Eugénie curtsied low to the Emperor, who was seated on the dais with the Imperial family. Then, with the Emperor's eyes following her every move, Eugénie headed for the benches along the wall where sat the privileged ladies of the Court. Madame Drouyn de Lhuys, wife of the Foreign Minister, stood up and whispered into Eugénie's ear that the area was "out of

---

* Apprised of this by her concièrge as she set out for the ball, Eugénie replied: "In Spain we always wear them; why should I not do so here!"

bounds to foreign adventuresses." The other ladies smirked with satisfaction. Eugénie froze in embarrassment. Sensing that an insult had been thrown, the Emperor rushed down from the dais and invited her to join him there.

It was a replay of the New Year's Eve Ball. The Emperor asked what had happened; Eugénie whispered that everyone was staring, that she would explain later. Everyone was indeed staring— especially the three Bonaparte Imperials, who were seated on the dais and all but frothing at the mouth. A few minutes later the Emperor invited Eugénie to dance a quadrille with him. During the quadrille, Eugénie sought an immediate Audience. The Emperor quadrilled her out of the ballroom and into a corridor, where he demanded to know what had happened.

At which point Eugénie, as they say, let it all hang out. In a strident voice that, had it gone any higher in decibel count, could have been heard only by a bat, Eugénie informed the Emperor that she had been publicly insulted, that her reputation had been ruined, that her honor had been besmirched, that her good name had been compromised, that all of France was speaking of her as an adventuress and a whore—and that she was leaving on the morrow, never to return to France.

After a long silence, the Emperor assured her that leaving Paris would not be necessary.

A formal request for her hand in marriage would be dispatched forthwith.

Having arrived at that decision, the Emperor took another three days to send the formal request; three days in which he had to endure the verbal assault of his family (Morny excepted) and his closest advisers (Persigny called it "suicide"), and accept the resignations of a few of his ministers. All discussion was ended when the exhausted Emperor announced: "I do not ask your advice; I merely state the fact. This marriage I have decided upon, and it will be accomplished!"

Palais des Tuileries
January 15th, 1853

Madame la Comtesse,
   For a long time I have been in love with Mademoiselle your daughter and have wished to make her my wife. I am today, therefore, asking you

for her hand, for there is no one so capable of making my happiness or more worthy to wear a crown.

I pray you, if you consent to this proposal, not to reveal it till we have been able to make arrangements.

Believe me, Madame la Comtesse, when I assure you of my sincere friendship.

Napoleon

It was decided that the civil marriage would take place on February 27, to be followed by the religious ceremony on the next day. An emissary was dispatched to Rome with the request that Pius IX travel to Paris to celebrate the nuptial pontifical mass.

Pius did not wish to insult the Emperor; French troops were stationed in Rome protecting him against the Romans bent on abolishing the Temporal Power. On the other hand, he had as little inclination to officiate at a Bonaparte wedding as he had had to officiate at a Bonaparte coronation. He sent back felicitations and regrets that "great age and infirmities" precluded his making the journey to Paris.

For the record: Pius survived Napoleon by five years.

Lord Cowley to the Foreign Office:

> The great one has been captured by an adventuress. To hear the way in which men and women talk of their future Empress is astonishing. Things have been repeated to me, which the Emperor has said of her, and others which have been said to him, which it would be impossible to commit to paper. In fact, she has played her game with him so well that he can get her in no other way but marriage, and it is to gratify his passions that he marries her.

The Princess Mathilde wept with rage that she was being displaced as Official Hostess by a foreign commoner. The Countess de Montijo wept with relief when Achille Fould advised that the Emperor had arranged a personal income of 250,000 francs per annum for the future Empress, that no dowry was expected, and that unlimited credit had been placed at her disposal for the bride's trousseau.

Only a few hours before Fould's visit, Madame Barenne had dunned the Countess with a writ.

Cousin Plon-Plon announced that he could never accept Eugénie as Empress (he never did) and that, as a mark of his contempt, he would wear black at the wedding (he did). Uncle Jerome announced that "for the first time in the family's history, the name Bonaparte has been dragged through the mud" (!) and then dragged himself off to brood in bed for a week. His celebrated prediction had come to pass: "Louis will marry, if she wishes it, the first woman who refuses him her favors!"

In all the drawing rooms of Paris it was decided to accept the forthcoming marriage. There was no other choice. A few of the more pragmatic aristocrats, along with those ministers (and their wives) who did not resign, became fulsome in their praise of Eugénie's beauty and the great contribution it was felt she would make to the Empire. Soon those aristocrats and officials were tripping over each other to be the first to offer the Emperor their appreciation of his great wisdom in having decided to give them Mademoiselle de Montijo as their Empress.

Prince William (later Emperor William I) of Prussia expressed the attitude of the European Courts: "The Montijo marriage is a relief to me, for now no European royal family will have to marry that *parvenu.*"

"My dear good sister," wrote Eugénie to Paca,

> I wish to be the very first to inform you of my forthcoming marriage to the Emperor. . . . He has fought and won. . . . He will announce it [officially] to the Chamber [of Deputies] in the speech from the throne. . . . Be kind enough to buy me two scarlet fans, the finest you can find; if none please you, send as far as Cádiz in search of them. Please try to find another sandalwood [fan] with silver filigree, and another one gilded, the most elegant you can lay your hands on. . . . I would also like a pretty Andalusian *mona;* I need it for a fancy-dress ball. It must be very light and very pretty. . . . I am very busy. Good-bye. . . .

No account of that fancy-dress ball has survived, which is a pity. A *mona* is a female monkey.

In his Speech from the Throne, the Emperor explained that the only way to bring France, the bastion of revolution and liberty, back "into the pale of the old monarchies" was through an "upright policy" rather than "by royal alliances, which give false securities and often place personal interests before those of the nation." Recalling how the previous seventy years had seen a succession of dreadful "foreign princesses as Queens of France," he pointed out that the only woman who "brought happiness" to the French people was "the modest and virtuous" Empress Josephine, who was not of royal blood. "When in the very face of Old Europe, one soars on the wings of a new principle to the heights of ancient dynasties," he continued, "it is not by making ancient one's coat of arms and by endeavoring to become allied to royal families *at any price* that one is accepted. It is rather by always calling to one's mind one's origin, by preserving one's character, and by boldly assuming before Europe the position of a *parvenu*—a glorious title when won by the free vote of a great people—that one would succeed."

Having thus put Europe's dynasties in their place for having rejected him through marriage, the Emperor next played to the emotions of the French people: "I have preferred a woman whom I love and respect to one whose alliance might have brought advantages mingled with self-sacrifices."

Admittedly, his bride-to-be was a foreigner, but she was "French in heart, in education, and . . . her father shed his blood for the Empire"; she was "a devout Catholic" who would "send up to Heaven the same prayers as myself on behalf of the prosperity of France." He had "every hope that her Court will be as renowned for its virtues as was that of the Empress Josephine."

The speech created an uproar.* The royal courts fumed; *he* had turned down *their* daughters in marriage? Queen Victoria found it all "in *very* bad taste!"; others found it worse. The French aristocracy resented the Emperor's having referred to himself—and, by extension, to themselves—as a *parvenu*. Too, his citing of the Empress Josephine's "virtues" caused many to wonder just how virtuous their next Empress really was.

But Louis knew what he was doing; in French memory Josephine was held, and justifiably so, as having been a greater helpmeet for Napoleon I than the Austrian-born Marie Louise. Besides, to Louis the Empress Josephine *was* virtuous.

---

* *About the only one who was not perturbed was Madame Howard. Said she philosophically: "He always was capricious, but he is subject to indigestion and will soon come back to me." He did come back to her soon. The night of his Speech from the Throne, as a matter of fact.*

His government and family might resent the marriage, but the Emperor felt that the people, whose opinion he coveted, would prefer that he enter into "a love match instead of a dynastic alliance."

It was a good try, but it did not wash with the people. Josephine's virtues (or lack of same) notwithstanding, she had still been French by birth.

There was no circumventing the fact that Eugénie was—as Persigny promptly labeled her—"that Spanish woman."

Eugénie and her mother moved into the Elysée, their official residence until the wedding. Barely had they unpacked when the Emperor sent word over from the Tuileries that the nuptials were to be put back one month "for reasons of State." The wags along the boulevards outdid themselves with that one.

The Emperor visited Eugénie daily (and visited Madame Howard nightly out at Saint-Cloud, whither she had retired to collect her personal belongings). Many people paid courtesy calls, aristocrats as well as foreigners. The Paris correspondent for *The Times of London* found Eugénie "wearing the incipient honours of her approaching rank as if she had the consciousness that they were not superior to her merits." Baron Hübner, the Austrian envoy, thought Eugénie "sparkled, not exactly with intelligence, but with that Andalusian charm which is one of her attractions."

Eugénie sought to ingratiate herself with her new subjects. She requested that the Council of the Seine take back their gift of a diamond necklace and donate its value (more than half a million francs) to the relief of the Paris poor. The Imperial family thought this was merely cheap grandstanding. It was a cheap shot on their part. The gesture was unselfish; Eugénie deserves that much. Unfortunately, it was wasted.

Knowledgeable as she was about her adopted country, it would take Eugénie a while to realize that the preponderance of Gauls learn xenophobia in the womb.

On the evening of January 29, the bride and her mother were escorted by the Imperial Master of Ceremonies to the Tuileries for the civil marriage. In attendance were the Imperial family, the diplomatic corps, and leading government officials and their ladies. Eugénie wore a magnificent gown of pink silk trimmed with precious lace; on her head she wore a wreath of jasmine. As the Imperial bride entered, everybody was literally bowled over by the picture she presented.

Everyone, that is, except the Imperial family. Princess Mathilde thought she looked "overdone"; Plon-Plon thought she looked "cheap"; uncle Jerome thought she was "a blot on the family's escutcheon." Baron Hübner reported that the bride was "pale and fatigued." (The Emperor, on the other hand, he found to be "gay and frisky.") Readers of *The Times of London* were informed that the bride's "demeanor throughout was of one accustomed to a high station," though it was noted that "she trembled for a moment before she took the pen to sign the marriage register."

After the register was signed, the bride's full array of titles was proclaimed. Mérimée had been drafted to compile the official genealogy. While it does not reach the literary sublimity of his *Carmen*, it is every bit as imaginative: "Marie Eugénie Ignacia Augustine de Guzmán y Porto Carrero et Kirkpatrick de Closeburn [!], Comtesse de Mora et de Banos, Marchionesse de Moya, de Ardales et de Oséra, Comtesse de Téba, de Ablitas et de la Santa Cruz de la Sierra, et Vicomtesse de la Calzéda."

The ex-King of Westphalia hissed to his son Plon-Plon: "It *still* does not add up to Bonaparte!"

The Imperial pair then retired for a bit of refreshment so that the bride might compose herself. At one moment she felt faint and reached out for Princess Mathilde's hand. Princess Mathilde gave her a foot. When the congregation reassembled, the bridal couple led them all into the *Salle des Spectacles*, where they were subjected to an overblown wedding cantata composed by Auber specially for the occasion. It was a spectacle in itself; half the auditors almost fell asleep.

After the cantata, the bride returned to the Elysée and spent her wedding night with the Countess de Montijo.

The bridegroom returned to Saint-Cloud and spent his wedding night with Madame Howard. (She was obviously taking her sweet time packing those personal belongings.)

Next day was a Sunday—the day of the week that would have the most significance for Eugénie, the one day of the week that she superstitiously came to fear.* After climbing into her "white silk, satin and velvet gown with a long train, ornamented with Alençon lace, the design of which represented violets," Eugénie dashed off a quick note to Paca:

> I am saying farewell to my family and my country, in order to devote myself exclusively to the man who has loved me sufficiently to raise me up to his throne. I fear the responsibilities that will weigh upon me, and yet *I am accomplishing my destiny. . . . I have accepted this greatness as a divine mission!*

Then, drawing about her waist a belt of diamonds and donning the crown that the Empress Marie Louise had worn on her wedding day, Eugénie set out for the Tuileries, accompanied by her now-hyperkinetic mother and the Imperial Master of Ceremonies. There she joined the Emperor—he was dressed in a military uniform that was, inexplicably, one size too small—for the grand procession to Notre-Dame Cathedral.

Paris was awash in pennants, banners and triumphal arches, all sporting Napoleonic eagles, Napoleonic bees, Napoleonic violets and the letters N and E intertwined. Aristocrats rubbed shoulders—distastefully, to be sure—with peasants who had flocked in from neighboring villages in donkey carts and with provincials who had availed themselves of the latest national novelty, the railroad.

Everyone was eager to have a look at the great beauty who was their Empress.

Attempting to keep order were troops in spanking new uniforms, cuirassiers in shiny helmets and breastplates, and mounted cavalrymen in feathers and plumes. Contributing to the tumult was the cacophony of bands at every intersection, blasting out marches dating from the First Empire.

The Cathedral's perennial grime had been covered over with precious stone-encrusted hangings depicting France and Spain, pennants representing the Empire's cities and provinces, and gigantic reproductions of the Bonaparte and Montijo coats of arms.

---

* *Among the catastrophic events that occurred on a Sunday were Paca's death, the Prince Imperial's death, and the overthrow of the Second Empire. Eugénie herself died on a Sunday—rather unexpectedly, her advanced age notwithstanding.*

To one foreign envoy it all added up to "loud colors, a profusion of flowers and candles, many flags, little taste—typically French."

Shortly after noon, the Emperor and Empress set out in the glass and gilt carriage that had taken Napoleon Bonaparte and Josephine to their coronation in 1802, and, in 1810, Napoleon Bonaparte and Marie Louise to their wedding. Drawn by eight white-plumed bays, the carriage was preceded by a squadron of the *Garde Impériale* and followed by a division of heavy cavalry.

As the procession passed under the archway of the Pavillon de l'Horloge and out onto the Rue de Rivoli, the Imperial crown of gold atop the carriage suddenly broke loose and clattered to the ground. The superstitious among the onlookers hurriedly made the sign of the cross.

The same thing had happened in 1810.

At exactly 1 P.M., amidst the roaring of a thousand cannons and the tintinnabulation of every church bell in Paris, the carriage arrived at Notre-Dame. As the pair entered the Cathedral, which was lit with 10,000 candles, they were greeted by the cardinals of France. All moved majestically up the aisle toward the high altar, while an orchestra of 500 played the Coronation March from Meyerbeer's *Le Prophète*. Baron Hübner found it "stupefying."

At the high altar, they were greeted by the papal legate, dressed as befitted the solemn occasion, and the Imperial family. Characteristically, the ex-King of Westphalia was attired as if he were on his way to a fancy-dress ball as Lord Chief Marshal of the Universe. Uncharacteristically, Princess Mathilde, the epitome of *haute couture*, was garbed in a plain, unimaginative gown, as if she were on her way to the welfare office as Charity Case of the Month. True to his word, Plon-Plon wore black evening dress as a sign of mourning.

During the hour-long rites, including a Te Deum intoned by a tone-deaf archbishop, the Empress, according to one eyewitness, rose "at the saying of the Gospel, made several crosses with her thumb—*à l'espagnole*—on her forehead, her lips and her heart." Baron Hübner felt that "Perhaps there was a shade too much dignity and religious fervor, but these were little mistakes she will correct as she gets used to the footlights."

Eugénie never did get around to correcting those little mistakes.

Among those present was Lady Augusta Bruce, a close friend of Queen Victoria's mother, the Duchess of Kent. Victoria had dispatched her to report personally on the wedding. Reported Lady Bruce:

> We saw her distinctly enough to be able to say that a more lovely *coup d'oeil* could not be conceived. Her beautifully chiseled features and marble complexion, the noble carriage of her head, her exquisitely proportioned figure and graceful carriage were most striking, and the whole was like a poet's vision! I believe she is equally beautiful when seen close; but at the distance at which we saw her, the effect was something more than that of a lovely picture—it was ethereal; ideal. . . . A sort of cloud or mist of transparency enveloped her . . .

At the conclusion of the rites, the Imperial bridal pair moved majestically to the west door of the Cathedral. Amidst the banging of drums and blowing of trumpets, these two protagonists in the eighteen-year Imperial charade on which the curtain had just gone up climbed into their carriage and returned processionally to the Tuileries.

They played to a mixed crowd.

One member of the British Embassy reported that "there was— for the Emperor—no enthusiasm expressed. . . . The novelty and the sex interesting them, the Empress was cheered everywhere by the people." But while thousands cheered, "coarse jests passed from mouth to mouth." Many in the crowd took to chanting some of the hastily composed ditties of the day, of which the following is a fair example:

> Montijo, more beautiful than wise,
> Heaps vows upon the Emperor.
> This evening, if he finds a maidenhead,
> It will mean that she had two of them.

The Emperor had told the nation that the Empress was as "virtuous" as Josephine. Many die-hard Republicans were prepared to take him at his word.

Early that evening, the pair left for a week-long honeymoon in the suburbs of Paris. They had planned to spend their wedding night at Saint-Cloud, but at the last minute the Emperor announced a change of plans. They went instead to the nearby lodge at

Villeneuve-l'Etang, scene of their first private meeting almost four years earlier.

The Empress thought this a charming sentimental gesture on the Emperor's part.

Actually, Madame Howard was still in the château at Saint-Cloud packing her belongings . . . one by one.

Of the Emperor's and Empress's nuptial night, nothing is known but much can be inferred.

The Emperor, a confirmed satyr, subsequently told his cousin Mathilde: "I was faithful to the Empress for the first six months of our union."

A few years later, when the Empress learned that one of her young Bonaparte in-laws was balking at marriage to a fifty-year-old widower, she said: "Tell the girl that after the first night, it makes no difference whatever whether a man is good-looking or ugly, and that after a week it comes to exactly the same thing!"

Part II: Sovereignty

Chapter 7
Imperial Court

The Napoleonic Court was a curious hybrid; it combined the rigid etiquette of the Habsburgs and Bourbons with the morality of the Jukes and Kallikaks.

Typifying the etiquette: Ushers in powdered wigs and plumed hats stood stiffly at doorways, ready to shout out *"l'Empereur!"* should Napoleon happen to sidle by, more often than not carrying his favorite rhinoceros-penis walking stick surmounted by a golden eagle. Every time Eugénie—always attended by six ladies-in-waiting and a chamberlain—sat down to dine, a pair of Nubians in Venetian garb stood at attention behind her chair; when Félix came to dress her hair daily, he appeared in knee britches and with sword.

Typifying the morality: One day as Persigny was complaining to a group of courtiers about his new bride's misconduct, he was interrupted by the Duke de Gramont-Caderousse with: "Monsieur! I cannot allow you to criticize my mistress in this fashion!"*

For the Emperor and Empress, it all took a bit of getting used to. Kind and attentive as he always was, particularly to women, Napoleon was incapable of playing the graceful and dignified sovereign.

---

* *When Persigny was ambassador to London, his wife, who enjoyed a predilection for embassy clerks, became the heroine of a popular jest: "Madame de Persigny is lost! It is impossible to find her!" "Well, have you looked carefully under all the furniture? The tables, the buffets—the secretaries?"*

He was stiff, gauche and easily bored; he seldom smiled, frequently yawned, always abhorred gossip and small talk. Eugénie was too accustomed to moving and doing as she pleased to be locked into a protocol-defined existence.

In time, the sovereigns, but especially Eugénie, would take to their roles. But at the outset of the reign it was left to the Imperial Grand Chamberlain, the Duke de Bassano, to prance through the drawing rooms dressed to the nines and cry aloud: "It is Their Imperial Majesties' wish that you amuse yourselves, *messieurs et mesdames!*" The *messieurs et mesdames* did as Their Imperial Majesties wished. They drank, dined, gossiped, waltzed and fornicated.

Remarked the Empress: "I watch over the virtues of the young girls [her ladies-in-waiting]. As to the married women, I care for neither their virtues nor their moral lapses."

The Imperial Privy Purse was 25 million francs per annum. There was, in addition, 5 million francs from the yearly rentals for crown lands that included all the Imperial palaces, the Louvre, several private mansions in and around Paris, and the Sèvres porcelain works. Certainly enough to finance the gilded epicenter of an eighteen-year regime of which Count Émile Félix Fleury, the Emperor's chief equerry, would recall in epitaphic nostalgia: "It was not exactly a proper empire, but we did have a damn good time."

The Court was literally acrawl with a superfluity of equerries, secretaries, aides, chamberlains, ladies-in-waiting, valets, butlers, chefs, gardeners, gamekeepers, wardrobe mistresses (especially wardrobe mistresses), and servants of every description and area of responsibility. The Imperial household was as overpopulated as New York City's welfare rolls.

Presiding as Imperial Grand Maître was one of the Emperor's Tascher de la Pagerie cousins. He also doubled as Court Buffoon. The Empress often enjoyed breaking into a conversation with the command: "Count Tascher de la Pagerie, do imitate a turkey cock for us!" The obliging Grand Maître would immediately gobble and strut about. He could also "do" (and often "did") the sun, the moon, a pregnant turtle, a braying jackass and—the Emperor's favorite—Louis-Philippe putting on his wig.

Another class act at Court was one by Count Duperré, the Prince

Imperial's equerry. His ability to flick bread pellets into the Prince's mouth from a distance of twenty feet was a marvel to behold.

The Court moved in a fixed orbit: the Tuileries from mid-December to Easter; Saint-Cloud in the spring; Fontainebleau in the summer; Biarritz for a few weeks in September; and then on to Compiègne until mid-December, when it was time to return to the Tuileries and start the round anew.

The Empress's favorite was the Villa Eugénie built for her by Napoleon at Biarritz as a wedding present. Situated near the Spanish border, it assuaged her occasional homesickness. The Villa Eugénie was hers and hers alone; she could invite whomever she pleased; she need not be subjected to the multitude of hangers-on who followed the sovereigns in and out of the other Imperial palaces.

It was at the Tuileries that the Court was most splendiferous and most pretentious. There were countless receptions, dinners, concerts and ballet and opera performances. Every Monday evening the Empress gave an Audience in her private apartments. (Baron Hübner advises that on these occasions she "flitted from one subject to another, like most Spanish women do; they are more vivacious than witty and more witty than profound.") Every Thursday evening the sovereigns hosted a reception for eight hundred. Four times a year, between New Year's Day and Lent, there was a Great Ball attended by upwards of five thousand.

On those occasions, footmen in powdered wigs and sumptuous livery, richly embroidered with the Napoleonic eagle and Napoleonic bees, moved about. Swiss Guards stood at attention in plumed hats and holding halberds. Lining the staircases were the *Cent-Gardes*, the richly caparisoned ceremonial bodyguard whose members were selected on the basis of size and looks (and who were "passed around" by the courtiers: some accommodated the ladies, some accommodated the gentlemen, some accommodated both).

The sovereigns wore gold-gilt Court dress to "receive" their guests. Military officers and foreign envoys wore embroidered uniforms; government officials and honored male courtiers wore knee britches and silk stockings. All the ladies wore enormous crinolines (it was the Empress's wish), low décolleté and elaborate coiffures. (Many dyed their hair in an attempt to emulate the Empress's auburn tresses and, given the chemicals they used, occasionally went bald in the process.)

Guests were led from their carriages to the foot of the Fontaine Staircase and then marched ceremoniously up to the *Salon des Maréchaux*. There, on gilded thrones on a dais, sat the sovereigns, surrounded by their attendants: men on the left, ladies on the right. At the foot of the dais stood the Duke de Bassano; at his side, three chamberlains. The nearest of the chamberlains would ask the name of the person about to be presented; the name was repeated by three pairs of lips, and then to Bassano, who, in his turn, would repeat it to Their Imperial Majesties. The guest would bow twice and then withdraw.

When the last guest had been presented, the dancing would be commenced. (Johann Strauss often wielded the baton.) As the guests waltzed about, the sovereigns remained seated, their attendants standing stiffly as if frozen in time. The Emperor sat in a slouched position, hand to chin, peering upon the entire scene through half-closed eyes, confounding dignity with boredom; the Empress sat rigidly erect, looking down impassively on the assemblage, confounding dignity with superciliousness.

After a respectable interval, the Grand Chamberlain would announce that Their Majesties were retiring for the evening (whereupon a few of the wags would mouth the words "But not with each other"). Their Majesties would rise as if on cue; the Empress would place her hand on the Emperor's arm; and the two would depart the premises ceremoniously—Eugénie majestically, as if both feet were on an air current, Napoleon grotesquely, as if one foot were in a ditch—followed by their attendants. It was like a platoon of mannequins come miraculously to life.

Their Majesties' days were less stultifying. After breakfast, the two met for an hour or so and then went their separate ways. Eugénie's mornings were given over to catching up on her correspondence, receptions for favorite courtiers, occasional Audiences, and visits to charitable institutions. Napoleon spent his days tending to government business, reading assiduously the daily press— concerned with his own popularity, he was pleased with what he read in the newspapers, which were all heavily censored—and making unescorted tours about the city to check up on Baron Haussmann's massive reconstruction program.

Every afternoon at four o'clock, weather permitting, the Empress—whom Nestor Roqueplan characterized as "the best kept kept-woman in all of France"—and the Emperor—whom Théophile Gautier described as looking "like a ringmaster who has been sacked for getting drunk"—would set out in an open carriage, escorted by a troop of *Cent-Gardes*, for their daily ride in the Bois de Boulogne. As they were driven slowly around the lake, the Emperor would tip his hat and the Empress would nod benignly to aristocrats and courtesans who were also "doing the Bois."

After the drive, the sovereigns would again go their own ways, not meeting again until seven, for dinner. There were usually no less than eighteen at table, often a hundred. After dinner, if there was no ball or reception planned, the sovereigns would lead their guests into a drawing room for coffee, light music and heavy chatter.

Living quarters in the Tuileries were dismal: dark, badly ventilated rooms. Only the Imperial apartments had any form of central heating. The corridors were gloomy: gas jets flickered and lackeys rushed hither and yon carrying great cords of wood for the palace's many fireplaces. The Emperor's private apartments were spartan; the Empress's—directly above, connected by a narrow winding staircase—were overcrowded.

There was no "Empress Eugénie style" in furnishing; just well-upholstered mishmash. According to Mérimée, Eugénie was given to "furnishing rooms so richly that there is no more space left in them for people." Visitors had to take caution not to stumble over chairs, bang into settees, fall against curio-laden tables, crash into screens, or trip over bibelots. Entering the Presence was like running a trash-strewn obstacle course. One courtier recorded:

> She is happy if she may change her salon about. She arranges four sofas, eight armchairs, and twenty other chairs along the sides of the room, small shelves in the corners, and small tables and cushions in the middle, so that no one knows where to turn! When once you are inside, you cannot find your way out! But that makes the Empress happy; that is a side of her character that you must touch if you want to gain recognition. You must praise the artistic arrangement. You must say that in her an interior decorator has been lost!

When not rearranging her apartments, Eugénie was rearranging her wardrobe. The little Spanish grandee to whom clothes were a matter of supreme indifference was now a French empress to whom clothes were an obsession. She began the custom of changing one's wardrobe twice yearly and changing one's costume seven times daily. She introduced pastel colors, high-heeled boots and, of course, the crinoline. (The "Eugénie hats" would not come until much later in the Empress's life, after she had lost her throne.)

Those crinolines were expansive as well as expensive. In the Tuileries, a freight elevator was installed so that the Empress would not have to negotiate the stairs. It was considered a great honor to share the elevator with Her Majesty. All the ladies vied for invitations—except the Princess Mathilde. Mathilde, who stayed away from Court as much as possible, allowed that she would "rather descend on a rope than share an elevator with that witch."

Thanks to the Empress's patronage, Charles Frederick Worth became the arbiter of women's fashion, and Paris became the fashion center of the universe. Women of means flocked to the House of Worth at 7 Rue de la Paix the way Attic initiates flocked to partake of the Eleusinian Mysteries. (The Goncourt brothers knew one woman who ordered the famed *couturier* to "make sure I always have something black at hand. You know I've got three sons at the Crimean front!") The Empress thought nothing of spending 30,000 francs on a cape or 60,000 francs on a gown at Chez Worth. And she purchased many a cape and gown.

The Emperor's wardrobe, on the other hand, was less extensive and less imaginative. Except on ceremonial occasions, when he affected knee britches, silk stockings, buckled shoes and an ermine-lined mantle embroidered with golden bees, he favored either a dark suit or his general's uniform, sword and riding boots.

When the Court moved on from Paris, life became more relaxed. At Saint-Cloud, balls gave way to *tableaux vivants*. In one, the storming of the Malakoff was "performed" to celebrate the conclusion of the Crimean War. Upwards of 100,000 francs was spent on the costumes and décor, enough to buy a week's supply of milk for every child in France. The Empress and her ladies-in-waiting defended a mound that represented the Malakoff Tower, which the Emperor and his courtiers "stormed." Next day it was whispered in horrified Orléanist drawing rooms that "the Emperor made the attack on all fours and caught hold of the ladies by their feet. The Empress was not amused."

Saint-Cloud was also the setting for numerous *bals-masqués*. There were the usual Pierrots and Pierrettes, Turks, Greeks, Neapolitan peasants, Parisian ragpickers, shepherds and shepherdesses, and the like; "the most dignified ministers and highest ladies of the Court," sniffed one observer, "spend an indecent fortune to dress up and make damn fools of themselves."

The Empress derived so much pleasure from these fancy-dress affairs, she often dressed up twice. At one, she spent the first half of the evening as Diana the Huntress, the second half as the wife of a Venetian Doge; the Emperor spent the first half of the evening as a knight in black and red, the second half in bed with one of his equerries' wives.

When carping tongues began to rail against "this whirl of festivities and pleasures and conspicuous waste" surrounding the sovereigns, criticism was forestalled—though not for long—by pointing out, in the *Moniteur*, that "the money spent on Court entertainments falls back in a rain of gold on the various industries." Dancing was a necessity; it gave employment to musicians. Banquets at which more was thrown away than consumed were beneficial to the food growers and purveyors, not to mention the employment it gave all those chefs and waiters. If the Empress and her female courtiers were to limit the size of their wardrobes, it was feared the silk weavers of Lyons might wind up in bankruptcy. One socially committed hanger-on, the Countess de Portales, did her part to keep the flower trade solvent by spending 50,000 francs to fill her vases every time she entertained.

"The chief item of news," wrote Tocqueville sarcastically to a friend in England, "is that the new Court ladies have already returned to trains and little pageboys, and the new courtiers go stag hunting with their master in the Forest of Fontainebleau, clad once more in the hunting costume of Louis XV with the plumed cock hat."

In addition to the fine hunting at Fontainebleau was the famous fishpond, where the courtiers whiled away many a summer hour boating about. The Empress enjoyed being poled hither and yon in a gondola that had been imported, along with a crew of gondoliers, from Venice's Piazza San Marco.

Another popular pastime at Fontainebleau was the Imperial picnic. Everyone would get all gussied up in Louis XV costumes—

green and crimson velvet with lace cuffs and tricornered hats—and troop out into the Great Forest, followed by a legion of hamper-toting lackeys, to watch that confirmed Hispanophile, Mérimée, make the *gazpacho*.

(Mérimée was made a Senator for life by the Emperor. He accepted at the insistence of Eugénie, but on the condition that Court activities not be allowed to interfere with his creative endeavors. Though he cared little for the Emperor, Mérimée admired his lack of pretense; the Emperor, for his part, did not particularly trust Mérimée—mainly because of his close friendship with the Empress—but admired his wit and erudition. In addition to accommodating the Empress with his avuncular presence, Mérimée kept her mother up to date on the carryings-on at the Napoleonic Court.

(The Countess de Montijo returned to Madrid—reluctantly—shortly after Eugénie's marriage. According to Filon, "Her son-in-law had made it absolutely clear to her that if she remained on in France she would be treated merely as a distinguished foreigner. I have found traces of her disappointment in the correspondence between Mérimée and Madame de Montijo, as all her letters written to him at this time are full of epigrammatical remarks about the Emperor, whom she calls 'Monsieur Isidore.' "*)

Once a year, to signal commencement of the "autumn season," the Imperial train—six parlor cars for guests, six first-class carriages for servants (Napoleon was considerate of his social inferiors), ten to twenty baggage cars (depending on the number of guests; each and every crinoline and hoopskirt had to be crated individually)—would set out from the Gare du Nord for the fifty-mile run to Compiègne, a magnificent château set amidst one of France's most beautiful game preserves. The train would be met at the station by horses and carriages whose postillions affected green and gold livery and powdered wigs. At the château, a pair of *Cent-Gardes* stood outside every door; a valet was placed at the service of

---

* *According to documents rescued from the Tuileries prior to its destruction during the Commune of 1871, the Emperor settled his mother-in-law's outstanding Parisian debts to the tune of 1,358,160 francs. On none of her visits was the Countess invited to stay at the Tuileries. As the Princess Mathilde remarked, "If the Emperor had wished to have an Empress Mother, he would have found her elsewhere."*

each guest; a footman was stationed behind every chair; a military band played during all meals.

Such was the comparative informality, the ladies rarely changed their costumes more than four times a day.

Invitations to Compiègne were highly prized: writers, artists and prominent scientists were often asked. There were four "series" of guest lists, defining status. On one occasion a rather patronizing *grande dame* asked one of the better-known Court doxies, "Are you in the Elegant Series?" and was told: "No, dearie, I'm in yours."

Other than the annual St. Hubert's Day Grand Ball in the Great Hall (November 3), evenings at Compiègne were more informal than at any other of the royal residences (Biarritz excepted). Dinner would be followed by dancing, billiards, table quoits (the Emperor's favorite game), spelling bees or Blind Man's Bluff (the Empress's favorite game). Sometimes, to break the monotony, one of the Parisian theatrical troupes would be brought out to give a performance in the château's five-hundred-seat theater.

Life at Compiègne was not to everyone's liking. Wrote Lord Cowley: "The Empress, instead of letting people alone, torments herself and them by finding it necessary to furnish constant amusements for them—such amusements generally suited to some people and not to others!" Among those amusements was *Cheval Fondu*—a favorite of Eugénie and Napoleon alike.

In this rather hilarious amusement, one gentleman would kneel on the floor with his head buried in some lady's pubic region, whereupon everyone would climb atop him until all fell in a droll heap. The Empress did not partake physically; she preferred to be hilarious from the sidelines.

At one *Cheval Fondu*, when the guests had all collapsed in the obligatory heap, it was noticed that the gentleman who had buried his head in the lady's pubic region was still thus interred.

It was, of course, the Emperor.

Throughout the early years of the reign, Eugénie would on occasion drop her Imperial pose and revert to the high jinks of her youth. According to a secret police report dated April 5, 1854:

She cannot forget the habits of extreme freedom contracted before her marriage. It even happens that sometimes she behaves in a childish manner curiously in contrast with her present elevation. The story is told that recently she went with the Emperor to visit a garden. During the walk he bent to examine a plant. The Empress thought it funny to push her august consort from behind, causing him to fall.

Her august consort's reaction was not recorded.

On another occasion, at Fontainebleau, Eugénie "conceived a mad desire to go to a rustic dance in the village." With one of her female attendants, she "drove in a carriage to the edge of the forest," where the two changed into peasants' costumes and then "ran to the village and entered the tent in which the lads made their lassies dance." When the Emperor learned that one of the lads had "put his arm around the Empress's waist," he scolded her roundly. "Eugénie defended herself by reminding him that Marie Antoinette had 'indulged in similar pranks'!"

Her courtiers liked Eugénie better when she behaved as the free and unconventional Mademoiselle de Montijo than when she stood on her Imperial dignity. Unlike Napoleon, who was thoroughly unpretentious and whose sanguine personality was constant, Eugénie became more imperious with each passing year. In time, she assumed a haughty and affected mien that most people found ludicrous and infuriating.

Ironically, she really did not intend to come across as such. Eugénie was a victim of her own pretentions. No one, save the favored few among her entourage, was permitted to approach without having been invited to do so by a chamberlain who was always in attendance. Whenever, during the course of the day, she wished to see the Emperor, Eugénie would ring a little bell. If the Emperor was in the vicinity, he would come trotting. If he was not, the Empress would throw a little fit.

On balance, it can be said that Eugénie did not learn how to behave like an empress until she had ceased being one.

The boulevard wits said that the only thing Napoleon inherited from his famous uncle was his insatiable sexual appetite. He once said, "Usually, it is man who attacks; as for me, I defend myself, and I often capitulate." It would seem that he spent half his waking hours capitulating.

Had his health been any more indelicate, the Emperor might well have capitulated himself into terminal exhaustion.

Within the Imperial Court were any number of women who threw themselves at the Emperor in order to advance the careers of their husbands or lovers or, in some instances, themselves. It was not easy being the most sought-after man in all of France. Princess Mathilde recalled:

> At a ball at the Tuileries, I noticed that he was very preoccupied, and I asked him the reason. "I have a very bad headache," he replied. "Moreover, I am persecuted by three women. I have a blonde on the ground floor, whom I try my best to get rid of. Then I have the lady on the first floor, who is still very beautiful, but bores me to death, and then there still remains the blonde on the second floor, who follows me everywhere. . . . I need these little distractions . . ."

Those "little distractions" were transitory liaisons, and are not to be confused with the various official mistresses he went through, at times concurrently.

"All those who knew this weakness of the sovereign—and there were very few who did not—used the most daring means to oblige him to come near," reports the Marquis de Taisey-Châtenoy. All were advised by Bacciochi that "His Imperial Majesty does not like to be kissed on the lips, but may be kissed anywhere else on his august person."

The Emperor's satyriasis was treated as a charming game by his courtiers, many of whom were similarly afflicted. When the Court was at Fontainebleau, he liked to fill a straw basket with trinkets, one of which had been secretly designated as "the prize." Elegant countesses and duchesses would gather, along with the transient trulls, for the "drawing" and would, amidst much hilarity, fight for "the prize"—which was, of course, the Emperor. The lucky winner's husband rarely raised a demur in light of his wife's good fortune.

More often than not, the Emperor's approach was less public and less subtle: he would simply sidle up to a lady who had titillated his appetite, twist the ends of his far-flung moustache suggestively, and murmur, "This evening." If the lady's husband was at Court and it was suspected that he might not be too happy about the whole thing, some pretext was found to dispatch him back to Paris or wherever. Napoleon knew what he wanted when he saw it, and is never known to have been rejected.

Occasionally, though, the randy monarch would get more than he bargained for.

One wintry afternoon at Saint-Cloud, he walked into a dimly lit drawing room and noticed a scented frock draped across a sofa. Drawing closer, he discerned that the frock was inhabited, and he pinched a calf. It belonged to the Bishop of Nancy, who had fallen into a wine-induced stupor.

During one *bal-masqué* at the Tuileries, intrigued by a voluptuous masked figure, the Emperor edged up to her, squeezed her hand suggestively, and then led her from the crowded ballroom. As he escorted the mysterious masked beauty toward his private apartments, the Emperor could sense that she was uneasy. Now in heat—he enjoyed the novelty that some lady might not be willing to bed down with him without at least the semblance of a struggle—the Emperor began to press himself on her. "Sire, I must implore you, you are mistaken. . . . I beg of Your Majesty to listen to me . . ." His majesty would not listen. He removed the mask—and discovered in his arms the young duke known as "Mademoiselle," who was the Imperial Court's resident drag queen.

In explaining to his cousin Mathilde that he needed those "little distractions," the Emperor added the qualificatory "but I always return to the Empress with pleasure."

It was certainly no pleasure for the frigid Empress; and after the birth of the Prince Imperial in 1856, the Emperor, at the Empress's insistence, did not even bother returning.

So far as Eugénie was concerned, he could have stopped returning within months of their marriage. In the archives of the Imperial Minister of Police, a report dated July 2, 1853 reveals that "the Emperor has completely resumed his relations with Miss Howard." (Which would indicate that he had indeed been faithful to Eugénie "for the first six months.") Toward the end of September, recuperating from her first miscarriage, Eugénie "told her august husband that she intends leaving France, if the Emperor has no greater regard for his dignity and does not realize the duty that he owes to the wife of his choice. Something of a scene took place. . . . The Emperor, always calm and gentle, even when he is in the wrong, ultimately succeeded in calming her anger by promising to break off all contact with the person in question. . . ."*

The august husband dispatched "a hundred and fifty thousand francs which Monsieur Mocquard [their go-between] thought were essential in order to keep Madame Howard quiet."

It took more than that to keep Madame Howard quiet. After a year or so of protracted negotiations, she agreed to get out of the Emperor's life upon payment of 5,449,000 francs, an estate and a title. Madame Howard proved over the long haul to have been Napoleon III's most expensive mistress by far.

But then, look what he had cost her.

Financing of the Imperial mistresses was nothing compared to the financing of the Imperial kinfolk. Just how much was drained from the public purse by the battalion of Bonapartes who flocked around the Emperor is unascertainable. The Jerome Bonapartes alone—including Mathilde, Plon-Plon and their half-brother "Bo"—accounted for more than 37 million francs. Before the Second Empire collapsed, upwards of two dozen Bonaparte first and second cousins were drawing pensions against the Privy Purse. An equal number had by then been given high-paying (and often meaningless) jobs, handsome grants from time to time, and, where necessary, handsome dowries.

Princess Napoleone-Elisa Bacciochi, daughter of the Emperor's aunt Elisa, accounted for 6 million francs. (Upon her death, she willed what was left to the Prince Imperial.) The five grandchildren of his aunt Caroline Murat Bonaparte averaged half a million each; in addition, the middle Murat grandchild, Princess Anna, later the Duchess de Mouchy (she was a favorite of Eugénie's), accounted for close to 3 million. Uncle Lucien Bonaparte's fourth (and rottenest) son, Pierre-Napoleon, known as "the Corsican Wild Boar," was good for 100,000 francs a year. (He would repay his cousin's generosity by helping bring down the Empire.)

---

* *Princess Mathilde: "The Empress did not want to sleep with the Emperor and did not want anyone else to either. But it was not jealousy on her part. She was not only frigid, she was of the conviction that everyone else should be frigid too. That woman belonged in a cloister!"*

In addition to the Bonaparte cousins, there was a whole flock of Beauharnais and Tascher de la Pagerie cousins. Mercifully, these were less of a fiscal nuisance than their Bonaparte counterparts; their combined take did not equal what it cost the Emperor to keep some of his relatives from further embarrassing the monarchy by dragging their squabbles into court.

For example, when uncle Jerome died in 1860, he left a will that set Mathilde and Plon-Plon at each other's throats. Only when they threatened to fight it out before a magistrate did Napoleon resolve the issue by settling 1.5 million francs on the two. At that, it was a bargain. When the Duke de Morny married, he was threatened with a suit by his long-time mistress, Madame Le Hon. Anxious to avoid a scandal, the Emperor settled 3.5 million francs on her. It was a mere pittance compared to what Madame Le Hon had spent on Morny and hoped to recover through litigation, but it sufficed to keep her out of court.

From all the foregoing, one might infer that this pair of Imperial adventurers were transmogrified by their elevated status into a pair of Imperial vampires who fed off each other to their and the Empire's mutual destruction. One might, but one shouldn't.

Both wanted what was best for France. Both had the interests of all Frenchmen at heart, poor and rich alike; indeed, both were more concerned with bettering the lot of the have-nots, probably on the assumption that the haves were quite capable of bettering themselves. Napoleon encouraged public works, patronized industry and science, sought to alleviate the plight of the poor through mass housing and the like. It was with good cause that Sainte-Beuve hailed him as Saint-Simon on Horseback (Saint-Simon the economic philosopher, not the biblical apostle).

In all this, Eugénie was supportive. She was president of all maternal welfare societies and founded a number of hostels for orphans and unwed mothers. Too, she pioneered coeducation in French universities and was an advocate of what today we call "women's rights."

The Emperor did more than indulge himself in his women and his relatives; the Empress did more than replenish her wardrobe and berate her husband for his chronic infidelity.

Basically, both were socially committed, inherently compassionate human beings who shared a vision—to succeed where Napoleon Bonaparte had failed, to make France the most prosperous as well as the preeminent Power on the Continent.

Though often at odds as to how that vision could be realized, they labored with equal determination and zeal.

The reason they failed miserably is not because both were out of their minds, but simply because both were out of their element.

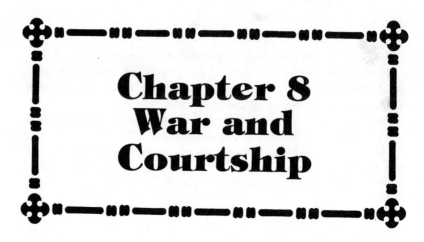

Chapter 8
War and
Courtship

What Napoleon I failed to accomplish through war, Napoleon III would accomplish through alliances, persuasion and political cunning.

Or so he hoped.

In allying himself with Great Britain, the leading liberal Power, against the tyrannies of Russia and Austria, he would wipe out the memory of Waterloo and the humiliations imposed by the Congress of Vienna.

Or so he hoped.

For assisting at the birth of such independent states as Poland, Italy and Rumania, he would be remembered as their benefactor.

Or so he hoped.

For offering his good services to a continent ruled by a few reactionary Powers whose component parts were destined to achieve independence, he would be "rewarded" by an extension of French territory on its eastern borders.

Or so he hoped.

None of Napoleon III's schemes in the area of foreign policy ever worked out quite as he had planned. In pursuing those schemes, he invariably wound up entangled in knots of his own making. Time and the tide of history were on his side. But he was too idealistic for his own good, too inherently decent for his own good—and too cunning for his own good. Of all Napoleon III's foreign adventures, only the first—the Crimean War—was successful.

Remarkably, it was the only adventure he himself did not hatch.

To dismiss the Crimean War as merely a religious crusade, as do so many less than recondite historians, is as fatuous as to dismiss the Vietnam War as merely an anti-Communist crusade. There was, to be sure, a religious question involved: Which among the major Powers—Catholic, Greek Orthodox, Protestant, Mohammedan— would "protect" the Holy Places of Palestine following the impending collapse of the Turkish-Ottoman Empire?

Religion, though, was only an excuse that diplomacy—and international inanity—transformed into a *casus belli*. Had the shrines been situated on an Arctic tundra, Europe would have found some other excuse to stumble into a needless, witless catastrophe that did not resolve the basic issue—Russian expansion toward the Mediterranean and influence in the Balkans—but merely postponed it. Over the long haul of history to date, the Crimean War stands as the only major conflict whose positive results amounted to little more than a universal appreciation for the humaneness of Florence Nightingale.

"We have on our hands a very sick man," said Tsar Nicholas I to the British envoy at St. Petersburg. It was a remarkably unoriginal diagnosis. The sick man—Turkey—had been in delicate health since the seventeenth century. That it was still alive in the nineteenth century was due only to the efforts of the major Powers, who hovered over the patient like a pack of mutually antipathetic physicians proffering rival prescriptions. By the 1850s, the sickness was terminal: miserable mismanagement and dismal decadence made the Ottoman Empire's eventual demise not only a historical inevitability but a historical necessity.

Nicholas—whose unstable mind rendered him unfit to cope with complex problems—concluded that the time had come to dispose of "the sick man of Europe" once and for all time. But the attending physicians wished to keep him alive until they were in a position to divvy up his possessions. Shortly after Napoleon came to the throne, the Tsar decided to enforce his assumed right as protector of Orthodox Christians in the Ottoman Empire by occupying Constantinople "temporarily."

At the same time, he proposed an agreement with Britain concerning the ultimate disposition of the vast Ottoman heritage. In return for being allowed to create—under Russian auspices—a few independent Balkan states, Nicholas would let Britain "have" Crete, Egypt and a few other choice parcels in the Levant. Reasoned the Tsar: Britain was not unfavorably disposed toward a Russian advance westward; Britain was apprehensive of French designs (might not Napoleon III pursue the policies of Napoleon I?); the other major Powers—Austria and Prussia—would support Russia, passively if not actively; Catholic France would never intervene on the side of a Mohammedan state.

The Tsar was a victim of chronic delusions. Protestant England was less concerned with who controlled the Holy Places of Palestine than with maintaining free access to the trade routes of the Black Sea.

While the British and Austrian governments both endeavored to persuade Nicholas to abandon his bullying attitude toward the Turks, the press began to whip up strong public opinion against Russia. The wily Persigny now saw an opportunity for Napoleon to emerge as guarantor of European peace.

Accordingly, on June 13, 1853, the French fleet was dispatched to Greek waters.

Napoleon's detractors maintain to this day that he deliberately engineered the Crimean War for the sake of military glory and international prestige. Nothing could be further from the truth. He realized that no one in France wanted war, there was no deep hatred for Russia, there was no enthusiasm for allying France with England, and pro-Turkish sentiment among the French was all but nonexistent.

Five factors militated in favor of his interjecting himself into the Russo-Turkish squabble: a desire to avenge Waterloo and the dynastic settlement imposed by the Russia-dominated Congress of Vienna; a desire to ally France firmly with England; a desire to bring about Rumanian independence (in line with his belief in the right of national determination); a need to hold the Catholic vote in France; and a need to win the liberal vote by destroying the might of autocratic Russia.

He sought to resolve the entire mess diplomatically. His dispatching of the French fleet was not so much a sign of intent as a gesture, in the face of Russia's invasion of the Danubian Principalities (later Rumania)—a gesture in which the British soon joined by dispatching their fleet.

As Europe slowly drifted into a war that no one really wanted,

Napoleon continued to press for a settlement of the basic issues. His attempt to convene a European congress was rebuffed by Russia. On January 3, 1854, at Napoleon's suggestion, the French and British fleets entered the Black Sea to protect the Turkish coasts and shipping. Later that month, in a personal letter to the Tsar, he made a frantic last-minute attempt to avoid hostilities.

When this came to naught, he joined with Queen Victoria's government in an ultimatum demanding evacuation of the Principalities. The Tsar ignored the ultimatum, France and England joined in an alliance with Turkey, on March 20 the Russians crossed the Danube, and eight days later Europe was at war.

Nicholas boasted that "Russia will prove that in 1854 she is still what she was in 1812." France rallied behind the Emperor to prove she wasn't. Most supportive was the Empress. She wrote emphatically to Paca: *"I regard the war as good."*

Characteristically, Eugénie saw the conflict in terms of the Christian West stamping out the Russian Antichrist. How she squared the idea of the Christian West stamping in collusion with the infidel Turks is best left to the imagination.

France assumed leadership of the Allies, supplying more than half the manpower, half the matériel, and half the casualties. Incompetence was assumed on a *pro rata* basis by all parties concerned.

Europe had not fought a war in forty years; a generation of young men who lacked even a clue as to what they were doing—or why they were doing it—were led by a generation of aged generals who were either inexperienced, sickly or downright inept. Mass confusion in logistics, impenetrable cold, periodic raging epidemics (notably cholera and typhus), appallingly unsanitary conditions—all militated against the troops' standing much of a chance. More men died in hospitals than in battle. Often the stretcher-bearers themselves collapsed and died at the side of the invalids they were bearing. At times the gravediggers collapsed and were buried in the very trenches they were digging for others.

Crimea did not end war on the Continent; it set the stage for future wars. It did not halt the encroachment of the "northern colossus"; it merely postponed the inevitable. England wound up with an excuse to fairly litter London with monuments to Alma, Balaklava,

Inkerman, Sebastopol and the lot. One hopes Florence Nightingale would have argued that such glory hardly justified the purchase price.

As for Napoleon III, Crimea gave him the fulfillment of a dream: to be the arbiter of Europe. Furthermore, it paved the way for the fulfillment of yet another dream: alliance with England.

Napoleon, in the words of Lord Clarendon, "made love to her . . . with a tact which proved quite successful . . . and as his love-making was of a character to flatter her vanity without alarming her virtue and modesty, she enjoyed the novelty of it without scruple or fear."

The object of Napoleon's love-making was Queen Victoria. More than enjoying the novelty of it, she succumbed to it. Napoleon did not woo her as an end in itself but as a means toward an end: to ally permanently their mutually antipathetic nations.

That mutual antipathy predated the Napoleonic era. It went back to the fourteenth century, when Edward III's claim to France led to the Hundred Years' War, which culminated in Edward's great-grandson, Henry V, conquering France. Though the conquest was short-lived, the animosity endured; successive English monarchs persisted in taking the regnal title King of France, though none set foot in that corner of his realm. Had one dared, he would have been shot.

Making common cause in the Crimea brought the two nations together. Napoleon let it be known through diplomatic channels that he considered the wartime alliance the first step toward perpetual alliance. The British government let it be known through diplomatic channels that the idea was hardly worthy of consideration. Lord Aberdeen, the Prime Minister, unenthusiastic about France to begin with, regarded an alliance with Austria as being in his nation's best interests. Prince Albert, to whom Napoleon was a "tyrant," argued that once the war was ended, the tide "that had been flowing very strongly in favour of France might flow the other way when our people saw that the Emperor continued to be a despotic ruler and necessarily an enemy of constitutional government."

In the summer of 1854, realizing that wooing the Prince Consort was a necessary precondition to wooing the Queen, Napoleon invited Albert to see the military camp he had built near Boulogne: "I need not tell Your Highness how . . . happy I should be to show you my soldiers. I am convinced, moreover, that personal ties will contribute to strengthening the union so happily established between our two great nations."

Albert accepted the invitation. He was not so much interested in seeing the Emperor's soldiers as in making sure they were not being primed to scale the white cliffs of Dover.

The four-day visit went down fairly well. While Albert deplored the Emperor's lack of musical appreciation and incessant cigarette-smoking, he appreciated the Emperor's readiness to converse in German, quote Schiller, swap student songs, and discourse frankly on any topic. Shrewdly, the Emperor gave the impression of being most attentive to his guest's verbiage-ridden political dissertations.

Albert looked upon Napoleon as an amateurish politician, one in whose mind churned an admixture of "very sound and many crude notions." He appreciated Napoleon's open honesty—the Emperor made no pretense of functioning as a constitutional monarch, though he did promise to be one when he felt the country was ready for it—while deploring so much of what he was told. When Albert astounded Napoleon by telling him the Queen read every dispatch to and from her Foreign Office, Napoleon astounded Albert by admitting that he preferred to rely more on his private agents than on his diplomats.

Though Albert returned to Windsor convinced that an Anglo-French alliance should not be dismissed out of hand, Victoria had her doubts. Once the war was over, might not Protestant England be seriously compromised by being tied to a Catholic, illiberal, unstable regime? Had the two nations anything in common, except that mutual enmity for Tsar Nicholas?

Napoleon refused to be put off. He sent word through his old friend Lord Clarendon that "nothing would give [me] so much pleasure as to visit the Queen." The Queen advised Clarendon—now cast in the role of matchmaker—that she "would wish no anxiety to be shown to obtain the visit" and then suggested "sometime in November."

It is not good form for one chief of state to issue a coeval such a casual, drop-by-the-palace-sometime invitation. The Emperor sent

back word that November was "inopportune." He was anxious to go
a-courting, but not with his hat in his hand. To sweeten the pill, he
suggested that "a better time would be later, so as to show [our]
friendship [has] suffered no diminution."

The Queen was furious: "His reception here ought to be a boon to
him and NOT a boon to *us!*" Months—and the war—dragged on,
and it looked as though the courtship would never get off the
ground.

Then three events transpired to bring matters to a head: Lord
Aberdeen's conservative coalition government fell, cousin Plon-Plon
disgraced himself (and France) in the Crimea, and the Emperor—
encouraged by the Empress—determined to lead the Allied armies
in the field.

Upon arriving in the Crimea to take command of a division,
Plon-Plon devoted his time to insulting the Turks, outraging the
British, antagonizing the French, and otherwise making a damn
nuisance—and public spectacle—of himself. A few months later, he
suffered an attack of dysentery. Instead of accepting this common
complaint in the Allied armies as part of a soldier's life, he went to
Constantinople to recuperate.

While awaiting permission from the Emperor to return to
France—permission which the Emperor repeatedly refused to
grant—Plon-Plon insulted the Sultan, railed against the Allied
leadership, bad-mouthed his Imperial cousin, and intrigued for an
attack on Austria—which Britain and France were desperately trying to bring into the anti-Russia coalition!

By the end of January 1855, Plon-Plon was back in Paris. The
official version: ill health. The popular version: cowardice. Quipped
the Duke de Morny: "If ever a bullet is found inside Prince Napoleon, it will be one that he has swallowed." About the only one who
came to Plon-Plon's defense was his father. Grumbled Jerome: "Oh,
these French people! *Throwing stones at this poor child who has not
seen his mistress for months!*"

Even before Plon-Plon's activities in the Crimea became widely
known, Napoleon had decided to take personal command. French
and British cooperation in the field had deteriorated. Worse, no one
could come up with a workable plan to reduce the Sebastopol fortress. Napoleon felt that only he could unify the Allies and capture
Sebastopol, thus ending the war. With Plon-Plon now having so

embarrassed the dynasty, Napoleon felt that only an act of courage on his part could atone for that embarrassment.

Meanwhile, in England, public opinion had swept the Aberdeen government from office; the new Prime Minister, Palmerston, pushed for Anglo-French *rapprochement*. Though Victoria hated Palmerston, she liked his thinking. What if the British army were to become "contemptible and weak in the eyes of the French army," while Napoleon led his troops to victory at Sebastopol? Palmerston suggested that Her Majesty personally discuss the war with the Emperor—and perhaps disabuse him of the notion of going East and stealing Britain's thunder. A proper invitation was issued for a five-day State Visit.

Napoleon and Eugénie arrived on April 16, accompanied by numerous government officials and personal attendants and tons of luggage (including the first crinolines seen in England).

Despite her natural assurance, Victoria was preternaturally shy when it came to meeting strangers. Napoleon immediately set Victoria at her ease. He allowed that the great, indeed God-given fortune England enjoyed in having Her Majesty at the helm was exceeded only by the great, indeed God-given fortune Her Majesty enjoyed in having the Prince Consort for husband and helpmeet. After the Imperial visitors had been introduced to (and made a proper fuss over) the royal children, and the two royal couples had parted to dress for the official welcoming banquet, Victoria was able to inform her journal that "everything has gone off beautifully."

In the general confusion of arrival, Eugénie's hairdresser, Félix, had somehow gotten mislaid, along with all the trunks containing her clothes and jewels. Eugénie suffered a *crise de nerfs*. Napoleon suggested she plead fatigue and skip the banquet. After a few minutes of hysterics, Eugénie rose to the occasion. She borrowed a simple gown from one of her ladies-in-waiting, hastily dressed her hair, and went off to join her consort in the Rubens Room.

When Victoria and Albert came to collect their guests, the dumpy Queen in her lavish, tasteless gown, bespattered with jewels, made a pitiful contrast to the Empress, a study in simple elegance.

Far from being jealous, Victoria was bowled over: "The profile and the line of the throat and shoulders are very beautiful, the expression charming and gentle, quite delightful," she later enthused to her journal. "The hair light brown [actually it was reddish gold], the face very pale, the mouth and teeth lovely!"

Having succumbed to the Empress's beauty, the Queen now succumbed to the Emperor's charm. While the two sat tête-à-tête at dinner, he recalled serving as a special constable during the Chartist Riots in 1848; he remembered exactly where he had stood in Green Park to watch the Queen set off to prorogue her first Parliament; he modestly recollected paying £40 for the privilege of seeing Her Majesty attend a performance at Covent Garden. The two recalled jointly a more prosaic occasion when their paths had crossed in 1848: at a public breakfast in the Fulham Road to raise money for public washhouses.

As the State Visit progressed—three days at Windsor, two days in London—Napoleon pressed the attack.

He dutifully hung on the Prince Consort's every word. He fussed incessantly over the royal children, for whom he had brought a cornucopia of extravagant gifts; learning that five-year-old Prince Arthur was his mother's favorite, the Emperor quietly opined that this must *surely* be "the most precious babe in all Christendom." He professed an inability to articulate adequately his admiration for the English way of life; *"L'Angleterre, c'est admirable!"* made its way past his lips with almost monotonous regularity. He even waxed poetic on the fecundity of England's cows and the greenness of England's grass.

The Queen confided to Lord Clarendon how "very extraordinary and unaccountable" it was that the Emperor seemed to "know *everything*" about her since she had passed puberty: where she had been and what she had done, why she had done it and even what she had worn while doing it. On ceremonial occasions—a parade, a military review, even a ride in Great Windsor Park—the Emperor would canter his horse over to the Queen's carriage and bend low to whisper pleasantries into the royal ear.

By the time the royals removed to Buckingham Palace, the Queen was hooked. As she confided to her journal:

> That he *is* a very *extraordinary* man, with great qualities there can be *no* doubt—I might almost say a *mysterious* man. . . . He is evidently possessed of an *indomitable courage, unflinching firmness of purpose,*

self-reliance, perseverance, and *great* secrecy; to this should be added, a great reliance on what he calls his *Star,* and a belief in omens and incidents as connected with his future destiny, which is *almost romantic*—and at the same time he is endowed with wonderful *self-control,* great *calmness,* even *gentleness* and with *a power of fascination,* the effect of which upon all those who become more intimately acquainted with him is *most sensibly felt.*

Napoleon could not have succeeded as he did with Victoria were he not the very type of man to whom she was always drawn tropismatically: the *"mysterious* man." That she truly loved Albert is unarguable; indeed, a good argument can be made for her having literally loved him to death.*

But, physical beauty excepted, Albert the Good lacked just about every quality Victoria subconsciously sought in a man. Save in a sexual sense, the men she allowed to play havoc with her emotions exuded mystery and sensuality, were rakish and raffish and exotically colorful, and flattered and fussed over her instead of taking her for granted (one of Albert's great failings). Notable among these were the worldly, witty, libidinous Lord Melbourne, her first Prime Minister; the *outré* Disraeli, her favorite Prime Minister ("We writers, Ma'am"); the sensuous, gruff Highland ghillie, John Brown (with whom some historians contend she entered into a morganatic marriage); and, in her twilight years, her exotic young Indian servant, the Munshi, for whom the Queen developed an attachment and defensiveness that almost forced her from the throne.

Napoleon III was, in a word, Victoria's "type": an accomplished seducer who carried with him a mysterious presence commingled with a scandalous, ergo glamorous, past—and who never allowed his ardent flirtation to exceed the bounds of propriety. Therein lay his fatal attraction for the Queen.

Albert was completely impervious to the Emperor's magnetism. He feared the Emperor might upset the peace of Europe in his quest for "spectacles to divert an impatient France." Even more alarming to Albert was the possibility of France's becoming too powerful; this

---

* Her biographers attest that Victoria resented her pregnancies because they interfered with her sex life, while Albert rather welcomed them as a respite from conjugal labors. When it came to physical passion, Victoria was a typical Hanoverian, Albert an untypical Coburgian.

would not be consonant with his overall ambition to make Germany the preeminent Power on the Continent.

Albert did, however, think well of the Empress. "Altogether," confided the Queen to her journal, "I am delighted to see how much he likes and admires her, as it is so seldom that I see him do so with *any* woman!"

But Albert merely admired Eugénie; Victoria fell in love with her. *"N'est-elle pas délicieuse!"* whispered she to someone as Eugénie glided by during a ball one evening in the Waterloo Gallery (which Victoria had renamed the Music Room in deference to French feelings).

Victoria often "fell" for people possessed of natural beauty (and often bemoaned the fact that so little of it was to be found in her own family)—provided those beauties "fell" for her. And Eugénie fell with a thud. Once she had overcome her initial nervousness at being a *parvenu* sovereign in this hidebound Court, and her clothes and jewels (and Félix) had turned up, the Empress relaxed. More, she came completely under the spell of the formidable Queen, only eight years her senior, who, for her part, was *"quite* unable to decide" what it was about the Empress that thrilled her most: her beauty, her talkativeness or her open (and sincere) admiration for the Victorian Court's high moral tone.*

Queen and Empress engaged in numerous little tête-à-têtes during the course of the visit, ranging over such topics as needlepoint, the scandalous behavior of Queen Isabella II of Spain (whose shenanigans would ultimately precipitate Eugénie's dethronement and exile), and having babies—the latter a subject on which Victoria could speak with authority.

Then, having established a close friendship that would end only with her death forty-seven years later, Victoria raised with Eugénie

---

* *Victoria was confident enough of her own heritage and station in life to become intimate with a woman who might look and behave like an empress but was not to the purple born. Perhaps nowhere was this basic difference between the two women more evident than at a performance at the opera. As they prepared to sit after acknowledging a standing ovation by the audience, the impeccable and elegant Empress turned to make sure her chair was in place, whereas the frumpy Queen sat gracefully without taking her eyes off the audience. She knew her chair was in place.*

the main reason for the State Visit: dissuading the Emperor from going out to the Crimea. Albert and the British Cabinet were not making much headway; Victoria presumed that Eugénie could influence him on a husband-wife basis.

Eugénie, who was all for the journey—the Sultan was already refurbishing a palace for them—replied tactfully that Plon-Plon's behavior had made the trip necessary.

Toward the end of the visit, emboldened by the knowledge that Napoleon's own advisers were against his going—would his reputation survive a military defeat? would the regime survive his prolonged absence from Paris? would British troops take orders from a Bonaparte?—the Queen boldly pleaded with him not to put "your precious life" in jeopardy.

The Emperor calmly assured her that he himself was having second thoughts about the venture, given the fact that Plon-Plon was still the Imperial heir. Perhaps this was a face-saving gesture on his part; perhaps it was a case of putting the Queen off. His answer did not give Victoria or her ministers (or *his* ministers) the assurance they wanted. But it gave them room for hope.

Not everyone in England was as taken with the Emperor as their Queen was. The press fulminated against him daily. Thomas Carlyle, "nauseated" by the hospitality Victoria was lavishing on the "*soi-disant* august pair," wrote that "the best that can be said" about the Emperor was that "he has not been shot hitherto."

But the cockney masses loved him; they shouted "*Vive le Hemperor!*" as he cantered ceremoniously through London to partake of a military review. (The Emperor was observed to be "visibly moved" and "strongly affected by the cheering," whereas the Empress was observed to be "condescending in her acknowledgments." Napoleon was at home in a crowd; Eugénie was most at ease in a drawing room.)

It was time to end Victoria's "dream—a brilliant, successful, and pleasant dream, the recollection of which is *firmly fixed in my mind.*"

The Emperor reminded the Queen of her promise to come over for the Paris Exhibition in August. The Empress burst into tears, flung herself into the Queen's arms, and swore that only the knowledge that they would soon be meeting again made their imminent separation even remotely tolerable. Emperor and Queen embraced each other twice. The royal children, who had a charming talent for bursting into tears on the slightest provocation, ululated commendably. The Emperor and Empress floated off to Dover on a wave of tears, and the Queen floated up to her study to record: "I cannot say *why*, but their departure made me so melancholy, I was near crying. . . .—all made me, I know not why, quite *wehmüthig*."

Victoria might be quite melancholy, but Napoleon was quite happy. He was not only returning home with the alliance he had so assiduously sought, he was returning home with the realization that the Queen of England considered him a fellow-sovereign—the first of the European royals to do so.

The Queen had inducted him into the exalted Most Noble Order of the Garter (during the course of which Napoleon had put the wrong arm through the ribbon and had a bit of difficulty rising from his knees). As the two sovereigns passed out of the Throne Room at Windsor following the investiture, Napoleon whispered to Victoria in his characteristic half-smiling, half-wry manner:

"At last, I am a gentleman."

While still a prisoner at Ham, Louis-Napoleon had determined to emulate the Emperor Augustus, who transformed Rome into a city of marble. Just as prosperity spread throughout the Roman Empire as a result of Rome's reconstruction, so must the Second Empire benefit from Paris's reconstruction. Napoleon's intention was to make Paris more than merely a stage-setting of beautiful buildings and broad boulevards. It was he who first uttered "the flattering yet truthful phrase: 'Everyone has two countries, his own and France.' " It was he who gave validity to that artful piece of propaganda.

There were already a few elegant areas: the Rue de la Paix and Rue Saint-Honoré on the Right Bank of the Seine, the Faubourg Saint-Germain of the Left Bank. But these were enclaves in a city of more than a million that was still quasi-medieval and agonizingly odiferous even by reduced Gallic standards. The core of Paris—"old Paris," before the incorporation of surrounding towns and hamlets—was a hornet's nest of tenements and wretched little shops, whose inhabitants and artisans lived in squalid little rooms in mud- and garbage-strewn streets that crisscrossed the city like filthy creases on a patriarch's hand.

Sanitation was at best rudimentary. Few buildings had running water, piped in from wells and nearby rivers. For drainage, most Parisians depended on cesspools that adjoined their hovels; at dawn could be heard the sound of dripping wagons lumbering off to the Forest of Bondy east of the city with their quotidian loads of human excrement. The Seine served as a sewer. Street lighting was such that those who lived in the enclaves had to run a gauntlet of scabrous thieves and pustulating prostitutes.

The Ile de la Cité, site of the Cathedral of Notre-Dame, the Prefecture of Police, and the Palais de Justice, was cluttered with narrow, malodorous, teeming streets. (When Baron Haussmann renovated the area, 25,000 denizens were evicted and a hundred streets became sixteen.) The Bois de Boulogne, once a private hunting preserve for the Valois kings, was a haven for footpads and gypsies. Rows of decaying houses with open, running sewers in front of them lined the area of the Rue Montmartre. One of the most wretched little slums in all of France was tucked neatly between the Louvre and the courtyard of the Tuileries. (Haussmann removed the courtyard and joined the two buildings.)

For those citizens in quest of sunlight or fresh air, there was a pitiful total of fifty acres of public park, of which half were breeding grounds for vermin.

Napoleon was not the first to deal with the problems facing this capital city so deficient in sanitation and housing, so much at the mercy of the traffic that cluttered its narrow streets and the hired assassins who stalked its even narrower alleys. A number of improvements had been undertaken during the First Empire and had continued under the Orléanist regime; but these measures were less to ameliorate the lot of the masses than to better the lot of the privileged few, and were patchwork at best.

Within weeks of becoming President, Napoleon was often seen doodling with different colored crayons on a map of Paris. He was sketching out a threefold dream: to better the housing and sanitary conditions of the poor, to generate economic prosperity through extensive public works (a prosperity that would echo throughout

France), and, of course, to create a splendid setting for the Empire he envisioned.

Shortly after coming to the throne, he named Georges Eugène Haussmann to be Prefect of the Department of the Seine. On June 29, 1853, he handed Haussmann that multi-colored map. Sixteen years and close to 3 billion francs later, the dream was a reality.

Except for the Palais de Chaillot, the Eiffel Tower and Sacré-Coeur, the Paris of today is the Paris of the Second Empire: 5,000 acres of public parks, great landscaped boulevards, extensive sewers and bridges and aqueducts, magnificent mansions and railroad stations, many fine hospitals, schools, houses, churches and synagogues, new markets and military barracks, such architectural gems as the Théâtre de l'Opéra and the Reading Room of the Bibliothèque Nationale—even the Louvre was finally completed after seven hundred years.

The total cost was half of what Americans pay for one nuclear-powered aircraft carrier, though for the time it was astronomical, exceeding by twenty percent France's entire national budget for the year 1867. Still, the Emperor—who rode herd on Haussmann every step of the way—built his splendid city of *son et lumière* without levying any new taxes. Money was raised through a variety of ways: bond issues, public loans, governmental subsidies, inflationary financing (long-term borrowing against future income and extension of credit).

The project had its critics. Conservative bankers threw up their hands in horror at Haussmann's reckless spending and unorthodox fiscal methodology. Provincial officials resented so much money being lavished on the capital city. Middle-class and aristocratic Parisians feared the influx of thousands of laborers. Perhaps the bitterest critics of all were the poor of Paris, who were evicted from their pestilential lairs to make way for the parks and boulevards.

The project had its scandals. Many attached to the Imperial Court used privileged information to enrich themselves through real estate speculation, especially on resale of condemned property *("Morny est dans l'affaire")*. Haussmann's financial vagaries—of which the Emperor was probably ignorant—became such that he was forced to resign in 1869, lest the tales that were coming to light damage further a by then mortally damaged regime.

When English reformer Edwin Chadwick visited France, he re-

marked to the Emperor: "May it be said of you that you found Paris
stinking and left it sweet."

The reconstruction of Paris was not Napoleon III's first dream;
nor was it his only dream to come true. But it was the only one of his
many dreams to endure.

The year 1855 had begun on a note of gloom: agricultural depression, economic recession, floods, a cholera epidemic that carried off
150,000 victims—and, of course, the tedious and sanguinolent pro-
longation of the war in Crimea. Napoleon's bad luck bottomed out
the last week in April.

A week after his triumphant return from London, he was riding
horseback along the Champs Elysées when a stranger named
Pianori approached as if to present a petition and fired a pistol from
close range. The culprit was subdued by police agents after a brief
scuffle—and after convincing the Emperor, albeit unwittingly, not
only of the latter's mortality but of the inherent disaster that would
face France were Plon-Plon to succeed to the throne.

Pianori, a follower of the Italian republican patriot Mazzini, resented the presence of French troops in Rome; his attempt on Napoleon's life was an intimation of how the fight for Italian unification
would soon plague the Emperor. Napoleon sought to spare Pianori's
life on humanitarian grounds, but gave in to the demands of his
ministers, who pointed out that the assassin had a record of political
murders in Italy. The incident was soon forgotten as Paris became
caught up in the *Exposition Universelle de 1855*.

Work on the *Exposition* had been going on for two years.
England had opened its International Exhibition at the Crystal
Palace in 1851. Napoleon was determined to go the English one
better. By May 1855, the "haussmannization" of Paris was underway in earnest: the great north-south artery, called the Boulevard
de Strasbourg (later renamed Sebastopol) and the great east-west
artery, formed by an extension of the Rue de Rivoli as far as the
Rue Saint-Antoine, had already been laid out; the old quarters of
Saint-Denis, Saint-Martin and Saint-Antoine, long the haunts of
insurgents, had been disemboweled; the Hôtel de Ville had been
renovated (the avenue leading to it would be named after Queen

Victoria); the Bois de Boulogne was in the final throes of landscaping. Members of the bourgeoisie were erecting houses of uniform style and height. Prosperity was returning to France.

The site of the *Exposition*—the first ever to be held in France—was a compound of three buildings between the Seine and the Rond-Point of the Champs Elysées. In the Palais des Beaux-Arts, foreign artists were exhibited along with most of the leading French artists of the day: Delacroix, Delaroche, Ingres, Horace Vernet. (The characteristically obtuse selectors rejected Courbet, leader of the nineteenth-century Realist school, much to the disgust of his patron, the Duke de Morny.) In the two buildings that comprised the Palais de l'Industrie were to be found such novelties as gas radiators, agricultural machinery and British lifeboats, and demonstrations of the commercial uses of rubber, food-processing and photography. While the Exhibition (5 million visitors) was but a shadow of the great Exhibition of 1867 (15 million visitors), still it adumbrated the prosperity and glory that was to characterize the Second Empire at its apogee.

The *Exposition Universelle* opened on May 15, two weeks behind schedule. Nothing was ready. President of the planning commission was Plon-Plon. By the end of June, when the show finally got underway, the Emperor was in so jubilant a mood he was prepared to forgive Plon-Plon anything.

The Empress was again pregnant, and Napoleon just knew that this time she would bear him an heir. So confident was he that he ordered his ambassadors to inform all foreign chiefs of state practically the moment Eugénie had ceased ovulating. First to be informed was Queen Victoria. Familiar with Eugénie's history of miscarriages, the Queen expressed "*grave* concern" and urged that "the dear Empress take *hot baths*."

Highlight of the season was the arrival of Victoria and Albert on August 18 for a ten-day visit. The Emperor went out of his way to be the perfect host. (Eugénie spent most of the summer at Eaux-Bonnes in the Pyrenees, undergoing a prolonged, painful treatment her physicians considered vital if she was to carry full-term.) The Queen went home in raptures over "my brother and faithful ally—and *friend*, Napoleon III—I may add, for we really are *great friends!*"

For Victoria, the emotional high point of the visit came when she went to the Hôtel des Invalides to pay her respects to the mortal remains of Napoleon I. "There I stood, at the arm of Napoleon III, his nephew, before the coffin of England's bitterest foe! I, the granddaughter of that King who hated him most, and who most vigorously opposed him, and this very nephew, who bears his name, being my *nearest* and *dearest* ally!"

One day, while sitting alone in the Empress's drawing room at the Tuileries, the Queen was suddenly seized with one of her periodic *wehmüthig* moods. Wrote she in her omnipresent journal:

> All so gay—the people cheering the Emperor as he walked up and down in the little garden—and yet how recently has blood flowed, and a whole dynasty [the Orléans] been swept away. How uncertain is everything still! All is so beautiful here; all seems now so prosperous; the Emperor seems so fit for his place, and yet how little security one feels for the future! All depends on him and on his too precious life!
>
> These reflections crowded on my mind, and smote upon my heart. . . .

Those reflections have a strangely prophetic ring.

Chapter 9
Annus Mirabilis

It is difficult to recall the Second Empire without recalling its clichés, and by 1856—Napoleon III's wonderful year—the clichés had been set. Reigning courtesans riding in elegant carriages through the Bois de Boulogne. Winsome flower girls peddling their blooms to nattily dressed speculators seated over ices on the terrace of Tortoni's. Raunchy nightly revels at the Bal Mabilé, where Pomaré and Rigalboche danced the cancan. And—the period's proto-cliché—opening night of an Offenbach operetta (he wrote more than a hundred) at the Bouffes Parisiennes.

Jacques Offenbach. To Rossini, he was "the Mozart of the Champs Elysées." To Wagner, he was the man who "released the odor of manure from where all the pigs of Europe had come to wallow." He was neither a Mozart nor a manure merchant. He was a brilliant parodist whose beguiling rhythms and infectious melodies made most palatable his putdowns of the vulgar ostentation and *arrivisme* with which the Napoleonic Court fairly reeked. Take, for example, his greatest success, *Orpheus aux enfers*.

The setting is Mount Olympus. All the gods are emulating the chief deity, Jupiter, who makes love to all the pretty girls, despite the constant carping of his jealous wife Juno. Pluto, god of the underworld, in hopes of escaping punishment for having abducted Eurydice, attempts to inflame the gods against him. Enter now Public Opinion, who demands that Orpheus prevail upon Jupiter to arrange the return of his beloved Eurydice. In a switch on the classical legend, Jupiter cannily resorts to a convenient legal loophole that compels poor Orpheus to renounce Eurydice and disappear—along with Public Opinion. Whereupon all the Olympians (Juno excepted), led by their chief god, revert to dissipation and drunkenness as they set out stumblingly on the road to hell.

For Jupiter, read the Emperor; for Juno, read the Empress. Public Opinion? The social conventions of faith, fidelity and honor. And is not Mount Olympus obviously the Tuileries? Lest anyone miss the point, there were as many topical allusions in the libretto as there were memorable tunes in the score. (The biggest laugh came when Juno berated Jupiter for his marital infidelity, and he walked out on her with the words: "I have an appointment with my architect!") Equally obvious was the moral of the piece: The great and powerful suffer no qualms in riding roughshod over public opinion.

After attending a command performance of this brutal satire, the Emperor sent Offenbach a note of thanks "for an unforgettable evening." He was able to laugh at himself.

The Empress's reaction, on the other hand, given her difficulties with French *opéra-comique*, was predictable: "Just as one is getting interested in what they are saying, they start singing, and when one is interested in their singing, they start talking!"

Offenbach's first success came during the 1855 *Exposition*, when he premiered his *Ba-ta-clan.** From *Ba-ta-clan*, the high-living Parisians of the Second Empire took as their inspiration the chorus: "Let us waltz! Let us polka! Let us leap! *Let us dance!*"

Their ballroom was an area that stretched from the Madeleine to the Place de la République and took in the so-called *Grands Boulevards:* des Italiens, des Capucines, and Saint-Martin.

Here they pranced against a cacophony compounded of the clip-clop of carriage wheels and the cries of street singers, organ grinders, wandering musicians (flutes, violins and the newly invented saxophone), and egg merchants and fishmongers hawking their wares *("À la coque!"* and *"À la barque!").*

Here they sat at sidewalk cafés, trading tales about their current mistresses (and often trading their mistresses), while magicians, jugglers, acrobats and dwarfs vied for their attention with charlatans purveying such elixirs as arsenic pills for rejuvenation. (The

---

* *Four months earlier, Alexandre Dumas* fils *had opened his play* Le Demi-Monde *and given the language a new term.*

Duke de Morny was one of the many who thus rejuvenated themselves into an early grave.)

Here were situated their favorite theaters, their favorite dance halls, their favorite restaurants. (The *Grand Seize* in the Café Anglais on Rue Marévaux was the most sought-after *chambre séparée* in all of Paris; noblemen and financiers booked the room months in advance to wine and dine each other's bored wives.)

Here the high-livers of the Second Empire promenaded, speculated, dined, entertained, were entertained, gambled, fornicated and otherwise comported themselves to the best of their natural abilities.

British diplomatist Lord Hertford called the area *"la clitoris de Paris."*

Leading the dance were the *Cocotés* and the *Ogresses*. The *Cocotés* (which translates roughly as "swells") were the approximately one hundred leading men-about-town; to belong, one had only to be financially solvent and pleasantly disgusting. Their unofficial leader was the Duke de Gramont-Caderousse, who once gave his love of the moment an enormous Easter egg that contained a splendid carriage and four prized steeds. Thanks to Plon-Plon and Morny, themselves *Cocotés*, Gramont-Caderousse and his cronies enjoyed entrée into Imperial court circles. The diarist Viel-Castel dismissed them contemptuously as "those gilded pimps."

The *Ogresses* were the approximately one hundred leading courtesans, the overwhelming majority of whom had ridden up on their backs from either obscure provincial origins or filthy Parisian cribs. They were a mixed bag. Many were admired as much for their gimmicks as for their beauty. Giulia Barrucci made it a practice never to say "No" to any gentleman who belonged to the right clubs. Anna Deslions made a practice of sending her trick of the evening a duplicate receipt for the gown she was going to wear, as an index of what she expected in the way of remuneration.

Many were admired as much for their upward mobility as for their beauty. Marguerite Bellanger made it from the *trottoirs* to the Tuileries as the Emperor's last official mistress. Céleste Mogador, who started in a provincial whorehouse and was a bareback rider with the *Cirque Français*, put in a spell as the most available number at the Bal Mabilé before marrying the fabulously wealthy idiot heir to the Count de Chabrillan.

Few, however, were known for their brains. The story is told of one *Ogresse*—it may have been Juliette Beau, another of the Emperor's transient "diversions"—who declined an invitation to ride in the Bois one afternoon because "I am now reading Renan's *Life of Jesus* and I am anxious to see how the story ends."

Unofficial leader of the *Ogresses* was La Païva, who bridged the worlds of the *demi-monde* and the *beaux-arts*. Born Therese Lackman in Moscow, on coming to Paris she married a Portuguese nobleman, the Marquis de Païva. On their wedding night, Therese informed the Marquis that she was keeping his name and title, but was dismissing him. When the Marquis asked why, Therese replied that he had amused her sufficiently; now she wished "to live as a whore."

To La Païva's magnificent *hôtel* at 25 Avenue des Champs Elysées came the leading writers and intellectuals of the day. All were as charmed by her mind and hospitality as by her eccentricities: La Païva loved to wander amongst her guests unwashed, in tattered gowns and a half-million francs in jewels.

Not all the great whores of the Second Empire lived by their bodies alone. Many came from the world of musical comedy (just as many of the more respectable kept-women came from the world of ballet). Interestingly enough, three of the foremost courtesans of the day—Cora Pearl, Hortense Schneider and Léa Silly—were Offenbach's leading ladies.

Cora Pearl—born Emma Crouch in London—spoke French with a cockney accent, was built like an odalisque, and swore like a demented sailor. Her going price was between 5,000 and 10,000 francs per customer. Cora liked to throw stag parties, at which she would bathe in champagne and dance in the buff on a carpet of orchids for the delectation of her guests.

At one such funfest, an admirer blew his brains out because Cora would not devote herself to him exclusively. As the other stags gaped in horror, Cora looked down at the mess and screamed: "That fucking pig has ruined my beautiful carpet!" Cora was all heart. That might explain why she put in a spell as Plon-Plon's exclusive property.

Hortense Schneider had more class than Cora Pearl. She was also a better singing actress. Among her many lovers were the Prince of Wales and the Tsar of Russia. Hortense's great rival was Léa Silly, who won the hearts of audiences by mimicking every one of la Schneider's theatrical gestures and mannerisms. Léa and Hortense shared the same lovers, though Léa could go her one better: Brigham Young wanted to marry her.

While touring America, Léa's troupe played Salt Lake City; the Mormon leader became instantaneously enamored of her, sought to convert her to the teachings of the prophet Moroni, and expressed the hope that she would become his twenty-fifth simultaneous consort.

Léa dined out on that offer for the rest of her life.

Offenbach was one of the two figures who most typified the Second Empire. The other was Princess Pauline von Metternich, who took Paris by storm in 1859, when her husband Richard became Austrian ambassador. Mérimée described Pauline as "two parts whore and one part great lady," which just about sums her up.

Her credentials were impeccable: she was both granddaughter and daughter-in-law of the great Metternich. She came by her zest for life naturally: her father, a wealthy Hungarian horseman known as Mad Moritz Sandór, liked to gallop around Vienna kicking dogs and smashing furniture.

Pauline had no illusions about herself: "I may look like a monkey [she did], but at least I am a fashionable monkey." That she was. Among the fashions she introduced was that of ladies dining in public restaurants—smoking cigars into the bargain. Viel-Castel complained that she "assumed the manners and the style of a strumpet . . . she drinks, she smokes, she swears, she is ugly enough to frighten one, and she tells stories." She also sang smutty songs, danced obscene dances, threw some of the raunchiest parties of the regime—in her bedroom—and liked to cruise with the tarts on the Boulevard des Italiens.

Pauline became the Empress Eugénie's closest female friend and confidante. That she was ambassadress of Catholic Austria was not the least of her attractions.

There are other clichés associable with the Second Empire: the *chiffonières*, those wretched ragpickers who lived near the Clignancourt Gate and slept under the Seine bridges; the thieves and prostitutes, who sat hunched over their absinthe in a pitiful stupor in some ramshackle, vermin-infested bistro; the multitudes who picked over garbage for a few scraps, often having to fend off an equally hungry stray dog or two. In Second-Empire France, the rich got richer and the poor got more desperate. Nowhere were the polarities more pronounced than in Paris.

One thirteen-year-old who earned a franc a week as a servant was sentenced to four years in the Saint-Lazare women's prison for stealing a bit of jam and syrup from her mistress. The presiding judge's rationale: "to imbue her with a moral sense." Not far from the Saint-Lazare, a fancy-dress ball was held at the Hôtel d'Albert at which first prize for the most imaginative costume went to one epicene nobleman who came as a turd—a 7,000-franc turd.

A common site in the Rue du Cherche Midi near the Boulevard Raspail was an undernourished pregnant woman picking through a garbage heap for scraps of cabbage and apple cores. Not far from the Rue du Cherche Midi, members of the Club des Grands Estomacs met every Saturday at the Restaurant Philippe to partake of an eighteen-hour gourmet meal.

In 1862, midway through the regime, four out of five Parisians lived below the poverty level. These included the thousands of masons, carpenters and artisans who flocked to the capital to work on its "haussmannization." They received between two and four francs for an eleven-hour working day. Prices rose along with prosperity, but wages and the standard of living among the poor remained constant.

At that, the laborers fared better than the beggars, cripples, ragpickers, thieves and prostitutes (half of whom were teenagers), who were the majority of the population.

The poor aped the rich. They strolled the streets adjacent to the *Grands Boulevards* and had their own dance halls and "restaurants." (One of the absolute worst of these establishments, La Guillotine, was situated three blocks from the Tuileries.)

And they resorted to crime. Imaginative entrepreneurs from the lowest socio-economic stratum organized schools for thieves, where children sold by their parents for a few centimes were given elaborate training. Beggars rented stolen babies with which they sought to evoke sympathy from strollers along the boulevards. The more sophisticated criminals hired themselves out as murderers. (The going rate was seven francs per contract.)

The government seemed less concerned with resolving all this misery than with persecuting those who forced all this misery on their attention. Flaubert was hauled into court on grounds of immorality for his *Madame Bovary;* Baudelaire—one of the greatest poets of the nineteenth century—was prosecuted for writing his masterpiece, *Les Fleurs du mal.* (Paradoxically, Eugénie offered to pay Baudelaire's fine but refused to read Flaubert's masterpiece: "I have heard it is indecent.")

The journalist-statesman Montalembert, a champion of the Roman Catholic Church, pontificated: "I only know of one means of making the poor respect property: they must be made to believe in God!" Napoleon III doubted deism was the answer. Wrote he, in his *Extinction du paupérisme:* "It is better to invest 300 million in organizing employment than 120 in building new prisons."

As he had demonstrated when he turned the confiscated Orléans fortune back to the people, Napoleon *was* concerned with the problems of the poor; he *did* want desperately to improve their pitiful lot. He encouraged industry and agriculture, financing them with the likes of the Crédit Mobilier, the Crédit Foncier, the Comptoir d'Escompte and numerous Sociétés de Dépôt, all backed by the Banque de France.

But little of the prosperity filtered down to the masses; at any rate, it all collapsed—on the eve of the Empire's collapse—because of overexpansion and corruption.

Veuillot, leader of the extreme Ultramontane wing of French Catholicism during this period, wrote in his *Les Odeurs de Paris:* "Poverty is the rule for a section of society; they must submit to a divine law." Some would dismiss this rule as arch cynicism, others as palpable pragmatism. A number of aspects of the Second Empire were truly unique. But its failure to bridge the gap between rich and poor was not one of them.

There was as little sexual intercourse as social intercourse between rich and poor. Still, gonorrhea and syphilis knew no class distinctions. While sexual morality was the Second Empire's fashionable pastime, venereal disease was its fashionable affliction—and common denominator. At no time were there less than 50,000 prostitutes on the streets, the majority of them daughters (often illegitimate) of the poor, the majority of them infected. Attempts were made by the police to supervise them with periodic medical examinations, but few bothered to report; at any given time, sixty percent of the women in the Saint-Lazare women's prison had gonorrhea or syphilis—or both.

Statistics among the rich are speculative at best: aristocrats rarely announce when they have caught the bug. It is known, though, that during one three-month period the *Garde Impériale*—whose members serviced only the aristocracy—lost over 20,000 duty days in the hospital being treated for syphilis.

To the poor, sex—and its attendant penalties—was more often than not a means of staving off starvation; to the rich, it was more often than not a means of staving off boredom. Homosexuality was prevalent among the higher social order. Many of the better-endowed studs of the *Garde Impériale* were passed around as male prostitutes; popular actresses and society women dabbled in lesbianism. One of the Emperor's aides was arrested by the police at a drag ball where half the Guardsmen present were decked out as nuns; one noblewoman passed along her spirochetes only to her closest female friends.

However, heterosexuality was still the norm. Wife-swapping was perfectly acceptable. A man whose spouse had become his close friend's mistress could look upon it all with equanimity; chances were that another close friend's spouse was *his* mistress.

On February 14 of her consort's *annus mirabilis*, the Empress wrote Paca: "I shall soon be obliged to make a fuss over the Plenipotentiaries of the Congress, and I fear that these state dinners and concerts will not do me much good in my present state, especially as [her pregnancy] will be over in a month's time." Eleven days later, the envoys convened at the Foreign Office in the Quai d'Orsay to write *finis* to the Crimean War.

It had taken as long to end the carnage as to start it. On September 11, Sebastopol fell to the Allies after 332 days, and Napoleon became anxious for peace. The conflict was unpopular in France, and the country was materially (as well as emotionally and morally) past the peak of its war effort. Napoleon's immediate aim in having gone to war—keeping Turkey and the Mediterranean area outside the sphere of Russian influence—had been realized. He now wished to forge a strong bond with Alexander II, Nicholas I's successor; he saw an Anglo-French-Russian alliance as the basis of peace and order for Europe.

England, on the other hand, anxious to see a weakened Russia, became more bellicose and wanted to continue the war she had never wanted to fight in the first place. Mercifully, no one else wanted to continue the slaughter. (Eugénie would not have minded—provided she was given a guarantee by God that Russia would disappear completely. While it would be a few years before she could sweep into the innermost councils of government, Eugénie had begun to put her foot in the door. She had also begun to put her foot in her mouth. At a state banquet hailing the fall of Sebastopol, she insisted that the Allies follow England in taking a stronger line with Russia. The others present agreed with the Emperor that "women in an advanced state of pregnancy often act silly.") On January 16, 1856, Russia threw in the towel.

Hosting the peace congress was a *parvenu* Emperor who only a few years previously all the Powers had hoped to exclude from the concert of Europe. Napoleon III had come a long way in a short time. To England, he was now a most trusted ally. To Russia, he was a powerful foe to be placated. To Sardinia-Piedmont (which had shrewdly entered the war so that she could be in on the peace), he was the one neighbor to be courted in the cause of Italian unity. To Austria and Prussia, he was an enigma to be treated with caution and respect.*

Because protocol precluded Napoleon's serving as conference chairman, the job fell to his cousin, Count Alexandre Florian Walewski, whom he had made Foreign Minister the previous May.

Walewski was the first Bonaparte Emperor's bastard by a beautiful Polish noblewoman who had become his mistress in hopes that he would liberate her nation from Russia. After inheriting his mother's estates, Walewski went to Paris, where, after taking French citizenship and informing everyone whose son he was, he failed at a

---

* *Though she remained neutral in the war, Prussia was invited to attend the congress in her capacity as a major Power. She was, however, excluded from the bargaining sessions. Leader of the Prussian delegation, forced to cool his heels in the anterooms of the Quai d'Orsay, was Bismarck—who little more than a decade later would reorganize Europe more to his liking.*

number of occupations before finding his vocation as a diplomat. In 1851, Napoleon made him ambassador to London. The London embassy was a success (he superintended the two State Visits between the French and British sovereigns). It was his only success.

British statesman-diarist Lord Greville dismissed him, accurately, as "an adventurer, a ready speculator without honor, conscience or truth, utterly unfit, both by character and capacity, for high office of any kind." When Walewski died in 1868, Napoleon admitted that this "mediocrity" was in no way a statesman—but that, on the other hand, no one else in France (himself excepted) was a statesman either.

Walewski rarely saw eye to eye with the Emperor. He did not mind that his wife was Napoleon's mistress, but he resented Napoleon's courting of Russia; Walewski had inherited his mother's Polish patriotism. Politically, he was a staunch conservative who opposed any weakening of the papacy. Eugénie made him one of her favorites—until, later in the reign, he supported the Emperor's program of liberal reforms.

Napoleon attempted to turn the congress into his favorite device, a Council of Europe. He hoped to effect a general revision of the 1815 (Congress of Vienna) treaties; in essence, he wanted to obviate the possibility of future wars. He ordered Walewski to insist on a discussion of just about everything under the sun, from attacks by the Belgian press on the Second Empire to the simultaneous evacuation of French troops from Rome and Austrian troops from Northern Italy. (Napoleon would not withdraw from Italy unilaterally.) He even permitted Cavour to raise the Roman Question.

The other Powers objected. Britain sided with Austria in wanting to maintain the status quo; Austria had no intention of abandoning her presence in Italy; Russia and Turkey joined Austria and Great Britain in reminding France that they had come to end the Crimean War only. Work moved apace, and within a month the treaty was on paper.* Napoleon allowed that "something must be done for Italy."

---

* *Turkey was admitted to the concert of Europe after promising to tidy herself up. Russia abandoned all claims to a protectorate over the Christians in Turkey, ceded the mouth of the Danube, agreed to the neutralization of the Black Sea, and recognized the Danubian Principalities as autonomous states under Turkish suzerainty. (Thanks in large mea-*

There was more to the Congress of Paris than bargaining sessions. There were grand balls at the Tuileries, galas at the opera, banquets at Saint-Cloud, receptions at the foreign embassies.

The Empress was not "obliged to make a fuss over the Plenipotentiaries," as she had bemoaned to Paca. Though she did not withdraw completely from society until a week before her confinement—her pregnancy was indiscernible under all those hoopskirts and crinolines—Eugénie did forgo most of the festivities.

It is doubtful that she was missed. The eyes of all were on an Italian intrigante who had been dispatched by her government to remind the Emperor that "something must be done for Italy." The Emperor did not need to be reminded. But he was never one to look a gift horse in the mouth.

The gift horse's name was Virginia ("Nini") Oldoini-Verasis, Countess di Castiglione. She was the nineteenth century's most outrageously beautiful, tyrannically egocentric, egregiously narcissistic and monumentally insipid trull. She was also Napoleon III's most incredible mistress.

By the time she was fifteen (1850), this daughter of a pair of unscrupulously ambitious Florentines was being celebrated as one of Western Europe's great beauties, and marriage offers were coming in daily. In 1854, she agreed to marry the fabulously wealthy, twenty-nine-year-old Francesco Verasis, Count di Castiglione, favorite aide-de-camp to King Victor Emmanuel. Nini told Francesco she would never love him. He did not care. It was enough that he could claim as his wife the one woman all men coveted (and many men had had).

It was not a happy marriage. Francesco resented her habit of proclaiming publicly "I am married to an imbecile," her refusal to sleep with him after the birth of their only child ("I do not wish to become pregnant a second time"), and her habit of spending his money. The two went separate ways within a year of their marriage. The Count wound up in debt; the Countess wound up in Victor Emmanuel's bed.

---

sure to Napoleon, they were united as Rumania five years later.) Also, four rules of international law were adopted, most notably the abolishment of privateering.

Ere long, Nini announced that she was bored and eager for adventure. Victor Emmanuel and his Prime Minister, Cavour, who was Nini's cousin, found adventure for her. They had determined that all of Italy must be incorporated into the Kingdom of Piedmont-Sardinia, and had concluded that Italian unification would require not only French sanction but French military aid.

Victor Emmanuel rushed over for a State Visit during the Paris Exhibition of 1855 and reminded Napoleon that Sardinia had been the first state to accord him recognition on his Imperial accession. The two randy monarchs became friends. Before returning to Turin, Victor Emmanuel mentioned casually that a beautiful young friend of his was coming over for the Exhibition; he hoped the Emperor would keep an eye out for her.

Nini departed for Paris in November 1855, leaving behind, in addition to the debris of her marriage, an infant son and a still loving husband, who had gone through his entire fortune and borrowed an additional 2 million francs in order to prove that love. Though he bombarded her with letters begging her to come home, the Countess would not see the Count again until 1867, at the wedding of Victor Emmanuel's son, the Duke of Aosta—which wedding precipitated the Count's funeral.

(From all accounts, it must have been history's most devastating wedding. The bride's wardrobe mistress hanged herself as she was dressing the bride; the majordomo who was to lead the procession from the palace to the church fell off his horse, a victim of sunstroke; and the gatekeeper was found dead in a large pool of blood. At the height of the nuptial mass, the best man blew his brains out. As the bridal procession rode toward the railway station, the court notary who had drawn up the marriage contract dropped dead from an apoplectic fit. At the station, the stationmaster became so excited he fell beneath the wheels of the approaching bridal train. The superstitious king, now beginning to suspect that his son's wedding was in some way jinxed, ordered everyone to return to the palace. The Count di Castiglione, who was cantering alongside the bridal carriage, fell off his horse and was crushed to death beneath the carriage wheels. His estranged Countess regretted publicly that she had not had the opportunity to bid her long-suffering husband a proper farewell—and remarked privately that it was "the most accident-prone wedding *I* have ever attended!")

The Countess di Castiglione made her debut in Second-Empire society on November 24, at a fancy-dress ball in the Tuileries. It was quite a debut. As she entered grandly on the arm of an old Court dandy named "Chinchilla," dressed—rather, undressed—as a Roman lady of decadence, musicians stopped playing, gentlemen climbed atop furniture for a better view, ladies reached for their fans, and servants tripped over their own feet. The Emperor, who was standing by in the garb of a Venetian nobleman, sidled over to the practically naked debutante and asked for the first waltz.

Napoleon's involvement with the Countess came at a time when his health had become a problem. He was suffering from nervous exhaustion, was unable to sleep, was plagued by intermittent intense pain in the cutaneous nerves in various parts of his body, and was bothered by hemorrhoids. At Dr. Conneau's insistence, a London expert was called in. The expert gleaned from the Emperor the admission that after sexual intercourse "he remained wakeful for the rest of the night, whereas previously he had found that it contributed to his sound sleep." The expert concluded that, on top of all his other ailments, the Emperor was on his way to becoming impotent.

The fair Nini rejuvenated Napoleon—so much so that one night, on arriving for a tryst at the house he had taken for her in the Rue de la Pompe, the Emperor became so keyed up with anticipation that he did not exit his carriage by way of the door but leaped nimbly out the window.

The damage was minimal—a sprained wrist, a bloody nose, a few facial lacerations—and that night, as on every other night that he romped with "my divine Countess," the Emperor found that once again sexual intercourse contributed to sound sleep.

Emperor and Countess did not rush into their affair precipitately. All evidence indicates that they did not bed each other down until the early summer of 1856—by which time Napoleon had given her a 100,000-franc emerald, a 442,000-franc pearl necklace, and that house in the Rue de la Pompe (among other precious gifts), and the anticlerical wits along the boulevards were proclaiming parodistically: "There is no Emperor but the one Emperor, and Castiglione is his prophet." The Emperor was too busy, what with hosting the peace congress and glorying in the birth of an heir, to commit himself to the Countess. For her part, the Countess was too busy reveling in the grand intrigues of an international diplomatic parley—and reveling in making a public scandal of herself—to commit herself to the Emperor.

The Countess sought to convince everyone (she had already convinced herself) that but for her, Sardinia would never have been admitted to the congress. She went to her grave convinced that only she had made possible the unification of Italy. Actually, all that she made possible was for other Italian agitators in Paris to enjoy casual access to her house in the Rue de la Pompe. It is significant that a number of assassination attempts were made on the Emperor during the course of his periodic visitations; those trysts were hard to keep secret. (It is also significant that all attempts on Napoleon's life were made by Italians—none by Frenchmen.)

Cavour and Victor Emmanuel had released a rabbit in the field, and the rabbit was running amok. She was highly indiscreet, not only with her body but with her mouth. Worse, she was antagonizing the French Empress, who was known to be pro-Austrian and vehemently opposed to any despoilation of the papacy—a despoilation that was the *sine qua non* of Italian unification.

Initially, Nini behaved herself in the Empress's presence; when invited to attend Eugénie's Mondays, she not only kept her mouth shut, she appeared dutifully in the crinolines and hoopskirts the Empress insisted all her female guests wear.

Feelings between the two women soured when Eugénie made known her displeasure over Victor Emmanuel's government's having passed some anticlerical legislation. In what must surely rank as one of the great non sequiturs of all time, Nini replied that any woman who would not appear in public without wearing a corset and brassiere should stay home.

The break was complete when Princess Mathilde—who, in addition to detesting (and being screamingly envious of) the Empress, favored Italian independence—pointedly took Nini to her ample bosom. Nini felt it safe to shed her crinolines and hoopskirts and otherwise do her number. Eugénie was happy to see her go—but was unhappy that she did not go far enough.

On February 17, she turned up at a *bal-masqué* given by Walewski, sporting little more than a smidgin of gauze ornamented with a few hearts scattered here and there in strategic places. Since the Empress, a guest herself, could not command the Countess to leave, she was compelled to satisfy herself with a well-aimed barb: after complimenting the Queen of Hearts on her rather extraordinary attire, Eugénie lowered her gaze to the culprit's pubic region and added: "Your heart seems a little low."

Shortly thereafter, egged on by Mathilde, the Countess coerced the Imperial hairdresser, Leroy (Félix's successor), to dress her hair exactly as he was going to dress the Empress's for a ball that night. For Eugénie, who wore her hair the way Stephen Crane's hero wore his red badge of courage, this was the unkindest cut of all. But there was little she could do, except break Leroy's heart by replacing him with his protégé, Alexandre. (Poor Leroy soon sickened and died of despair.) After all, the Countess was a cousin of the Prime Minister of Sardinia—as well as the Emperor's mistress.

Nor was there much Eugénie could do when, during a command performance by the Comédie-Française out at Compiègne, the Countess abruptly excused herself from the royal box on grounds of a headache and the Emperor rushed after her solicitously—except to sit with egg on her face before the amused and knowing courtiers.

Castiglione lasted as the one Emperor's prophet for about a year, which was about the limit of his endurance. He found the Empress's screaming about "that Mediterranean fungus" as unnerving as that fungus's flamboyance. Besides, he had by then taken a fancy to his cousin the Foreign Minister's wife.

Madame Walewska was a beautiful Florentine noblewoman who was as ardent an Italian nationalist as the Countess di Castiglione and as adept at intrigue. (Mérimée: "I do not know if it is true, as the Walewska *claims*, that her family originates with Machiavelli; what is certain is that *she* descends from him!") Madame Walewska's saving grace: she was subtler in her methods and more tolerable to her contemporaries. It is a mark of her talents that she became the only one of the Emperor's acknowledged mistresses to win the Empress's favor. Perhaps the Empress felt indebted to her for paving the way for the Countess di Castiglione's fall from favor.

With the outbreak of the Italian War in 1859, the Countess was deported to Spezia, near Turin, where she spent long hours sitting stark naked in front of a gigantic mirror, trying her damnedest to comprehend what could have *ever* prompted God Almighty to create such a perfect creature. It was her conviction that, vis-à-vis all the great women of history, "I am their equal in birth, their superior in beauty, their judge in intellect." Indeed, she used this conviction as a superscription on all portraits of herself.

The Countess was permitted to return to France in 1861, at which time there was a reunion with the Emperor. But she was no longer the official mistress, just one of his many "little diversions." It was the Princess Mathilde who made her return possible.

She returned the favor by adding Mathilde's resident lover Nieuwerkerque to her string of admirers. Her other admirers included the Jewish bankers Charles Laffitte, Ignace Bauer, and the father-and-son combination of Barons James and Gustave de Rothschild. Nini was partial to Jewish bankers. She kept an album, entitled *Book of Testimonials*, in which her admirers were invited to inscribe a formal statement of her glory. The Emperor declined to inscribe a testimonial, though he did remark to Mathilde: "She is very beautiful, but she has no brains."

It was probably inevitable, certainly symbolical, that the Countess di Castiglione's end should come with the collapse of the Second Empire. In 1877, she went into virtual seclusion in a ground-floor flat in the Place Vendôme. She kept the place heavily shuttered and ventured out only after dark, to stand silently outside the mansions and palaces that had been the settings of her past triumphs. Her only companions were her pet dogs Kasino and Sandouga, whom she taught to waltz.

Nini went out with the century she had helped to light up. In her will, it was stipulated that she was to be buried in "the Compiègne nightgown"—a fond recollection of her days (rather, nights) as mistress to the Emperor of France. Though she insisted that her burial site was to be kept secret, the Italian Embassy buried her in the Père Lachaise.

Till the day she died, the Countess di Castiglione was convinced that "Had I arrived in Paris earlier, France would have had an Italian rather than a Spanish Empress." The conviction holds little water. But it is worthy of contemplation.

Eugénie gave birth early in the morning of March 16—Palm Sunday—after fifteen hours of agonizing, near-fatal labor. On learning it was a boy, Napoleon ecstatically embraced those nearest him

among the Imperial family and Court and State officials who had
been summoned to witness the accouchement from an anteroom.
Everyone shared the Emperor's joy over the birth of an heir—
except Plon-Plon. He was determined to play the role of the bad
fairy.

When everyone filed past the exhausted Empress to tender congratulations, the Empress's last impression as she drifted off to
sleep was of Plon-Plon peering down from behind a monocle with
unmitigated hatred. Later, in his capacity as First Prince of the
Blood, he balked at signing the birth register. It may have been on
this occasion that the Emperor lost his patience: "You consort with
all the enemies of my government!"

To which Plon-Plon replied: "I never drop my old friends."

Salvoes of guns boomed out the news all over France. As a sign of
the esteem in which the French Emperor was now held, the token
Allied forces left in the Crimea also fired salvoes, as did the Russians. From the Tuileries came word that every child born in France
that day (there were more than 3,000) would be given a gift. A total
of 100,000 francs was distributed to the poor, and 10,000 francs to
each of the mutual benefit societies. Political prisoners were amnestied; four generals were made Marshals of France. In Paris, people
snake-danced along the boulevards; firecrackers were set off between the Madeleine and the Place de la Bastille.

Within the hour, the good news had been telegraphed to all the
crowned heads of Europe. First to be informed was Queen Victoria.
("Excellent news of the dear Empress, but *distressing* ones [*sic*] of
her confinement which MUST have been an *AWFUL* one.") Congratulations poured in from all the sovereigns; the pope telegraphed
his blessings (marking the first time that the electric wire was
deemed appropriate for the transmission of a papal benediction). It
was announced that the pope and the Queen of Sweden (a Beauharnais cousin) were to be the infant's godparents.

It was also announced that the infant would be named Eugène
Louis Jean Joseph Napoleon and would carry the title Prince Imperial. Within the family he was known as Louis. The Emperor called
him "Lou-Lou" (a nickname the Empress hated).

Eugénie's first reaction on examining her son: "Louis will be
dreadfully ugly; already he has a nose like a man's." She did not care
for children very much. But she cannot be said to have been a bad

mother. She was an impatient mother. She expected her son to be as well developed at the age of four months as a child of four years. Eugénie was one of those mothers who come to appreciate their children only when they have reached adulthood. She gave the Prince Imperial as few kisses and maternal hugs as she had received from her own mother. But she loved him in her own fashion.

Napoleon, on the other hand, loved his little son to distraction, sought to spoil him mercilessly, and devoted more time to him than to anyone else. Eugénie disapproved of the Emperor's habit of having the boy near him in his study when he was working on State matters, and taking him to Cabinet meetings. ("But, Ugénie, I like to hear his opinions!") She also made it known that the Prince was never to be praised; she feared he would become "too vain and too proud of his Imperial position."

Eugénie looked upon him not as a son but as heir to the Napoleonic tradition, and considered his education and development only in that context. It was rough on poor little Lou-Lou, as the following scene should demonstrate:

One day at teatime the Emperor brought the boy, dressed as a huntsman, into the Empress's drawing room and said: "Ugénie, here is a clever hunter who would like to greet you." Eugénie asked the boy to recite for her guests a fable of La Fontaine. He began to do so, became embarrassed, and forgot his lines. Eugénie became impatient. One of her guests sought to save the situation by suggesting that the Prince start again. He did so, quickly became nervous, and ended by standing mute, buttoning and unbuttoning his vest, under the baleful glare of his mother and the empathetic gaze of his father.

That the Prince favored his father and understood his mother is reflected in an anecdote related by the Princess Mathilde, who loved the boy as if he were her own: "The Emperor and Empress had a violent discussion in the presence of the Prince the other day at lunch. Afterwards, the Emperor took his son to his study, and there the boy said to his father: 'It seems to me that Mama speaks foolishness.' The Emperor hugged him and agreed."

The Prince Imperial was baptized in Notre-Dame by the papal legate, Cardinal Patrizzi. To the maternal grandmother back in Madrid, whose presence had not been requested, Mérimée wrote:

"The Empress was in great beauty and wore a diadem of diamonds worth no doubt about two or three kingdoms. The Emperor also looked very impressive, and when after the ceremony he held up the child in his arms to present him to the multitudes, the enthusiasm was genuine and great."

Later there was a great banquet at the Hôtel de Ville, at which Cardinal Patrizzi presented to the Emperor a golden spray of flowers, a gift from Pius IX to his godson. The Empress was presented with the Golden Rose—a magnificent twenty-four-carat-gold rosebush on a thirty-inch-high lapis-lazuli and silver-gilt base—in papal recognition of her piety and purity. She was overcome with gratitude—until she learned that the previous year Pius had sent an identical Golden Rose to Isabella II of Spain, a woman not noted for her piety and purity.

Eugénie's recovery from the ordeal of childbirth was a painful and prolonged one; numerous cauterizations were involved, and it was not till May that she could walk unsupported. Her physicians warned that another pregnancy might prove fatal. Eugénie seized upon this as her rationale for ceasing all conjugal relations.

The Emperor accepted this. Eugénie had given him an heir; she could do no wrong in his eyes. He was beginning to listen more and more to her political views. When they did not jibe with his own— and they rarely did—he could always "blame the Empress" in the eyes of his less conservative courtiers. While it is unarguable that he "used" her, nevertheless Napoleon sincerely admired her; with all her faults, Eugénie was a beautiful woman, and she "wore well" in the Imperial scheme of things. The Emperor saw no problems in allowing his Empress a voice in the government. He assumed he could always keep her in check.

It was a fatal assumption.

Napoleon III was riding a terrific high. He had given Europe peace. France had emerged from isolation and allied herself with her powerful hereditary foe. She was the richest nation in the world, her capital the financial center—and envy—of Europe. Her Emperor had not only ended an unpopular war, produced an heir, and stifled all political opposition, he had won over all the people.

When flooding of the Rhone and the Loire caused devastation, the Emperor appeared in the stricken areas—where, ironically, hostility toward him and his Empire had always been most pronounced—and was, in Mérimée's words, "received like a God." When bumper wheat crops came in that year, the farmers thanked not God, but the Emperor.

Had Fate decreed that Napoleon III die in 1856, he would have gone down in history as one of France's greatest benefactors.

But Fate decreed otherwise, and he went down in history as one of France's greatest failures.

Napoleon assumed that the year 1856—his *annus mirabilis*—marked the end of the beginning of his beautiful dream.

Actually, it marked the beginning of the end.

Chapter 10
Shadows

The three men who were to cast the longest shadows over the Second Empire all appeared in Paris when the Empire was at its brightest: Bismarck, Cavour—and the Archduke Maximilian of Austria. Maximilian had been dispatched by his brother, Emperor Franz-Josef, to pave the way toward a better understanding between Austria and France. It was his first important diplomatic mission.

It was also his first step on a road that would end, a decade later, before a firing squad.*

---

* His arrival (May 1856) could have proven embarrassing for Napoleon, though there is no record of any concern on that score. If the rumors still circulating on the Continent were true—that Maximilian was the natural son of "Napoleon II"—then he was the rightful heir of France, Napoleon III the usurper.

The truth concerning Maximilian's paternity has never been established to the satisfaction of historians. It is known that the ambitious Archduchess Sophie, whose favorite son Maximilian was, had been excessively empathetic with and overly fond of the Duke of Reichstadt; his last years as a romantic prisoner at the Austrian Court coincided with Sophie's early years as the wife of the imbecilic Archduke Franz-Karl. And it is known that, at her specific request, Sophie was buried between the Duke of Reichstadt and her beloved Max. Furthermore, if the Lamarckian theory on the genetic transmission of acquired traits is operative here, it could have been from the Duke of Reichstadt that Maximilian inherited the liberal bent and elevated intellectuality that set him apart from all other Habsburg troglodytes.

Maximilian's liberalism and intellectuality notwithstanding, he was every inch a Habsburg. He found the *parvenu* French Court "absolutely lacking in tone." He was "distressed" to find an "inconceivably mixed" society, wherein wealth counted for more than quarterings and the Imperial suite was composed of "amateurs who are not very sure of their parts." He considered it "shocking" that the Empress "exhibited a hearty friendliness" toward her social inferiors and was given to loquacity, which did "not always seem to please her Imperial husband." (At one banquet, the Empress "babbled away" on international politics, while the Emperor "pulled a long sour face and fidgeted and haw-hawed in his seat.")

It was for the Emperor that Maximilian reserved his pithiest lines. With his "bow legs and sidling walk, the furtive look out of half-closed eyes," he seemed to the Archduke "not so much an Emperor with a sceptre as a circus master with a riding crop"; he was "lacking in all nobility and breeding," and had "a nasty habit of running after every pretty woman [which] makes a rather disagreeable impression and detracts from his Imperial dignity."

Within a week of his arrival, Maximilian was singing a different tune: "Napoleon is one of those men whose personality does not attract at first but who gains on knowing through his quiet charm and great simplicity."

The twenty-four-year-old inexperienced diplomat was no match for a congenital intriguer twice his age, whose talents at confiding duplicitously in those he wanted to flatter was positively awe-inspiring.

Napoleon got him to believe—and thus pass on to Franz-Josef—that Austria and France between them could settle the peace of Europe. He praised fulsomely the Archduke's brother, "who, in spite of his youth, has already accomplished so much" (which, in truth, wasn't all that much). As to the Crimean War, the Emperor admitted, "It might have been better to have carved up the Turkish Empire, instead of trying to save it"—as Austria, fearful of antagonizing Russia, had fondly hoped to see done. Even more outrageously, Napoleon convinced the Archduke that he "appears to be delighted with the humiliation of Russia."

Poor Maximilian had no way of knowing (nor had Eugénie, for that matter) that Napoleon was even then preparing to send the

Duke de Morny to St. Petersburg to lay the foundation for a Franco-Russian, ergo anti-Austrian, alliance.

Throughout their many talks ("I breakfast every day with the Emperor and Empress"), Maximilian tried to get his host's ideas on Italy. The host would only commit himself to the extent that the major Powers owed Sardinia "a debt of gratitude" for her "heroic participation" in the recent war. On the night before his departure, in desperation, Maximilian—encouraged by the Empress—drew the Emperor aside and asked him point-blank whether France was prepared to "cooperate with Austria in settling the Roman Question."

The Emperor assured him France had every intention of working hand in hand with Austria and would "never allow the Italians to come between us."

In reply to a "Dear Franzl" letter reporting on his talks with the French Emperor, the Austrian Emperor sent a "Dear Maxrl" letter, in which he congratulated his brother for having "managed the French Emperor with great cleverness and tact and thereby improved Austria's position in Europe."

Neither Franzl nor Maxrl could have suspected that Napoleon *had already decided* on the inevitability of a war between France and Austria over Italy.

The Imperial yacht *La Reine Hortense* was placed at Maximilian's disposal for the voyage from Le Havre to Antwerp; he was going to pay a courtesy call on Leopold, King of the Belgians. Eugénie, who knew that "our dear Max" was in the market for a bride, urged him to consider Leopold's sixteen-year-old daughter Charlotte; she was not only a beautiful, marriageable princess, she was a good Catholic princess. Maximilian took Eugénie's advice.

It was advice they would all come to regret.

The archducal visit was followed with visits by a number of other royals, all of whom wished to pay their respects to—and get a closer look at—the Emperor on whom European diplomacy was now centered and his gorgeous, gregarious wife. Often the conversation would devolve upon matters of a nonpolitical nature. Spiritualistic séances had become the rage among the higher social order, and celebrities were given to comparing notes on who among them had experienced the most rewarding ectoplasmic manifestation.

Napoleon and Eugénie learned of an extraordinary young Scotsman named Daniel Dungals Home, who was making the rounds of the major European courts, manipulating furniture, raising the dead, and levitating in and out of palace windows.

When Home manifested himself at the Tuileries around the beginning of 1857, the preternaturally superstitious Eugénie welcomed him as a true believer would welcome the Parousia. As for Napoleon, himself superstitious, he wanted to "believe" but had to be convinced.

The Empress informed Home that he could dispense with levitating himself (or anyone else, for that matter); she was "more concerned with communing with the spirits than watching live people fly about." Home obliged her. One morning, at Fontainebleau, Eugénie asked him to make a table talk. After a long pause, the table growled in an angry voice, "What are you doing here? It is Sunday, and you should be in Church!" The petrified Empress jumped up and fled off to mass.

The Emperor was not convinced.

Nor was he convinced when Home resurrected the Empress's father. As she described it in a letter to Paca:

> No one but me knew what anniversary that was [the death of the Count de Montijo]. When we sat down at the table, a hand took hold of me. I was astonished and asked, "You love me very much?" and immediately I was answered, and my hand was pressed. "Did you recognize me?" asked the spirit. "Yes," I answered; "tell me the name you bore on earth." The hand answered by letter, and said: "Today is the day of my death!" "Who can that be?" the others asked. "My father!" I cried, and immediately the hand pressed mine again and made the sign of the cross on my hand.

The Emperor still had his doubts. He could not explain why the late Count de Montijo spoke French with a Scottish burr.

A few days later, at a séance in the Tuileries, Home gave the Empress a bell to hold, and asked the Emperor to hold an accordion. Suddenly some spirits removed the bell from the Empress's hand and began to play "charming airs." Then, as a footstool galloped toward him from the opposite side of the room, the Emperor felt the accordion fly out of his hand, identify itself as the Empress Josephine, and begin to play some airs. (They were not "charming.")

Before the Emperor could even begin to grasp such incredible happenings, the table suddenly rattled about spastically and—in the name of his dead mother Queen Hortense—told him how proud she was that he had fulfilled his destiny.

The Emperor was convinced. (He was also unmindful—or uncaring—that his mother spoke not only with a Scottish burr, but in a baritone.) Home was soon on intimate terms with the sovereigns, offering advice of a political nature, in addition to summoning "Queen Hortense" and "Empress Josephine" to offer their own prognostications. The Emperor, who was not prepared to accept advice from corporeal matter, was hardly about to do so from a Scot, much less from an accordion and a table.

Still, he was convinced that Home was definitely more than a charlatan. He was particularly gratified when Queen Hortense jumped about excitedly one day and announced that she was happily in Heaven. His joy knew no bounds.

Demands were made among the Emperor's entourage that a stop be put to Home's hokus-pokus. Count Walewski led a delegation of ministers who threatened to resign unless the charlatan was evicted from Court. The Princess Mathilde berated her Imperial cousin for being an Imperial fool, and condemned Eugénie, whose protégé Home had become. He never left her side, following her to Saint-Cloud, to Fontainebleau, and to Compiègne, making tables speak and footstools gallop and chairs dance.

It was openly bruited about that the Empress was consulting the dead on political matters.

The Emperor began to have his doubts when Walewski convinced him Home was "a spy, in the service of foreign powers." (He wasn't.)

At length, Viel-Castel was able to inform his diary: "The famous Home, the man with second sight . . . who turned tables and . . . conjured up dead people before the Emperor and Empress, has been sent to the prison of Mazas as a thief and moral leper, and finally expelled from France."

Home's downfall came when he informed Their Majesties that the Prince Imperial would never sit on the throne of France.

It was the only prediction he made that came true.

❖

Great Britain was greatly perturbed with the French Emperor. She feared that he had sent Morny to St. Petersburg for the express purpose of putting an end to the Anglo-French alliance. It was no secret that Morny, a pronounced Russophile, hoped for a Franco-Russian alliance as a bulwark against Britain and Prussia, both of which nations he openly detested. Was Morny reflecting the aspirations of his half-brother?

Actually, no. Napoleon was intent on bringing about an Anglo-French-Russian alliance (something the English cared as little for as a Stuart restoration). But first he wanted to make sure French and not British interests got a head start in exploiting the enormous potential of industrially backward Russia.

He sought to reassure Victoria that nothing would be done that might in any way jeopardize Anglo-French amity. Victoria was not reassured. Her original enchantment with Napoleon had been dampened, thanks to Lord Cowley's keeping her fully abreast of the Castiglione affair. The Queen was "quite anguished" and "*betroffen*" over one report, dated July 1, 1856, in which Lord Cowley advised that

> All Paris is scandalised by His Majesty's late proceedings with the Castiglione. Even the Court entourage talk of a *fête champêtre* the other night at Villeneuve-l'Etang, where . . . His Majesty rowed the said lady in a small boat alone and then disappeared with her in certain dark walks during the whole of the evening. The poor Empress was in a sad state—got excited and began to dance, when not being sufficiently strong she fell very heavily. It was a regular orgy, the men dancing with their hats on. All this is very sad. It does the Emperor an infinity of harm politically speaking . . .

Reasoned Victoria: if the Emperor could "cause the *dear* Empress such *Verlegenheit*," what might he cause for England? (To which Albert harrumphed, "What indeed!")

On the advice of Persigny, who had replaced Walewski at the London Embassy, Napoleon made known his desire to visit England "in order to clarify his own ideas, to guide his policy, and to prevent by personal communications with the Queen, his Royal Highness [Albert] and Her Majesty's Government the dissidences and misunderstandings which the Emperor thinks will arise for want of such communications." An invitation was duly extended, and the French sovereigns arrived at Osborne on August 6, 1857.

Noted Lord Clarendon: "A very black cloud hung over the alliance when the Emperor came here; but all was sunshine before he departed." Napoleon broached his perennial theme: a revision of the 1815 treaties. Albert, who always took Victoria's place when it came to the conduct of State affairs, argued that however inadequately the Congress of Vienna had reorganized Europe, it had at least given the Continent forty years of peace after twenty-five years of French-induced bloodletting.

Napoleon assured Albert that he had no desire to upset Europe but was convinced that some changes could be made without endangering peace. However, he did not press the issue; he was anxious to maintain Britain's friendship at all costs, even though he was now made to realize that England had no intention of getting caught up in any alliance with Russia. The Anglo-French alliance was secure.

Though the Emperor pulled his usual ingratiating tricks with the Queen, it was the Empress who came in for the lion's share of compliments in the royal journal this go-around. Gone was the nervousness Eugénie had exhibited during the previous exchange of State Visits. Victoria was "much enlivened by the Empress's cleverness and originality," found her "full of spirit and *good* sense," and felt "*sure* the Emperor would do *well* to follow *her* advice."

Eugénie had made known her disapproval of any Franco-Russian *rapprochement*. For the British royals, it was "a comfort" to know that the Empress of France—"Albert's ally"—was more conservative than the Emperor in her outlook. And less devious.

After the visit, when acknowledging the Emperor's thank-you letter, Victoria advised her "*cher frère*" to lend more of an ear to his dear wife's opinions. "In a position so isolated as ours," she wrote sententiously, "we can find no greater consolation, no support more sure, than the sympathy and counsel of him or her who is called to share our lot in life, and the dear Empress, with her generous impulses, is *your guardian angel*, as the Prince is *my true friend*."

The Emperor must surely have gotten off one of his wry zingers on receipt of this advice. Lamentably, it has gone unrecorded.

On the evening of January 14, 1859, the Emperor and Empress were riding along the crowded Rue Lepelletier toward the Opéra to host a well-advertised gala, when suddenly the air was rent by three successive deafening explosions. Coachmen, horses and nearby escort riders were flung to the ground; tiles, slates, shards of glass, and fragments of masonry rained down on the panic-stricken onlookers. In the darkness—every gas lamp in the vicinity had been blown out—could be heard the groans of the injured and the screams of all others. Eight people were killed, 150 injured.

As police agents came rushing to the scene with torches, the sovereigns were seen disentangling themselves from the twisted wreckage of their coach. Incredibly, though one of the bombs had burst directly before their carriage, the two suffered no more than a grazed eye and a cut eyelid.

"Don't bother with us," said the Empress calmly, as police agents scrambled through the debris to lend a hand. "Such things are our profession. Look after the wounded."

To prevent a panic in the theater, where the noise of the explosions had been heard above the music (Rossini's *William Tell*), the sovereigns—their clothes bespattered with blood and detritus—rushed to the royal box, to be greeted with a standing ovation. During the intermission, they appeared on the balcony outside the theater and were rapturously cheered by the crowds in the street below.

Baron Hübner noted that the Emperor "seemed completely demoralized, whereas the Empress was admirable in her intrepid calm."

Writing to Paca of the event, Eugénie admitted that "I might have cried, but the public was present and *nobody* can say that they saw a single tear in my eyes!"

The assassination attempt was the work of one Orsini and three cohorts, all of whom were in police custody before the curtain went down. Indeed, one of them was in police custody before the curtain went up. He had been arrested with a bomb in his possession, along with a forged passport, outside the opera house a half hour before the Imperial cortège arrived. Perhaps the police are to be forgiven for doing no more than detaining him as a suspicious alien.

Never before in history had a bomb been used in an attempt on the life of a sovereign.

The conspirators intended not to bring the French Emperor into the Italian struggle against papal and Austrian tyranny, but to kill him for having failed to come in sooner. (Cavour's first comment on hearing of the attack: "Let's hope it's not Italians!") The plot had been hatched in London; the bombs had been made in Birmingham.

Mérimée, reflecting the national mood over this latest outrage, wrote the Countess de Montijo: "Working people are saying that if the English won't hand over [all other resident Italian revolutionists], it will be necessary to go fetch them." The Duke de Morny did his damnedest to keep anti-British emotion—which in France was always easily inflamed—at a fever pitch. Walewski, violently opposed to any Sardinian attempts to weaken the papacy, stirred up public opinion against Victor Emmanuel's government.

Official representations were made to London and Turin; both governments refused to accede to Walewski's demands that all subversives be expelled from, and anti-Bonapartist newspapers be suppressed in, their respective capitals. The Emperor gave his assent to these representations. But behind the back of his own government, he told Victor Emmanuel's envoy: "Assure him that in case of war with Austria, I will come and fight beside my faithful ally."

To another ally whose friendship he valued, Queen Victoria, he wrote in confidence: "In the first flush of excitement, the French are determined to find accomplices everywhere. I find it hard to resist the demand for extreme measures which I am asked to take, but this event will not make me deviate from my habitual calm."

He did not deviate from his habitual calm. Nor did he find it hard to resist the demands for extreme measures. The government passed the *Loi de Sûreté Générale*, the most odious legislation of Napoleon's entire regime. In essence, anyone who in any way disagreed with the government was liable to arrest; all provincial prefects were given monthly quotas. The government hoped to put a check on its enemies at home; the Emperor hoped to deflect public opinion away from London and Turin.

In the Chamber of Deputies, Emile Ollivier fulminated: "You have ruled for nine years. You are at peace with the monarchs of Europe. You have a strong and war-like army, an able police force, an enormous budget. Strategic roads cross the capital and you have erected formidable citadels. There is no freedom. The greatest freedom of all, that of the Press, consists merely in the right of saying things which do not displease [the government]. *Where will you stop?"*

Napoleon would not "stop" until, *in extremis*, he was forced to call upon Ollivier himself to save the Empire. But by then the Empire was past saving.

Napoleon had been awaiting a propitious moment to set into motion one of his pet schemes: the liberation of Italy under French auspices and the concomitant reduction of Austrian influence on the Continent. Now was hardly a propitious moment to move; with Russia not yet fully reconciled and England growing suspicious, to challenge Austria would be to court disaster.

But Napoleon saw himself as a Man of Destiny. He followed a Star. To his superstitious mind, the Orsini plot was a sign from his Star that the moment had come. Thus, while lack of propitiousness posed problems, they were not insurmountable ones—for a Man of Destiny. A Man of Destiny who thrived on intrigue.

Nowhere is Napoleon's talent for intrigue more—intriguing is the only word that comes to mind—than in the manner in which he set into motion a war between Austria and Italy. It began with the Orsini attempt. It ended—contrary to Napoleon's expectations—in the unification of Italy. And it paved the way for the collapse of the Second Empire.

Eugénie pleaded that Orsini be pardoned; a martyred Orsini, she argued, was potentially more dangerous to France than a forgotten Orsini—it could lead to further assassination attempts.

Napoleon also wanted to see Orsini pardoned. Or so he led everyone to believe. Being an old revolutionist himself—had he not fought with the *Carbonari?*—Napoleon felt Orsini should not be made to forfeit his life for having acted out of noble convictions. Or so everyone theorized. But his government argued that a man who had blown up a number of people was hardly entitled to compassion.

With a great show of reluctance, the Emperor compromised to the degree that he decreed that Orsini had to be given a fair trial.

(The other culprits were relegated to minor roles; Orsini, the most articulate of the lot, was the star attraction.) Furthermore, Orsini was to be given as his defense counsel Jules Favre, the most eloquent advocate of the day.

Highlight of the trial came when Favre read in open court a letter from Orsini that ended with the impassioned words "May Your Majesty not regret the last prayer of a patriot on the scaffold! Let him liberate my country, and the blessings of its twenty-five million citizens will follow him through the ages!"

The sensation caused by the trial—which included many outbursts on the autocratic subjugation of the Italians by Austria in the north and the Church in the Papal States—was as nothing compared to the sensation that ensued when the Emperor announced he was going to exercise the royal prerogative of mercy for the condemned man.

He changed his mind—with extreme reluctance—only after his ministers threatened to resign en masse.

The following day, another letter bearing Orsini's signature was released for public consumption: "I declare with my last breath that though by a fatal mistake I organized the attempt of January 14th, assassination for whatever cause is not part of my creed. Let my compatriots, instead of relying on this method, take it from me that the liberation of Italy can be achieved only by their restraint, their devotion, and their unity!"

Another sensation. The condemned Orsini was calling upon his compatriots to stop going after innocent European royals.

Two days later, Orsini and his accomplices went to the guillotine.

It would be many months before word got out that Orsini's letters had been written to express the sentiments of the Emperor, as transmitted through his Prefect of Police.

Napoleon had wanted a public trial that would do what the Peace Congress of 1856 had failed to do: make the European Powers accept the inevitability of Austria's expulsion from Italy. Too, he had wanted the European monarchs to "see" that supporting the idea of Italian liberation did not run for them the risk of assassination.

Having gotten what he wanted, Napoleon now moved with extreme furtiveness to ally France and Sardinia, secure the neutrality (if not the active support) of England and Russia—and maneuver Austria into starting the war.

Through Dr. Conneau—the only one he felt he could trust—
Napoleon arranged a secret rendezvous with Cavour at Plombières
on July 20. Within four hours, the two schemers had decided that
Austria was to be somehow maneuvered into declaring war on
Sardinia—*as a result of which France was to intervene in the role of
protector of the oppressed against the aggressor.*

At Napoleon's insistence, the war was to be localized in Northern
Italy; when Austria had finally been driven beyond the Alps, Italy
was to be divided into a four-state confederation under the
presidency of the pope. As a mark of gratitude, France was to be
ceded Nice and Savoy.

This projected division of Italy was not exactly to Cavour's liking. He wanted but one state, and that under the flag of Victor
Emmanuel. But, no mean intriguer himself, Cavour saw the Emperor's proposal as a logical first step toward overall Italian unification, especially after the Emperor agreed to provide 200,000 troops
to Victor Emmanuel's 100,000.

To cement their agreement, it was further agreed that the
Emperor's cousin Plon-Plon would marry the King's youngest
daughter, Princess Clothilde. Victor Emmanuel found the idea of
marrying off his fifteen-year-old, excessively pious child to the
thirty-six-year-old detestable rake odious, even though the rake
favored Italian independence. But Sardinia needed that alliance
with France.

Having thus committed their respective countries to a policy that
would initiate a new era of wars on the Continent, the two plotters
shook hands, swore each other to secrecy, and went their separate
ways: Cavour to build up Sardinia's armies, Napoleon to prevent
England and Russia from interfering.

In August, Napoleon invited Victoria and Albert to visit
Cherbourg—ostensibly to show them his new harbor works, but
really to quiet their suspicions. Word had gotten out by now that the
Emperor of the French and the Prime Minister (and Prime Man-
ipulator) of Sardinia had been seen walking through the countryside
near Plombières arm in arm.

Napoleon assured his British visitors that he had gone to Plombières only to take the waters; that it was coincidental that Cavour
should have happened to be taking the waters there at the same
time; that he and Cavour had only discussed the waters. His British

visitors were not reassured. Albert expostulated to one of his aides: *"That man is a walking lie!"* Victoria reluctantly agreed.

Next, Napoleon took Plon-Plon into his confidence; he cautioned him that the Empress, above all, was not to be told a thing (this Plon-Plon found to his liking), advised him of his forthcoming marriage, and dispatched him on a confidential mission to St. Petersburg.

Plon-Plon got Tsar Alexander II—whose armies were the most effective check on Austria and Prussia—to agree that, in consideration of a "benevolent attitude" on France's part toward his own "aspirations" in Poland, he would guarantee nonintervention, so far as concerned Prussia and Austria, if France would do the same on the side of England.

Napoleon then drafted the secret *pacte de famille* with Victor Emmanuel that formalized the Plombières agreement. The King and Cavour objected to some terms added by the Emperor: Sardinia was to pay for the French troops as well as her own, while the Emperor was to be overall commander of both armies. But they declined to risk an alliance so essential for them on what amounted to a "side issue."

During his 1859 New Year's Day reception at the Tuileries, Napoleon sidled up to Baron Hübner, the Austrian ambassador, and said: "I regret that our relations with your government are no longer so good as in the past; but I beg you to tell your Emperor that my personal sentiments for him have not changed."

With Sardinia and Austria now on an apparent collision course—Cavour made it obvious that Austria's continued presence in Italy was intolerable—England began working for a peaceful solution to the Roman Question. Pretending to prefer it that way ("Certainly I want peace; but sometimes one is carried along by circumstances"), Napoleon announced that France would not support Sardinia *unless Austria were the aggressor.*

On January 30, Plon-Plon married Princess Clothilde at Turin, after he and Victor Emmanuel had signed the still secret *pacte de famille.* The marriage won Eugénie's wholehearted endorsement: she liked the idea of a Bonaparte—even so reprehensible a Bonaparte—marrying into a bona fide royal house. Along the boulevards, the bride was referred to as "the first casualty" of the coming war. Lord Cowley found it "positively horrible to see that poor little frail creature by the side of that brute (I can call him nothing else) to whom she has been immolated." Clothilde went to her immolation in a shroud of piety: "It is the Lord who wished it. That is all there is to say."

On February 4, Napoleon published an article in the *Moniteur* that set forth his allegedly peaceful intentions. Praising Sardinia and attacking Austria's suzerainty, he called for Italian independence based on ideas first put forward by Napoleon Bonaparte on St. Helena—a federation of states under papal presidency. "But whereas the Emperor Napoleon I thought it right to conquer peoples in order to liberate them, Napoleon III wishes to liberate them without conquering them."

Three days later, in a speech opening the Corps Législatif, the Emperor asseverated his intention "to rely on the strength of the French army," but promised he "would not be easily provoked."

A week later he wrote to Queen Victoria, disclaiming any responsibility for the rumors of war that were sweeping Europe's chanceries and denying that any military preparations were being taken by the French.

With all Europe (Sardinia excepted) now branding him a warmonger, Napoleon found support in, of all people, Eugénie. The idea of Italy's being united under the hegemony of the pope was for her too delicious to contemplate.

Meanwhile England pressed the Austrian and papal governments to reform their regimes in Italy, in order to deprive the French Emperor of a *casus belli*. (Few in London disagreed with Clarendon's evaluation of the Austrian-supported papacy as "the most detestable government in the world.") Prussia threatened a counterattack along the Rhine if her own interests were imperiled by war. Russia—now having come to realize what it was she had been asked not to intervene in—pushed for a conference of the major Powers. This won the support of England.

Napoleon, less anxious for delay than for the appearance of it, consented to such a congress. "In order to divide my enemies and win over part of Europe to neutrality," he wrote Plon-Plon, "I must make loud profession of my moderation and of my desire for conciliation."

On April 8, Lord Cowley asked him point-blank if he desired war or peace. Reported Cowley: "The Emperor replied that he would be very glad if peace could be maintained, but that he was not afraid of war, and he added that his inmost conviction was that war was unavoidable."

It certainly was. Austria expressed willingness to enter into a congress—provided there was no question of territorial changes, and, furthermore, that Sardinia, which she wanted excluded from the congress, was disarmed beforehand. Cavour quite naturally refused to disarm unless Austria followed suit. On April 19, Cavour agreed to a plan that both sides demobilize. Austria rejected this and, on April 23, sent Sardinia an ultimatum directing her to demobilize within three days.

This gave Cavour the provocation he needed. The ultimatum was rejected, and Cavour and Napoleon got the war they wanted and on their terms: Austria had been maneuvered into the role of aggressor.

Few people were fooled. Victoria recorded in her journal: "People here are now excited against Austria, although *we* know that the *whole* [war] is caused by the Emperor Napoleon!"

France declared war on Austria on May 3—nine days after the first French contingents had departed for Genoa by way of Marseilles.

In his proclamation to the nation—it was also his justification to the major Powers—Napoleon explained that he had "drawn the sword not to conquer, but to liberate." Purpose of the war was "to give Italy to herself, not to make her change her master." He was not going to Italy "to foment disorder or overthrow the power of the Holy Father whom we have restored to his throne, but to free him of that alien pressure which is weighing on the whole peninsula."

A week later, vowing to free Italy "from the Alps to the Adriatic," the Emperor left the Empress as Regent and departed for the battlefields where his uncle had first gained fame sixty-three years previously. The entire country was behind him, the opposition not excluded. As the first Bonaparte had said cynically: "Just speak to the French of *la gloire* and they are seduced at once."

One is sorely tempted to deal frivolously with this war, which had about it the air of an Offenbach operetta. There were only two major battles, Magenta and Solferino; both came about because the rival armies literally stumbled into each other's path, both saw disor-

ganized leadership on the part of the contestants, and both ended
indecisively.

The Emperor threw himself into the conduct of the war with the
zest of his uncle Napoleon and the talent of his uncle Jerome. He
was "always in his shirt-sleeves, writing at his desk, sometimes
smoking a cigar, but always at work; for he saw to almost everything himself, and did not spare either fatigue or trouble."

Yet he lacked the vaguest idea as to the disposition of his army,
was unable to read a field map intelligently, and otherwise behaved
in so incoherent and confused a manner that he made sure all rec-
ords of his orders were destroyed at the campaign's end.

At the Battle of Magenta (June 4), which the French won by
default—the Austrians were first to retire in complete
confusion—when General Frossard exclaimed, "Sire, what a glorious victory!" the Sire confessed: "A victory, you say? And I was
going to order a retreat!"

But to equate this war with an opera spoof would be to commit an
obscenity. The battles were murderous *mêlées* in which both sides
demonstrated just how little military science had advanced since the
Middle Ages. Disease accounted for more casualties than the
fighting itself.

And—of far greater consequence—in warring against Austria,
Napoleon committed perhaps his greatest long-term blunder.
When, little more than a decade later, he went to war with Prussia,
he could not count on the support of a large Austrian army that
wanted nothing so much as Prussia's annihilation.

While the Emperor was acquitting himself questionably on the
battlefront, the Empress was acquitting herself admirably on the
home front. Three times weekly she presided over the Council of
Ministers. Daily she prayed publicly—often at as many as five
churches at a clip. Every evening she gathered her ladies together
to make bandages for the wounded. She thrived on being Regent:
reading dispatches from the front, concurring with ministerial decisions, receiving foreign ambassadors, functioning as her consort's
surrogate. Small wonder that, ere long, she would lament to her
ladies-in-waiting that she found the idea of sitting and rolling bandages "boring."

At the end of May, under the pretext of offering birthday congratulations, Eugénie wrote Queen Victoria: "I have received good

news from the Emperor. Thanks to the attitude taken by friendly powers, he hopes to localize the conflict, for a general conflagration would be an incalculable evil for the whole world. . . . We count on Your Majesty, who always has the peace of the world at heart, to use her personal influence . . . on Prince Albert, whose word carries such weight in Germany, in order to arrive at this aim . . ."

Prussia was looming large in the Empress's—and everyone else's—thoughts. Daily, reports came in of troop concentrations along the Rhine. Prussia was not about to allow the Austrians—fellow-Germans—to be defeated by a Bonaparte. It was Eugénie's hope that the pro-German Prince Consort might take it upon himself to be a tempering influence on his and Victoria's son-in-law, the Prussian Crown Prince Frederick.

Prince Albert wrote to Frederick: "May God destroy the wicked French!"

By the time the Battle of Solferino ended (June 24) in bloody indecisiveness, Napoleon had realized that in conniving to "liberate" Italy he had connived himself into an untenable position. Victor Emmanuel and Cavour had no intention of settling for a four-state confederation under papal presidency; they were going for total unification—which would present France with a rival Power in the Mediterranean.

Further, were Napoleon to chase the Austrians—who had retired across the Mincio into their Quadrilateral—he would almost certainly find himself at war with Prussia, France's hereditary enemy. Russia could not be expected to check a Prussian advance, Tsar Alexander's prior assurances to the contrary; a champion of legitimacy, Alexander was viewing with distaste the disappearance of "legitimate" monarchies up and down the Italian peninsula, as one state after another deposed its petty Bourbon rulers in favor of republicanism and unification. And Great Britain, pro-Prussian in any event, would be tempted to sit by and watch France brought down.

Napoleon decided he had better end the war immediately. In this he was encouraged by Eugénie, who was now sending along hysterical letters daily, decrying the Prussian build-up along the Rhine and "advising" he bring the French army home on the double.

Without notifying Victor Emmanuel, Napoleon proposed an immediate armistice to Franz-Josef, who was equally anxious to end the war. On July 11, the two emperors met at Villafranca and agreed that most of Lombardy was to be ceded to France and then retroceded to Sardinia (a little face-saving gesture here on Austria's part); Venetia, which Sardinia coveted, was to remain Austrian; and the deposed Italian princes were to be restored to their thrones "subject to amnesty of their revolting subjects [sic]."*

Cavour resigned in a rage, but Victor Emmanuel accepted the French Emperor's defection. He was not too sorry to see Napoleon go. Napoleon had been hogging all the glory (such as it was), and Victor Emmanuel was kind of touchy when it came to glory. Furthermore, he was confident Italy could carry on, now that the Austrians had been pushed back beyond the Mincio.

On taking leave of his allies, Napoleon explained that he had signed the armistice because "I would have needed 300,000 men to carry on, and I do not have them." He tried to reassure Cavour that, as regarded the Italian states still under Austrian control, "I will plead their cause." (No pleading was promised as regarded the Papal States.) Then, tacitly admitting he had not kept to his end of the bargain, Napoleon magnanimously agreed to forgo the compensation he had expected: the annexation of Nice and Savoy.

Within the week, Napoleon was back in Paris. His claim that by the annexation of Lombardy to Sardinia "the cause of national liberty and reform" had been "brought home to all Italy" had a hollow ring to it. But France was glad the damned war was over and done with. It had brought the country no added departments, no added taxpayers, no new conscripts for her armies.

A few days after his return from Italy, Napoleon hinted to his generals that the magnificently uniformed French army was suffering imperfections. France had fought two major wars—each of which had been ended by a timely peace, neither of which could have ended victoriously through further fighting. His generals assured the Emperor that his army was up to snuff.

After the generals had gone, Napoleon suffered a sort of moment of truth. He was now fifty-one years old—the age at which his uncle had begun his apotheosis on St. Helena, long after having conquered

---

* *The Treaty of Zurich (November 10) put the stamp of approval on these provisions.*

Europe. He could still hear that Parisian laborer who had cried out, as the Imperial train was departing the Gare de Lyon for the Italian war front, "Old moustachio is stronger than the enemy; he has the plans of his uncle!"

Old moustachio had the plans of his uncle; but that was *all* he had of his uncle.

Napoleon was beginning to suspect that things were not quite working out according to expectations.

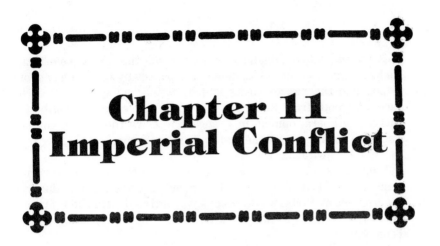

Chapter 11
Imperial Conflict

One night in 1856 while descending the grand staircase of the Tuileries after a reception, the poet Alfred de Musset looked over his shoulder and remarked sanguinely to a companion: "It is all beautiful today. Yes, for the moment very beautiful. But I would not give you two sous for the last act."

The period that followed the Italian War was the intermission before that last act; a period during which, no matter in what direction Napoleon turned, he alienated half his constituency.

"It is always public opinion that wins the last victory," he wrote. As the Empire reached its midpoint, he set out to court public opinion. But public opinion in France was a bifurcated monster; courting it was like courting mutually antipathetic Siamese twins.

In order to woo the political opposition, Napoleon instituted a limited program of parliamentary reform; this not only had the inevitable effect of giving his Republican opponents added impetus, but, and worse, it put him in bad odor with his own Bonapartist supporters.

And then there was the Cobden Treaty he concluded with England (January 1860), whereby France obtained valuable concessions in the reduction of English duties on fish products, silks, wines and fashion goods, in return for the opening of French markets to British products. This made him popular with the fishermen, silk weavers, vintners and fashion designers—and incurred the wrath of the industrialists and bankers.

His most profound dilemma, however, was the Roman Question. He had either to continue to defend the papacy by force of arms, or to abandon the papacy to its fate by withdrawing those French garrison troops from Rome. To follow the first course would be to antagonize liberal opinion in France. To follow the second course would be to antagonize clerical opinion in France—and, into the bargain, his own Empress.

While Eugénie was prepared to concede that the papal government was in need of reform—she prayed that the archreactionary government at Rome would become "penetrated with the Spirit of the Gospel"—she was not prepared to concede any vitiating of the Temporal Power.

And Eugénie was not one to keep her opinions to herself.

Napoleon hoped that his favorite device—a congress of the major Powers—would resolve the problem. But 1856's arbiter of Europe was 1859's bogeyman of Europe; the major Powers were having no truck with any of the French Emperor's congresses. Even if they had, no international settlement of the issue would have extricated Napoleon from the crossfire of liberal and Catholic opinion at home.

The Emperor would certainly have been familiar with the old French proverb "He who eats the pope will die of it." Nevertheless, he decided to do a bit of nibbling. He had no choice.

In December 1859, he published pseudonymously a pamphlet entitled *Le Pape et le Congrès*, in which he advocated a reduction of the papal territories to a minimum: "The smaller the territory, the greater its sovereign. The pope will be more powerful then in his weakness than in his strength."

It was not until the 1929 Concordat that the papacy could bring itself to accept this paradox. But Eugénie could never bring herself to accept it; indeed, she could not bring herself to accept that her consort had proposed it. (Lord Cowley to Queen Victoria: "The Empress is in despair about the pamphlet, but will not believe that the Emperor has written it.")

The pamphlet had predictable results. Napoleon's liberal constituency was pleased; his Catholic constituency was enraged.

In the midst of this firestorm, yet another firestorm engulfed the Emperor. Cavour, by now returned to power in Sardinia, proposed that Napoleon annex Nice and Savoy, in keeping with their Plombières agreement; in return, France would pay the cost of the late Italian campaign.

Cavour's was a shrewd move. Not only were the Sardinians unable to meet the outstanding war debt, Nice and Savoy were by sentiment and interest more than half French—and Cavour had no guarantee that Napoleon might not at some future date go ahead and annex them anyway. Napoleon agreed to the transaction—and agreed to overlook the incorporation of Tuscany and Emilia into the Kingdom of Sardinia.

In England, he was again the implacable foe. Even his old friend Palmerston suffered a change of heart:

> Till lately I had strong confidence in the fair intentions of Napoleon towards England, but of late I have begun to feel great distrust, and to suspect that his formerly expressed intention of avenging Waterloo has only lain dormant, and has not died away. He seems to have thought to lay his foundation by beating, with our aid or with our concurrence or neutrality, first Russia, and then Austria, by dealing with them generously to make them his friends in any subsequent quarrel with us.

Palmerston was overreacting, though he had no way of knowing so. Napoleon was not out to "avenge Waterloo" by destroying England. He sincerely wanted peace in Europe, and he sincerely wanted England's friendship. Unfortunately, he had a dismal way of showing it.

"Really it is too bad!" wrote Victoria to her uncle Leopold at Brussels:

> No country, no human being would ever dream of *disturbing* or *attacking* France; everyone would be glad to see her prosperous; but *she* must needs disturb *every* quarter of the Globe and try to make mischief and set everyone by the ears; and of course it will end some day in a *regular crusade* against the *universal disturber* of the WORLD! It is really *monstrous!*

Chief among those whom the universal disturber set by the ears was his own consort. On November 13, 1860, Lord Cowley wrote to Lord Clarendon:

> Various motives are attributed to this somewhat extraordinary proceeding—grief—ill-health—jealousy. The Emperor says that the

> Empress's nerves are in such a state that she will not recover nor resume her usual avocations until after an absence. Some people say that she . . . wants to consult *privately* Dr. Simpson [a noted diagnostician] of Edinburgh. . . . it is whispered that the [return] of the beautiful Madame di Castiglione at Paris has something to do with Her Majesty's absence. . . .

The "somewhat extraordinary proceeding": Eugénie's abrupt flight from France.

The "various motives" all played their part. But the basic motive was that the Emperor and Empress had reached a climacteric in their relationship. After seven years as husband and wife—and is it not true that climacterics usually come at the end of seven-year cycles?—it was probably inevitable. It was no secret in the better Parisian drawing rooms that the word "divorce" had been ricocheting off the walls of the Tuileries of late and that the Empress had on more than one occasion threatened to "take our son and leave France forever."

Napoleon knew they were idle threats. Eugénie was not about to leave him, less because of her staunch Catholicism—Pius IX would have gladly granted her an ecclesiastical separation—than because she *liked* being Empress of the French. She was hardly about to give up her sovereignty, now that she had begun to hit her stride.

As historian David Stacton has pointed out in his witty, brilliant omnibiography of the entire Bonaparte clan,

> Napoleon had two virtues which amounted to vices. He was inordinately kind, and incredibly patient . . . and seldom if ever did he put Eugénie in her place. At the most he would make some ironic remark, and she was beneath the reach of irony. She was emotionally jagged, and had only three techniques: she could storm like a virago, always in private, she could charm, always in public, and if she could not get what she wanted any other way, she cried.

It was the third technique that the Emperor found most unbearable. "Every time it happens, I am almost ill," he confided to the sympathetic Princess Mathilde. "I cannot see the Empress weep. When she does, I give in and do everything she wants just to dry her tears."

Well, not quite everything. All the tears in the world were not going to make the Emperor give up his mistresses and "little diversions"—or give in to Eugénie's demands that, come what may, "France must do everything within her power to maintain Pius IX in his Temporal Power." (Superstitious as he was, Napoleon dismissed Eugénie's reiterated fear that their son would die if his papal godfather lost Rome.)

Notwithstanding Napoleon's faults—and God knows he was blessed with a plenitude—it is Eugénie who must stand condemned for turning a basically incompatible marriage into a misery for herself and a trial for her mate. ("Dearest Paca: . . . I am so disgusted with life; the past seems so empty, the present so full of danger, and the future perhaps so short (at least I hope so!) that I frequently wonder whether it is worth fighting on . . ." "Dearest Paca: . . . I am prepared to wear a mask and show a smiling face, but that is the extent of my ability. Sorrow, insomnia, madness almost, that is all that remains of me . . .")

Not only did Eugénie overlook the fact that she had come to the throne by marriage and not by election, she played upon her husband's weaknesses in hopes of strengthening her own position.

To his credit, Napoleon not only showed Eugénie the utmost respect, he demanded that all others do likewise (at least in his presence). Further, he showered her with jewels, crinolines—anything she desired. It was not a case of Napoleon's hoping to buy her off. He was a truly generous man. Too, he could not do enough for the woman who had given him an heir and thus (or so he believed) assured the dynasty.

When it came to political matters, though, all the tears and all the tirades could not bring him around. As the Second Empire moved toward de Musset's last act, Emperor and Empress were, in Lord Cowley's words, "hardly on speaking terms."

Added to Eugénie's daily litany of connubial crimes her consort was committing—the Emperor was "wilfully embarrassing" her by sleeping around with "the scum of the earth," she was fed up with his "*crapule* [debauchery]; I can stand it no longer!"—was a new crime, perhaps most heinous of all in her eyes: Louis-Napoleon Bonaparte was "a Godless *heretic!*"

The heretic was granted respite from domestic aggravation in late July, when his sister-in-law arrived in Paris. Eugénie's attentions were all centered now on Paca, who was suffering—and agonizingly so—from some mysterious back ailment that had all her physicians baffled. (It is today assumed that the malady was cancer of the spine.)

On August 22, the sovereigns left on a tour that took in the new provinces of Nice and Savoy and a visit to Algeria. For Eugénie the journey was a personal agony. Her thoughts were continuously on Paca, who now lay in her house on the Champs Elysées so ill that she could no longer walk and had to gasp for every breath. Eugénie knew her beloved sister was seriously ill, but did not realize the illness was terminal.

The farther from Paris she traveled, the more her fears increased: "I am now in Lyon . . . We were received with an enthusiasm that is difficult to describe; it was almost madness. . . . The only thing that makes me sad is the thought that I am not there to relieve the tediousness of your couch." "I am in Annecy, a charming little city. . . . I pray devoutly, so that it seems my prayers *must* be heard . . ."

And from Grenoble: "They say twin sisters, if separated, are united by some mysterious bond, so that one feels the physical pain of the other. I too feel your pain physically, but my heart feels it a thousand times more, for my love for you is infinite. I am in great despair that I can not be with you . . ."

A disturbing telegram awaited Eugénie when the sovereigns landed in Algiers on the seventeenth. Eugénie wrote her mother, who had joined Paca in Paris: "The thought that Paca is worse and I am so far away makes my life a burden. I am frightened to death. I have prayed so much that it seems to me almost impossible that my sister should not get well. . . . This anxiety is frightening!"

Next morning, Napoleon received a telegram that Paca had died. He decided to withhold the news from Eugénie; a great ceremony had been planned in which the native beys and chiefs of North Africa were to pay their homage.

"The festive day ended in an apotheosis," recorded one observer. "Admiration for the Empress's beauty was reflected on the bronzed faces of the Algerian chieftains who prostrated themselves before her." One member of the Imperial suite found that "this pleased the woman in her."

That evening, Napoleon told Eugénie that Paca's condition appeared to be hopeless, and proposed they cut short their journey and depart for home the next day. It was not until they arrived back in Marseilles on the twenty-first that Eugénie was told Paca had died the previous Sunday.

Her grief was inconsolable. On the day-long journey back to Paris and for weeks on end, she wept, she cried, she sobbed, she moaned, she prayed. Most of her courtiers were astonished to discover the Empress was capable of such deep emotion. She demanded that the house in which Paca had died be razed to the ground: "No one must live in the room in which my sister died!" Fears were expressed for her sanity.

By November, the grief Eugénie felt over Paca's death had slowly given way to the fury she felt at Napoleon's having kept the news from her. There is no denying that she was being slightly unfair here; for Napoleon to have canceled the Arabian festival could have had political repercussions.

But Eugénie refused to listen to reason; by now she had all but lost her reason. She felt she had been betrayed—betrayed by a Godless heretic.

Whereupon the heretic committed an unsupportable indiscretion: he indulged himself another "little diversion" with the recently returned Countess di Castiglione.

For Eugénie, this was the last straw. She "threatened her husband with the divine wrath and the most appalling torments in this world and the next"—and left abruptly for London.

A statement was issued to French diplomatic missions abroad: "Owing to the effect on Her Majesty of the death of her sister the Duchess de Alba y Berwick, the doctors have recommended a change of air. The Empress will visit Scotland in the strictest *incognito*."

Immediately rumors flew in and out of Europe's major capitals: "The Empress has had it with the Emperor's love affairs," "The Empress cannot forgive the Emperor's treatment of the pope," "The Empress wants a divorce," "The Empress has lost her mind." King Leopold snidely wrote his niece Victoria that he "never heard Scotland recommended for winter excursions."

Eugénie opted for Scotland because she wanted reassurance from the eminent Dr. Simpson at Edinburgh that she was not suffering from the same disease that had carried Paca off. Dr. Simpson assured Eugénie that her health was perfect. (He also advised her to stay away from French doctors.) She returned to London on December 2; two days later she journeyed out to Windsor. Confided Queen Victoria to her journal:

> She looked thin and pale and unusually melancholy . . . when she spoke of her return from Algeria, her eyes filled with tears and she said it was only since she had come here that she had been able to sleep and eat again. She only mentioned the Emperor once and that was *d'offrir ses compliments.* . . . she gave me a melancholy impression, as if some deep grief and anxiety weighed upon her. Poor thing, one must feel for her. . . .

A week later, Victoria visited Eugénie at her hotel and found: "She looked very pretty, and was *in very good spirits*, but again carefully avoided any illusion [*sic*] to her husband . . ."

Eugénie had been wined and dined by London society and publicly fussed over; she had been reminded—if, in truth, she needed reminding—that she was still Empress of the French. Small wonder she was *"in very good spirits."* By the time Eugénie returned to Paris (December 12), her grief had been mitigated; she was now ready to resume the role for which Destiny had designated her—as she read Destiny.

Assumedly in an attempt to appease his Empress, the Emperor had reshuffled the Cabinet during her absence. Achille Fould was forced to surrender his two hats, Ministry of State and Ministry of the Imperial Household. Eugénie had not forgiven Fould for not delaying Paca's funeral until after her return from Algeria, nor for what she considered the rather parsimonious manner in which the rites were held. (They weren't really all that parsimonious.) Into the Cabinet came Count Walewski, who had been forced out because of his opposition to the Italian War and whom Eugénie favored because of his pro-papacy stance.

It was not really much of an appeasement. Fould was given the Ministry of Finance (where he properly belonged); Walewski was as easily managed in one office as in another. Furthermore, Persigny was brought back from the London Embassy to take over the Ministry of the Interior. He and the Empress felt a mutual detestation: Persigny was the most rabid anti-papist in all of France.

Eugénie's return from England marked the turning point in the lives of the sovereigns. They passed each other, moving in opposite directions: the Empress began to grow progressively stronger, the Emperor progressively weaker.

Ostrich-like, Napoleon seemed to find more solace in working on his eminently forgettable *Histoire de Jules César* than in coping with the problems of government, many of which were of his own manufacture. He was not giving up, though obviously he was beginning to lose his grip.

He was still following his Star—which at this point was not pursuing a straight trajectory but dancing a celestial jig. Napoleon was still confident that whatever he did was the right thing. But he was not *as* confident as when he had first latched onto that capricious Star.

Eugénie found it rather easy to insinuate herself into the highest councils of government. She began to attend all Privy Council meetings. Ere long, she would be attending all Cabinet meetings.

The Court became polarized: there was the "Empress's Party"—a camarilla of clerical conservatives—and "Plon-Plon's Party"—to which rallied those whose political philosophy was more republican than Bonapartist.

The Emperor, after his fashion, belonged to neither faction and both factions. He touched base with those influential anticlerics who had coalesced around Plon-Plon, wanting them to know he was indeed in complete political harmony with them; and he let the conservative Bonapartists believe he was in truth trying to work to their advantage by allowing his Empress to stand as their champion.

Barring the occasional tears and hysterical outbursts, Eugénie's passions were subdued. Her innate loquaciousness returned. She had an opinion on anything and everything. She was increasingly concerned with how she came across to people whose attitudes she shared. ("I have just seen the Nuncio," she told one courtier. "I would like to know what impression my conversation with him made. Try to find out.")

The Emperor consulted with her from time to time, seeking out her opinion on matters of State. If their opinions dovetailed—as in the case of the disastrous Mexican adventure—no problems obtruded. If their opinions diverged, Eugénie accepted in a quiet fury that the Emperor's will had to prevail.

Could she have suspected that her time was coming?

In their private lives, Napoleon remained the ever considerate husband. Eugénie's every wish of a material nature was indulged. Though he had by now begun to find the social aspects of emperor-ship troublesome, he acquiesced in Eugénie's seeming compulsion to preside over countless Court balls ("Often I would return to my apartments so exhausted, I barely had the strength to remove my jewels"). He dutifully accompanied her to countless receptions given by the accredited envoys in Paris—and stood by, smiling sphinx-like, as she made known her views and, more often than not, made herself foolish in the eyes of many.

Throughout this period, the Emperor was creating a true empire—one that included overseas possessions. The conquest of Algeria, begun during the reign of Louis-Philippe, had been completed; this new department was three times the size of Metropolitan France. In the Pacific, a "protectorate" had been established over the Loyalty, Wallis and Society Islands (the latter including Tahiti). Within a few years, Madagascar and French Somaliland would come under the Imperial flag. The capture of Saigon in 1859 marked the founding of France's eastern empire in Indo-China. Even as Napoleon was attempting to extricate himself from the mess he had made of things on the European Continent, France was meeting with success in the Levant, where a need to protect the Christian Maronites from Moslem Druse persecution gave Napoleon an excuse to establish French influence in Syria and Lebanon.

He had by now constructed an empire that would outlive the Second Empire itself.

There were other adventures, most notably France's colluding with the major European Powers to enforce the "rights" of Christian missionaries in China. In 1860, an Anglo-French fleet landed a "punitive expedition" that occupied Peking and dictated the terms under which China was at last opened to Western "diplomacy, religion and culture." As part of their Westernization program, the Europeans burned the "Summer Palace," looting or destroying property valued conservatively at ten million dollars. "Culture" and "Christianity" came to China—and museums and private collections throughout Europe were enriched by the exquisite treasures of an ancient, artistic, raped "heathen" civilization. (A few of the choicer vases found their way into Eugénie's drawing rooms, where they

reposed, somewhat incongruously, in contiguity with all the Marie
Antoinette memorabilia.)

A continent that had enjoyed forty years of peace had within five
years known two major wars. In both, Napoleon III had played a
paramount role. Though in neither case could he be considered the
aggressor—rather, he was the champion of the oppressed—still
Europe felt that his motto *"L'Empire, c'est la paix"* had a hollow
ring to it.

Poor Napoleon! He had irritated Russia and Prussia, alienated
Austria, antagonized Italy and Great Britain, infuriated Pius IX,
and condemned himself to losing the support of at least half of
France no matter which way he turned.

Having outraged the Old World, he now set out to outrage the
New World as well.

Chapter 12
Anatomy
of a Fiasco

The idea of putting an Austrian prince on the Mexican throne did not originate with the French sovereigns. But though neither Napoleon nor Eugénie was guilty of starting the whole sordid business, both were guilty of not stopping it when wiser heads urged them to.

Given Eugénie's religious bigotry, Napoleon's duplicity and their combined ignorance of political reality in the New World, it probably could not have been otherwise.

Mexico was like a beautiful maiden who has been subjected to a vicious gang-rape. The rape—which stretched over three centuries—was perpetrated by the Spanish *Conquistadores* and their Creole descendants, in collusion with the Roman Catholic Church. As the nineteenth century approached midpoint—and Mexico approached total exhaustion—civil war broke out between the Conservatives and the Liberals.

The Conservatives were the land-holding aristocrats, few of whom had any autochthonous Indian blood. The Liberals, all of aboriginal derivation, lined up behind Benito Juárez, whose political philosophy can be reduced to a simple apothegm: Mexico belongs to the Indians, from whom it has been stolen and to whom it must be returned.

Supporting the Conservatives were the Church bishops, who owned one-third of the maiden's body and three-fourths of her mind. Juárez had little going for him except the support of the masses, half of whom—four million Indians—lived in conditions as primitive as those under the *Conquistadores*. It was enough.

By 1853, the Liberals controlled the vital port (and customs revenues) of Vera Cruz, the country's lifeline to Europe. The Conservatives controlled the inland areas, centered on Mexico City. Except for the United States, which had helped bring Juárez to power, all the major Powers recognized the Conservative government as the official one.

In 1855, Juárez outlawed Church possession of the land. In hopes of conciliating the nation's power structure and thereby obviating further bloodshed, he offered monetary compensation for the expropriated land.

The bishops preferred further bloodshed; they not only wanted to hold onto their properties, they wanted to perpetuate the inflow of tithes exacted shamelessly from even the poorest of their parishioners.

Franciscan and Dominican monasteries were converted into entrepôts for the amassing of munitions of war; gold and silver ornaments were taken from the sacristies and melted down to finance the armies of their chosen Conservative champion, Miguel de Miramón.

It was not one of the Church's finer hours.

For years, a mere handful of Conservative émigrés had been seeking a European prince who would ascend the throne of a nation that had no monarchical tradition, in the hope that an imported dynasty would deal a death blow to American influence in the Western Hemisphere and, more to the point, protect their (and the Church's) vast holdings. The European Powers did not care to involve themselves in Mexico's chaotic politics.

But that did not stop the émigrés, two of whom stand out in bold relief: José Maria Gutierrez d'Estrada and José Hidalgo.

Wealthy landholders by inheritance, both had spent most of their lives abroad; both advocated foreign intervention in a land where, thanks to centuries of foreign conquest and exploitation, xenophobia was a national trait. They belonged to a breed that has yet to vanish: dedicated patriots who are happiest living outside the land of their birth, which they profess to love and refuse to understand.

Gutierrez d'Estrada, elder and more insufferable of the two, was popular in Vatican circles; through marriage, he became popular in Austrian circles. His mother-in-law was the Countess Lutzoff, mistress of Maximilian's household; it was the Countess Lutzoff who first suggested Maximilian for the Mexican throne.

Hidalgo was even better connected in monarchical circles: he was an intimate friend of the Empress of France.

The friendship dated back to Eugénie's pre-Imperial phase, when Hidalgo, at the time attached to his country's diplomatic mission in Madrid, was one of the regulars at the Countess de Montijo's *salon*. It was resumed in 1856, when Hidalgo was transferred to Paris. The witty, charming bachelor of means was quickly drawn into that charmed circle of Ultramontanes who gravitated satellite-like around the Empress.

Politically and philosophically, émigré and Empress were soul mates. Both considered republicanism a heathen concept; the idea of Mexico falling into the United States's sphere of influence they found unsupportable. (As far back as 1853, Eugénie had opined that "the day will come when the French will find themselves fighting the Americans.") Hidalgo argued that Mexico's salvation lay only in a strong Catholic monarchy, and that it was incumbent upon France to come up with the right monarch. Eugénie agreed. She began arranging little dinner parties for Hidalgo and the Emperor.

When word came that Maximilian (Eugénie's "dear Max") had been approached and was amenable, Eugénie pulled all stops.

The idea of France's expanding into the New World had never been far from Napoleon's mind. Should not France become the great civilizing influence in the region and, into the bargain, grab the lion's share of Latin America's markets? Today Mexico, tomorrow the Western Hemisphere. Also, it might be in his own best interests to come to the aid of the Church in the New World, and thus mitigate (he hoped) the Holy Father's holy wrath over France's equivocating on the Roman Question.

The timing seemed favorable. The United States was on the verge of dissolution. Furthermore, his Minister in Mexico City, Count Dubois de Saligny, was sending back glowing reports: the Liberals would not retain their power; the Mexican people resented Juárez's separation of church and state; practically everyone wanted a European monarchy; were French troops to debark at Vera Cruz, they would be welcomed with open arms; the time was ripe for a French move into North America.

Adding her own encouragement was the Empress; she felt Saligny could be relied upon to send back honest reports. Saligny was a protégé—actually, a tool—of the Duke de Morny. Would he, argued the Empress rhetorically, have any reason to misrepresent the truth?

Would he ever!

The Miramón government had borrowed some money from the Swiss banker J. B. Jecker in exchange for bonds valued at seventy-five million francs. When Juárez triumphed over Miramón, he suspended payments on that debt. Now finding himself on the verge of bankruptcy, Jecker made a deal with Morny whereby the latter, in exchange for his influence, would receive thirty percent of whatever Jecker recovered on those bonds. Unless France became involved in Mexico, Morny would wind up with thirty percent of nothing.

Napoleon read Saligny's reports with great interest, agreed with Morny that France's manifest destiny had now taken a westward turn, and listened sympathetically as Eugénie implored that France come to the rescue of Hidalgo's pitiful motherland—a motherland, it may be noted, in which Hidalgo had spent no more than three or four years of his entire life.

Much to Eugénie's impatience, Napoleon inclined toward caution. France, he argued, could not undertake an overseas expedition without the cooperation of the world's greatest maritime power, England. And Protestant England was not in the habit of creating Catholic monarchies.

In the spring of 1861, with his country's finances an utter shambles, Juárez had no choice but to declare a two-year moratorium on the payment of all foreign debts. Saligny, acting in concert with the Spanish and British envoys, broke off diplomatic relations with the Juárez government and threatened armed intervention. As Napoleon waited to see what England and Spain would do, Eugénie—whose love of playing at politics was by now an obsession—moved decisively.

While the Emperor was at Vichy taking a cure, the Empress had Count Walewski send a confidential letter to Richard Metternich, at the time on home leave in Vienna, advising him that "government circles in Paris [favor] the establishment of a monarchy in Mexico and [are] prepared to give *moral* support [italics in the original] to the nomination of Archduke Ferdinand Maximilian." An early reply as to whether the Austrian government favored the idea was solicited. If the reply was in the affirmative, France was "willing to take the initiative" in gaining British and Spanish support. One way or the other, Metternich's response was to be communicated directly to the Empress—who was taking "a personal interest in the matter."

Maximilian toyed with the idea of becoming Emperor of Mexico for the same reasons the well-meaning Countess Lutzoff had suggested it. He was bored: there was little to do, outside of fulfilling ceremonial obligations, for an Austrian archduke who was not direct heir to the throne. He was frustrated: there were few outlets for him to express the liberalism that set him apart from—and antagonized—his reactionary brother the Emperor.

Besides, his wife Charlotte wanted to be an empress. Charlotte had the backing of her father, King Leopold, who had already infested Europe's royal houses with Coburg princelings and was anxious to pollinate the New World as well.

Adding encouragement was Franz-Josef, who, simply stated, wanted his liberal brother out of Europe. Not only was Maximilian their mother's pet, he was the people's pet. Franz-Josef would never forget how on his return from Solferino he had been greeted with shouts of "Abdicate!" and "Long live Archduke Max!" But since Austria could hardly qualify as a maritime power, Franz-Josef would not give his needed sanction to Maximilian's candidature without French and English backing.

Napoleon sought to convince England that a "properly governed" Mexico would serve as "a powerful bulwark" against American encroachment, "as well as providing new markets for European commerce." He conceded that Britain "may have hesitated in the past for fear of endangering her relations with America," but now that the Civil War was raging, it was "impossible for America to interfere," while Mexico's suspension of foreign debts "justified intervention."

Such logic fell on deaf ears. Though rooting for the Confederacy, the Palmerston government could see that, given the superiority of the Union in manpower and industrial capability, the Civil War would end on President Lincoln's terms, and that once peace came, the United States would be able to redirect her efforts toward keeping Europe out of Mexico, in accordance with the Monroe Doctrine.

On October 30, 1861, as a follow-up to the action taken by their envoys in Mexico City, the three maritime Powers—England, France and Spain—signed the Treaty of London.

England, suspecting France of ulterior motives, insisted that none of the signatories was to undertake personal aggrandizement in Mexico or interfere in any way in that country's internal affairs.

So far as England and Spain were concerned, the three Powers were undertaking a debt-collecting expedition and nothing more.

So far as Napoleon was concerned, it was the first step in his creation of a French-sponsored Mexican Empire.

He had to move furtively. The deposed Miramón arrived in Paris and declared there was "no monarchist party in Mexico." Eugénie and Hidalgo succeeded in slandering Miramón. (Metternich: "The Empress hates Miramón and says the Emperor will not see him.")

But they could not keep Miramón away from the French opposition leaders and the anti-Bonapartist press. Disapproval of the Mexican émigrés' activities began to take on aspects of a ground swell. The Quai d'Orsay became highly suspicious of the Emperor's true motives in signing the London protocol.

The French debt-collecting expeditionary force was initially 2,000 marines. Eugénie pleaded that Napoleon send along "a few red blouses as well." Five hundred Zouaves and a field battery were added to the contingent. Then Eugénie learned that 6,000 Spanish troops, commanded by the ambitious General Juan Prim, had landed at Vera Cruz without waiting for their British and French allies. She became, in Metternich's words, *"fuchstëufelswild"* ("hopping mad").

Fearing that once Spain's honor had been satisfied as regarded those outstanding debts, Prim, a man of democratic principles, would come to terms with the Juárez government, Eugénie insisted that an additional 2,500 French troops be dispatched. She got no argument from the Emperor.

She was, after all, pushing him in a direction he had already anticipated.

Vice-Admiral Jurien de la Gravière, commander of the French naval squadron, was ordered by the Quai d'Orsay only to occupy the strategic Gulf ports in conjunction with his British and Spanish counterparts. Napoleon, however, gave him a secret set of instructions.

Now deluded into believing that a strong monarchist party would rise in support of the allied landings, Napoleon—in direct contravention of the Treaty of London—ordered Gravière to contact Conservative leaders in Mexico City with a view to gathering an assembly of "notables from the various states," thereby to pave the way for Maximilian's "elevation" to the phantom cactus throne.

Once on the scene, Gravière was convinced that the Emperor had been completely misinformed; that for France to continue along its present course in Mexico would mean involvement in a major—and unwinnable—war. He tried to warn the Emperor of how Saligny was pushing France into an untenable position. But, thanks to Morny, abetted by Eugénie, Saligny was in a position to discredit Gravière back in Paris.

On April 8, anxious to get out while the getting was good, Spain and England withdrew their troops from Mexico. Wrote General Prim to Napoleon: "It will be easy for Your Majesty to get the Archduke Maximilian crowned as Emperor. But once you recall your troops, he will not have a chance to survive."

Napoleon refused to heed Prim's warning. Saligny had convinced him that Prim was actually in league with Juárez. Eugénie argued: "Maximilian's presence in Mexico will be worth an army of 100,000 men!"

A few weeks later, a French force of little more than 6,000 men set out from Vera Cruz to occupy a hostile country three times the size of France.

Meanwhile Maximilian was being urged to withdraw his candidature. No Mexican of any importance inside the country had declared for a monarchy. President Lincoln issued a blunt warning in accordance with the Monroe Doctrine. The Viennese press editorialized against the idea of an Austrian archduke becoming a Bonaparte vassal.

The French sovereigns sought to reassure Maximilian. Eugénie advised that Saligny's reports were to be "given more credence than the opinions of those not on the scene." Napoleon advised that he had "studied" the United States while "sojourning there" following his Strasbourg attempt, and could "guarantee" that the Confederacy would "never rejoin the Union."

Also, there was marvelous news to pass along. General Lorencez, commanding the French troops marching on Mexico City, had sent along assurances that France was gaining adherents among the Mexicans daily; it was "only a question of weeks" before he expected to be in Mexico City. Lorençez was now approaching Puebla, the main stronghold of the Church, where he was assured the French would be met "with nothing but flowers."

Influenced by Saligny, Lorençez failed to mention the difficulties he was having in maintaining his supply lines against incursions by Juárista guerrillas; that yellow fever had begun leveling his troops within hours of their landings on the coast; and that out of 6,000 men marching inland, less than 5,000 were ambulatory.

The French were met at Puebla (May 5) not with flowers but with grapeshot from 4,000 shabbily clad, half-starved Mexicans, who had little going for them but true grit and some obsolete weapons left over from Waterloo and purchased years before from the British.

When news of the Puebla disaster reached the Tuileries, the Emperor succumbed to black depression, the Empress to hysteria. Everyone on all sides urged Maximilian to withdraw; the British envoy in Mexico City urged him not to "venture into such a hornets' nest"; and in France itself, public opinion was turning against what was not officially billed as the Franco-Mexican War.

But Europe's finest soldiers, veterans of Sebastopol and Magenta and Solferino, had been defeated by a pack of illiterate, ill-kempt Indians. This was insufferable. The honor of France was at stake. Encouraged by the Emperor and the Empress, the Duke de Morny prevailed upon the Corps Législatif to vote unanimously to recoup that honor.

Reinforcements aimed at bringing the expeditionary force up to a total of 30,000 men were given their sailing orders.

As the months dragged on, the Emperor was "very depressed by the heavy losses suffered by the French army . . . and confidence will only be restored with the capture of Mexico City" (Metternich's words). Compounding the Emperor's depression, condemnatory letters from the French troops began arriving in Paris, telling a different—truer—story of what was going on there. General Lorençez took it upon himself to complain about Saligny's intrigues; Admiral Gravière arrived home to defend himself against Saligny's delation and supported Lorençez's evaluation.

Napoleon entertained the notion of extricating himself from the quagmire. Eugénie argued to the contrary. Ere long, she was able to flash Napoleon a triumphant I-told-you-so. Juárez, whose armies were scattered all over the countryside, abandoned the defense of Mexico City and moved his seat of government north to a small provincial capital. (It was not a retreat, but a strategic withdrawal in the purest sense of the term.) Concurrently, General Robert E. Lee scored a series of successes against the Union army.

"Eugénie was radiant while Napoleon wept with joy," reported Metternich—who, along with just about everyone else within the French and Austrian governments, was opposed to the whole dynastic adventure. (Not privy to Napoleon's thinking, Metternich had assumed that the idea of enthroning Maximilian all boiled down to "a harebrained scheme on the part of the Empress and a handful of self-serving Mexican émigrés.")

Meanwhile in Trieste, Maximilian was beginning to suspect that the Mexican émigrés dancing attendance upon him lacked any knowledge of what was really happening inside their country. It never dawned on him that they had been feeding him with a pack of lies all along. But any ideas of abandoning the venture were obviated by Charlotte, who, encouraged by a steady barrage of letters from the French sovereigns, shored up Maximilian's courage.

Eugénie wrote Charlotte: "We hope that news we shall soon receive will be of such a kind as to hasten the departure of Your Highness, for none but a strong and vigorous hand can carry the work of regenerating the country to a successful conclusion." The "news" arrived in the first week of August 1863.

On the eighth, the archducal couple received a joyful telegram from Napoleon: a national assembly convoked in Mexico City had proclaimed Maximilian as their Emperor; "what the capital proclaimed today, the country will proclaim tomorrow"; it would not be too long now before Maximilian "was summoned by the whole nation to assist in its regeneration."

Unbeknownst even to Eugénie—he doubted her ability to keep from prating; discretion was not the Empress's long suit—Napoleon had given a secret set of orders to Lorençez's replacement, General Forey. Under Forey's protection, General Juan Almonte—a self-serving Conservative who had rushed back to Mexico after a long diplomatic exile in Paris—had summoned an assembly of Neanderthals that proclaimed Maximilian emperor. Napoleon could now "assure the world" that his purpose in going to Mexico had "not been to force alien domination on the people. They have made their own decision." (Supported by French bayonets, of course.)

Having done his duty, General Forey warned the Emperor that the ploy would not work.

The Emperor already knew it would not work. He wanted only two things: to get Maximilian to Mexico as quickly as possible so that the "Mexican Emperor" could assume his share of the burden, as a result of which France would recoup some of her losses; and to get his own troops out of Mexico.

In March 1864, Maximilian and Charlotte arrived in Paris and were given the royal treatment. Support among the French for the whole project had now dwindled to a small, influential circle of enthusiastic Bonapartist politicians and pro-Church public-opinion molders who were "delirious with joy at the prospect of a glorious end to the Franco-Mexican War."

The Empress, "determined to take all the credit for being the founder of the Mexican Empire," confided to her old friend, Duke Ernest of Saxe-Coburg, that within a scant few years "our dear Max" would be "one of the most influential rulers in the world."

Adds Duke Ernest: "No one shared this view more strongly than my unfortunate cousin Charlotte, who had never appeared in better looks or spirits, whereas Max looked much older than when I had seen him last and did not give the impression of having ventured on this dangerous enterprise with any of the enthusiasm of youth."

Maximilian's confidence rose when a telegram arrived from Almonte: "Three-quarters of the total territory of Mexico and four-fifths of her whole population have declared for a monarchy. Your arrival is awaited with eagerness and impatience." Eugénie and Charlotte danced with joy. Napoleon was more restrained.

He knew—given his own sources of information on the spot—that less than a seventh of the country was in French hands, and that only one in twenty of the three million people living in that area was a monarchist.

Furthermore, the French "military victories" were ephemeral at best. Since the French were incapable of garrisoning every town and village, as soon as they moved on, Juáristas would appear from out of the hills and retake the area.

Scanning the factitious reports that came out of Mexico is like scanning the reports that came out of Saigon during the heyday of America's involvement in Vietnam.

Maximilian had been warned by his Belgian father-in-law that "it is you who are helping the Emperor to pull his chestnuts out of the fire, and in return you must get him to put into writing the exact period for which the French troops are to remain in Mexico. The longer the better, as they constitute your chief support."

Napoleon promised Maximilian that French troops would remain on for at least three years, by which time, it was presupposed, Maximilian would have built up his own army "from amongst your countless loyal subjects" and would thus be in a position to protect himself. (Eugénie questioned what Maximilian had to protect himself *from*. Was it not *obvious* that *all* the Mexicans wanted an emperor?)

Furthermore, Napoleon promised that 8,000 men of the French Foreign Legion were "to be at the disposal of the Emperor of Mexico for another six years." And, lest Maximilian *still* doubt France's probity, Napoleon secretly pledged that—and this cannot be overemphasized—*"whatever happens in Europe, France will never fail the new Mexican Empire."*

Having thus made promises he knew he had no intention of keeping, Napoleon raised one rather niggling detail: finances. The Mexican government—Maximilian's government—was to pay 260 million francs toward the cost of France's expeditionary force, plus any outstanding claims of French nationals in Mexico for damages suffered during the war, *plus* the original debt that Juárez had suspended.* Thus was the Mexican Empire condemned to bankruptcy even before it had been launched.

But then, Maximilian had a reputation for being unable to balance his own checkbook. That might help explain why the Archduke was now being derided on the Continent as the Archdupe.

---

* *Now included in that debt were the Jecker bonds; at Morny's suggestion, Jecker had taken out French citizenship. To help ease the burden, Napoleon undertook the floating of a 200-million-franc Mexican loan, to be negotiated by a consortium of English and French financiers. The wily English bankers had nothing to lose; the guileless shareholders were almost exclusively French citizens.*

Eugénie and Napoleon gave Maximilian and Charlotte a grand sendoff as the two returned to Trieste to pack for the voyage out to their empire. One wonders if the two suspected that their French friends had assiduously kept them away from Napoleon's own government functionaries, who were so opposed to the whole venture.

A few weeks later the roof fell in at the Tuileries with the arrival of a telegram from Trieste: Maximilian was about to refuse the throne! Franz-Josef had insisted he surrender his perquisites as an Archduke and renounce his Imperial appanage as well as his rights of succession, something Maximilian was loathe to do. What if the Mexican throne were to fall? What had he to look forward to if he had to come running back to Europe?

Napoleon was furious. Eugénie was beside herself with rage. And Maximilian was on the verge of mental collapse. Pulling at him from all directions were his brother Archduke Leopold, who had orders from Franz-Josef not to return home without Max's signature on the Act of Renunciation; the Mexican deputation, who were doing their damnedest to convince him that the Mexican crown more than compensated for the loss of his Austrian appanage; and Charlotte, who refused to accept the loss of her throne and who was, furthermore, convinced she could persuade Franz-Josef to revoke his decision. (Charlotte's conviction is admirable; Franz-Josef absolutely detested her—as did the rest of the Habsburgs.)

The crisis was resolved when a letter arrived in Trieste from Napoleon, attacking Maximilian in his most vulnerable spot: his honor. Writing under what he confessed was "the influence of strong emotions," Napoleon argued: "What would you think of me if, once Your Imperial Majesty had arrived in Mexico, I were to say that I can no longer fulfill the conditions to which I have set my signature?" and perorated: "It is absolutely necessary in your own interests and those of your family that matters should be settled, for the honor of the House of Habsburg is at stake." He concluded the letter with: "Forgive me for this somewhat severe language, but the circumstances are so grave that I cannot refrain from telling you the whole truth."

Napoleon should have sought forgiveness for more than his "somewhat severe language." He had by now decided that within two years he would be openly repudiating those guarantees of

French support to "Your Mexican Majesty." He had no intention whatsoever of fulfilling "the conditions to which I have set my signature."

Maximilian was not about to have his honor sullied. Instead of going off to a psychiatric ward, where they both belonged, he and Charlotte went off to Mexico. Eugénie sent them a going-away note of reassurance: even were the Union to emerge victorious in the American Civil War, she and the Emperor were "positive" that the United States would "accept a Catholic monarchy on her southern border."

Napoleon kept his mouth shut. As heretofore indicated, he was cursed with an inchoate conscience.

Chapter 13
Moving Toward a Fall

"The Emperor is governed neither by passions nor principles," remarked Drouyn de Lhuys, the pro-papacy, pro-Austrian career diplomat whom the Empress insisted be named Foreign Minister. "Whereas most men seek to mold circumstances to their own views, he is content to await events and mold his views and designs to circumstances as they arise."

Napoleon's talents at molding had worked well during the period when he was bluffing his way to power. But soon that bluff had to be called. When Bismarck first met him, during the 1855 Peace Congress, he concluded: "I have the impression that the Emperor Napoleon is a judicious and amiable man, but not so shrewd as the world thinks him."

Others were coming to that same conclusion.

The first signs of turbulence came early in 1863, when the Poles rose against Russia, which had destroyed their Constitution in 1831 and spent the next three decades in an attempt to destroy their national identity and culture. The plight of the Poles aroused the sympathy of all Frenchmen, regardless of political or religio-philosophical persuasion. The two nations had enjoyed a close relationship dating back to the sixteenth century. Of all the major Powers, only France could be considered Poland's traditional friend.

Yet Napoleon—the champion of Polish independence—feared to lose Russia's friendship. He called for a European congress not only to settle the Polish Question but—his pet desire—to rescind the

1815 treaties and redraw the map. Half of Europe, especially England and Austria, was quite content with the 1815 treaties. At any rate, no one was interested in any of Napoleon's congresses.

Instead of remaining neutral—no one was coming to the aid of the Poles; their insurrection was foredoomed—Napoleon joined in a series of Notes to the Tsar. When the Tsar put down the rebellion, France—the traditional champion of the underdog—stood convicted of impotence in the eyes of the world. Worse, Napoleon's vague and fruitless efforts to satisfy public opinion had alienated Russia, thus ending his hopes for an alliance.

Next came Napoleon's involvement in the incredibly complex Schleswig-Holstein Question. Palmerston told Parliament, only half jestingly: "There are only three people who have understood this Question: the Prince Consort, and he is dead; a German professor, and he is insane; and myself—and I have forgotten all about it!" Whether Bismarck, that supreme master of *geopolitik*, understood the Question is academic. He certainly had the answer.

"Germany" was a confederation (Diet or *Bund*) of kingdoms, duchies, principalities and palatinates, those in the south under Austrian hegemony. Bismarck had outlined his program to Disraeli in 1862: "I shall seize the first good pretext to declare war against Austria, dissolve the German Diet, subdue the minor states, and give national unity to Germany under Prussian leadership." (To which Disraeli commented: "He means what he says!")

Until Napoleon III made it both possible and profitable, it was Bismarck's intention not to destroy France but to finesse France. His main concern was that France not war on Prussia while Prussia was warring on Austria. Thanks to Napoleon's inability to cope with events, especially now that Bismarck was calling the shots, it was not a question of "Won't you come into my parlor? said the spider to the fly" but rather "May I come into your parlor? said the fly to the spider."

Napoleon took the first step into Bismarck's parlor in 1864, when, having abandoned Poland, he abandoned Denmark, to whom the contested duchies of Schleswig and Holstein belonged. That union had been guaranteed by the 1852 London Settlement—with France assuming the role of major guarantor. When Bismarck prompted the German Diet to invade and seize the two duchies on grounds of

irredentism, England called for a European congress to resolve the
issue (presumably in Denmark's favor). Napoleon vetoed the idea.

"I am the only one who knows what the foreign policy of France is
going to be," Napoleon told Bismarck's ambassador to Paris, Herr
Von der Goltz. Napoleon was not so much formulating foreign policy
as ad-libbing it.

The Schleswig-Holstein Question now gave way to the
Prussian-Austrian Question, the question being when the inevitable
war would break out between the two German nations. Everyone
suspected Napoleon was up to something, but no two people could
agree on what it was.

In fact, Napoleon was banking on Austria's keeping Prussia in
check, so that he would be in a position to win Bismarck's consent
for France's annexation of the Left Bank of the Rhine, thus to
out-flank Belgium, a land Napoleon coveted but was in no position to
go after aggressively.

In the meantime, to strengthen his own position at home, Napoleon decided to resolve France's ludicrously contradictory position
vis-à-vis the papacy. He was maintaining troops in Rome to defend
the pope against the ambitions of Sardinia, which was France's ally,
and was thus protecting the papacy against the revolution aimed at
unifying Italy, while supporting that revolution everywhere else.

We need not go into the rather embarrassing particulars of Napoleon's proposed resolution of the Roman Question; suffice it to say, it
antagonized not only the pope but Victor Emmanuel. Worse, he
pushed Italy—which needed the Austrian-held Venetia in order to
complete her own unification—into Prussia's arms.

Napoleon now decided he had better "deal with Prussia."

French public opinion was already prepared to accept the idea of
German unity: "We do not fear a kingdom of 25,000,000 Italians,"
said journalist Edmond About, reflecting the national consensus,
"so why should we fear 32,000,000 Germans on our eastern border?"

But the Empress felt otherwise. In the face of everyone opposed
to the idea—including Austria itself—Eugénie pushed for a
Franco-Austrian alliance with a pertinacity that verged on fanati-
cism. (The harassed Richard Metternich was obliged to tell her: "I
cannot in all honesty say that you possess diplomatic subtlety, a
feeling for the finer shades and a sense of the right opportunity

which to me are the first necessity in politics and an essential prerequisite to success.")

The Empress's favorite quotation ("my motto")—which she loved to haul out from time to time—was Polonius's rather sententious advice: "This above all: to thine own self be true, and it must follow, as the night the day, thou canst not then be false to any man."

She must have been unaware that Polonius also told his son Laertes: "Give every man thy ear, but few thy voice; take each man's censure, but reserve thy judgment."

Bismarck was no stranger to Paris, where he had served briefly (1862) as Prussian ambassador before being recalled by his king, William I, to become Prime Minister. In October 1866, he visited Napoleon at Biarritz. Bismarck was anxious not to proceed against Austria without assurance of neutrality on France's part.

"The best interests of the Tuileries," Bismarck avowed, "can best be served by supporting the national mission of Prussia; Prussia, on the other hand, wretched and abandoned, would be driven to seeking in central and northern Europe for allies against her powerful neighbor in the west"—that is, France.

He then dropped vague hints that if France were to remain neutral in the upcoming struggle between Prussia and Austria and were to recognize Prussia's claim to headship of the German Confederation, he might support French designs on the Rhineland and Belgium.

Napoleon pledged France to strict neutrality in the upcoming war—which he saw fitting in with his own design. "War between Austria and Prussia," he confided to Walewski, "is one of those unhoped-for happenings that never seemed likely to occur, and it is not for us to oppose warlike intentions which contain so many advantages for our policy."

Translation: Napoleon assumed that the Prussian-Austrian conflict would be a drawn-out affair, with Austria emerging as the ultimate, albeit exhausted, victor, at which point he would step in and arbitrate the peace—to France's advantage.

It was not difficult for the wily Bismarck to see into Napoleon's mind ("the man is an incapacitated mediocrity"). So far as he was concerned, though, let the Emperor scheme. Bismarck's greatest fear—that Prussia, while fully occupied with Austria, would be stabbed in the rear by 300,000 French troops on the Rhine—was obviated.

As Bismarck went home to oil his saber, Napoleon pulled another trick from his sleeve. He encouraged Eugénie to pursue her witless talks with Metternich aimed at a Franco-Austrian alliance. Eugénie plowed ahead full-steam, in the belief that she had at last brought Napoleon around to her way of thinking.

Actually, as he confided to Persigny, the Emperor was not looking for an alliance but for a Sword of Damocles which he might dangle over Prussia, "should complications arise."

Next, in hopes of restoring his lost prestige among the Italians, Napoleon suggested that Victor Emmanuel make an alliance with Prussia, the purpose being to frighten Austria into ceding the province of Venetia, which Italy coveted.

Victor Emmanuel went Napoleon one step better. On April 8, he concluded with Bismarck an offensive and defensive alliance whereby Italy was to join Prussia if war broke out between Prussia and Austria within three months, with Venetia as a reward.

Thus the scheming Emperor—albeit unwittingly—gave Bismarck a much-needed ally. Without Italy to engage Austrian troops on the peninsula while Prussian troops engaged them elsewhere, Bismarck not only could not have won the war, he could not have *started* it!

Two days later, Prussia and Austria began to mobilize.

Eugénie made a last-ditch effort to force Napoleon into a military alliance with Austria as the only chance of stopping Prussia. "I shall go to bed one night a Frenchwoman," she screamed metaphorically, "and wake up the next morning a Prussian!" Napoleon brushed aside her hysteria with one of his sphinx-like smiles. He was confident that everything was going to work out exactly as he had planned.

On June 12, Napoleon secretly guaranteed a panicking Austria that he would remain strictly neutral. In exchange, Austria promised to cede Venetia to France, which in turn would retrocede it to Italy. Two days later, the Austrian-Prussian War broke out. Napoleon sat back to watch the two German nations beat each other to a standoff.

He assumed the war would last four years.

It lasted seven weeks.

A fortnight after hostilities began, Napoleon received a telegram from Vienna pleading that he abandon his "passive neutrality" and warning that "only French armed intervention can now prevent Prussia from achieving exclusive domination over Germany." On that day (July 3), the Austrians were routed at Königgratz (Sadowa) to the tune of 24,000 killed and wounded and 13,000 taken prisoner.

Napoleon urged the Prussian and Italian monarchs to make an armistice with Austria. King William, anxious to crown his victory in the field with a triumphal entry into Vienna, backed down only because Bismarck feared a French attack on the Rhine. Victor Emmanuel, preferring to receive Venetia by conquest rather than by dotation, halted hostilities only when Napoleon threatened a naval demonstration against Venice.

Neither of the sovereigns forgave the French Emperor for interjecting himself.

Nor, for that matter, did Bismarck.

Two days later, a meeting of the Privy Council was hurriedly called. The Emperor was in a black funk; the Empress was in a white heat. At issue was what attitude France should take toward the victorious Prussia.

The anti-Austria clique (headed by Persigny and Plon-Plon) argued that the Emperor was himself responsible for the alliance between Italy and Prussia; to come to Austria's aid would cause him to be branded a turncoat. Furthermore, France was hardly in a position to fight a major war, what with her troops bogged down in Mexico and Indo-China.

The "Empress's Party," which included Drouyn de Lhuys—the only Foreign Minister in all of Europe who never knew what his sovereign was up to—urged an immediate military demonstration on the Rhine as a means of cowing Prussia.

As the Emperor sat noncommittally, Eugénie carried the day (and wound up with a hoarse throat in the process). The Council voted to mobilize, to move 50,000 troops to the Rhine area at once, and to send a Note to Berlin warning that France would not permit any territorial changes on the Continent without her consent.

During the night, however, Napoleon countermanded the decisions of the Council. Next morning at breakfast, when she learned of this, Eugénie threw such a monumental fit "she had to be hauled back to her private apartments like a crinoline-clad sack of potatoes."*

With his Cabinet now trying to pull him in all directions, his wife hectoring him, his army unready to move, and himself suffering the agonies of indecision and an inflamed gall bladder, Napoleon decided the best course for the moment lay in accepting the terms Prussia had dictated to Austria: Hanover, Hesse, Nassau and Frankfurt were to be incorporated into Prussia; Austria was to be excluded from Germany (thus ending the *Bund*); the German states north of the Main River were to form a North German Confederation under Prussian leadership; and the South German states were to remain independent but were to be permitted to form a separate confederation.

Thus ended the first phase of the unification—and rise—of modern Germany. It was a process that owed its success as much to Napoleon III as to Bismarck.

"The Emperor seems to have lost his bearings entirely," observed the Prussian envoy, who saw him practically daily.

More than losing his bearings, the Emperor was slowly losing his Empire.

On July 26, the very day Bismarck was dictating peace terms to Austria at Nikolsburg, Eugénie told Metternich: "I assure you, we are moving toward our fall, and the best thing would be if the

---

* *Whether Napoleon was right or wrong in backing off is arguable. Undoubtedly a French advance on the Rhine would have been effective—though such an advance would have been more effective before Sadowa.*

A decade later, in private conversation, Bismarck admitted retrospectively that such an advance by the French would have led to an anti-Prussian uprising in South Germany, the reinforcement of the hard-pressed Austrian army in Bohemia by an Austrian army tied down in Italy, and, worse, a Prussian withdrawal to protect Berlin.

But, over the long haul, was it a mistake? There is no reason to believe the French army, its numbers notwithstanding, was in any better shape at the time than it proved to be four years later at Sedan (or, for that matter, during World Wars I and II).

Emperor suddenly disappeared. . . . He can't sleep or walk, and he can hardly eat. For two years he has been living in utter prostration, has not occupied himself with the government, but written *Julius Caesar* instead!"

Hardly the sort of thing your average empress would tell the ambassador of a foreign Power. But then, Eugénie was hardly your average empress. (Reported Metternich to Vienna: "Never since I have known the Imperial couple have I seen the Emperor to be so completely *nothing* and the Empress take our interests to heart with such fury and zeal!")

Napoleon, accepting with reluctance the collective refusal of the major Powers to gather at yet another of his congresses, took it upon himself to salvage what he could from the chaos for which he was in a way responsible. He demanded compensations from Prussia for having remained neutral—compensations that Bismarck contemptuously dismissed as "gratuities" and "innkeepers' bills." Prussia was requested to hand over the Left Bank of the Rhine as far as and including Mainz.

Bismarck shrewdly passed on the French Emperor's "request" to the press. Its publication (August 11) had a disastrous effect on European opinion. The old fears of French aggression were revived. Queen Victoria's "universal disturber" appeared to be at it again.

In desperation—was he attempting to persuade himself that France *still* held the diplomatic initiative?—Napoleon instructed his ambassador to Berlin to ask Bismarck for a Prussian promise to permit French annexation of Luxembourg (at the time suzerain to the King of Holland), to be followed in due course by that of Belgium.

Bismarck suggested, instead, a secret treaty: in return for France's recognition of the recent enlargement of Prussia—and the eventual, inevitable confederation of the northern and southern German states under Prussian leadership—Bismarck agreed to "facilitate" the French acquisition of Luxembourg, and to come to France's aid "in the event of her being led by circumstances to march into Belgium or to conquer the country."

Napoleon agreed, on the presupposition that by the time Bismarck had achieved that total unification of the German states, France would be ready both to conquer Belgium and to stand up to Germany.

The Prussian leader made one stipulation: the agreement was to be put on paper—in Count Benedetti's (the French ambassador) own handwriting. Napoleon agreed and sent Benedetti orders to sharpen his quill. Bismarck took the document and put it into his safe.

Four years later, he would pull it out—and use it to drive the all-decisive nail into the Second Empire's coffin.

These were dark days for the French Emperor. The recent war had not gone as he had anticipated; he was presiding haphazardly over a government whose ministers were spending more time arguing with each other than tending to their ministries; his Empress was giving him the evil eye; his health was rapidly declining.

Certainly the last thing he needed to cope with was the Empress of Mexico, who materialized at Saint-Cloud, en route to total insanity.

The decisive factor in Maximilian's going to Mexico when his instincts urged otherwise—honor—proved to be the decisive factor that kept him there when common sense dictated that he give it up as a bad go. The French expeditionary force was already in the process of a phased-out withdrawal. With the American Civil War now ended, Washington was in a position to demand that the Mexican Emperor withdraw too.

Instead of returning to Europe, Maximilian took Charlotte's advice: *she* would return to Europe and seek support for their throne, a support which she deemed to be nothing more—and nothing less—than a moral obligation.

On learning of her arrival in France unannounced, Napoleon, unwilling—and, given his present physical and emotional state, unable—to be reminded of all the promises he had made and broken, took to his bed at Saint-Cloud.

"If the Emperor refuses to see me," Charlotte told Eugénie, "I shall break in on him." On August 11, she rode out to Saint-Cloud and did just that.

"I did everything that was humanly possible," she later wrote Maximilian. Alternately pleading, cajoling and threatening, she argued for the continuation of monthly subsidies to pay the bedrag-

gled army Maximilian was trying to build and for the retention of
France's expeditionary force in Mexico for another three years.

But "though the Emperor spoke a lot about Mexico, he had already forgotten about it"; he "appeared to be utterly helpless, with
tears pouring down his cheeks, continually turning to his wife for
support." Napoleon ended the interview by promising to "consult
with my government" and invited Charlotte to remain for lunch.
Charlotte, in a state of repressed hysteria, ordered her carriage.

Ambassador Metternich called on Charlotte and advised sympathetically that "the French Emperor has been degenerating both
physically and mentally for the past two years, and is no longer
capable of making a decision" and that the Empress, in attempting
to direct the course of State affairs, had done "more harm than
good."

But Charlotte refused to take Metternich's well-intended, subtly
veiled advice that she abort her mission. Believing she could
"shame" Napoleon into acceding to her "proposals," Charlotte returned to Saint-Cloud a few days later.

It was a scene to which only an Ibsen or a Strindberg could have
done justice. Storming into the Emperor's study, she dramatically
thrust at him the fatal letter he had written convincing Maximilian
that he had no choice but to accept the Mexican throne: *"What
would you think of me if, once Your Imperial Majesty had arrived
in Mexico, I were to say that I can no longer fulfill the conditions to
which I have set my signature?"*

The Emperor stared at the letter; his Empress atomized her
handkerchief; their visitor stared them both down. Finally, reported
Charlotte with contempt, the Emperor "wept even more than before."

Frantic to put an end to the painful scene, Eugénie managed to
get Charlotte out of the Emperor's study and into her private
apartments, where the Ministers of War and Finance, summoned at
Charlotte's request, were waiting to continue what she had herself
billed as "a working visit."

Charlotte screamingly accused the Minister of Finance (Achille
Fould) of colluding with the French bankers and financiers in mis-
appropriating part of the Mexican loans, and raised the matter of
those sordid Jecker bonds: "Who are the persons whose pockets are
filled with gold at Mexico's expense?" she demanded.

Fould contested every one of Charlotte's accusations with counteraccusations—he did not hesitate to call the Mexicans "dishonest, distrustful and ungrateful"—and advised that there was a limit to the sacrifices France could be called upon to make in Mexico's behalf and declared that limit had already been surpassed.

At that point, the "working visit" ended in a melodramatic shambles. Eugénie burst into tears, flung herself onto a settee, and swooned in simulation of a fainting fit. The by now uncontrollably raging Charlotte was dragged away by her embarrassed attendants.

Next day, the Privy Council voted unanimously against any further Mexican credits and in favor of immediate evacuation of the remaining expeditionary forces. Maximilian was to be left to his own miserable devices.

Charlotte refused to accept this decision from anyone but Napoleon—who, in order to avoid any further personal contact, had fled immediately to Châlons. He hoped that by the time he returned to Paris, Her Mexican Majesty would be gone.

But Her Mexican Majesty was not going to leave Paris without seeing him once again. During the week that ensued, she exhausted (and made a public spectacle of) herself interviewing bankers, economists, politicians—anyone who would see her—all to no avail.

Eugénie kept her distance, but made sure baskets of flowers and fruit were delivered daily to Charlotte's hotel and put an Imperial coach and escort at her disposal. The gestures were ignored. Charlotte, whose hatred of Napoleon was now monumental, was in the first stages of the persecution mania that would condemn her to sixty-two years of irreversible insanity. She accused Eugénie of attempting to poison her.

Unable to stay at Châlons indefinitely, Napoleon returned to Paris and made his way trepidatiously to the Grand Hôtel for the courtesy visit the Empress of Mexico regarded as her due. Charlotte suggested that the Emperor summon immediately his Corps Législatif and request an immediate 90-million-franc loan to Mexico.

Napoleon told her quite bluntly that she was indulging in fanciful illusions. Charlotte screamed, "Your Majesty is as much concerned in this affair as we are, so it would be better if you did not indulge in any illusions either!" Napoleon eyed her a brief moment, bowed to her coldly, and left the room.

Next day, as Charlotte was preparing to leave Paris, she received formal notification that "the Emperor of the French is unable to comply with your requests." A few days later, Napoleon wrote to Maximilian:

> We had the great pleasure of receiving the Empress Charlotte, yet it was painful for me to be unable to accede to her requests. We are in fact approaching a decisive moment for Mexico, and it is necessary for Your Majesty to come to a heroic resolution; the time for half-measures has gone by. I must begin by stating to Your Majesty that it is henceforward impossible for me to give Mexico another ecu or another soldier. . . .

Thus did the gambler cut his losses and get out of a game that he should never have gotten into in the first place—a game that for him was not yet ended. . . .

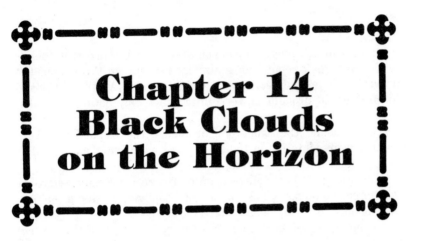

Chapter 14
Black Clouds
on the Horizon

The turbulence of international waters was exceeded only by the turbulence of the home waters in which Napoleon III was not so much sailing as wallowing. There was a growing demand for reform. Prior to 1866, he had drifted toward his ultimate goal—liberalization of the regime—because he could. Now, as sickness overtook him and shadows overtook his regime, Napoleon drifted toward that goal because he had to.

In the process, he collided head-on with Eugénie.

Eugénie's ideas on liberal reform extended little beyond bettering the lot of the pauper class through education and improved living conditions. Such ideas were noble, as were her efforts in that area. But they were not enough.

In the autumn of 1863, sensing Napoleon's intentions and determined to check them, she prevailed upon him to name Eugène Rouher as Minister of State, a position that was the equivalent of Prime Minister in other governments. Rouher was the conservative who had ground out the autocratic Constitution of 1851 in twenty-four hours. Like Eugénie, he was determined to halt the regime's liberal drift.

Both Eugénie and Rouher failed to see—or chose to ignore—the Emperor's precarious position. The Catholics, whose support he had lost over the Roman Question, were now allied with the manufacturers, whose support he had lost over the free-trade (Cobden) treaty. There was a marked revival of republicanism and radicalism, and a growing epidemic of strikes and widespread trade-unionism. The

Emperor could no longer depend on the good will of his "true friends in the cottages"; republican sentiment had spread throughout the provinces. France's involvement in the Prussian-Austrian War and in Mexico had brought no territorial gain—only national humiliation.

To compound the Emperor's problems, the Republicans were gaining representation in the legislature with every passing election, despite Persigny's attempts to rig those elections.

Morny urged that Napoleon grant reforms willingly before he was forced to do so; it was the old philosophy of getting a jump on your enemy. But Napoleon seemed paralyzed.

In the spring of 1866, more than forty members of the *government majority* broke away and formed the Third Party, which asked the Emperor "to further the natural development" of those paltry few concessions he had granted in 1860. In desperation, Napoleon turned to the man who was his most articulate detractor in the legislature: the Third Party's leader, Emile Ollivier.

The Empress found Ollivier pleasant enough, but admitted that the principles of liberalism he expounded "make no sense to me." Napoleon liked his ideas, especially those on freedom of the press and unhampered elections. Eugénie and Rouher sought to convince him that Ollivier was no more than an ambitious politician out for personal aggrandizement.

Napoleon's congenital inertia combined with his periodically painful kidney stones and inflamed bladder (he was now passing blood occasionally) and with the hectoring of Eugénie and his conservative courtiers to rob him of the vitality necessary to follow anything but a do-nothing policy. He took an immense liking to Ollivier, heard him out—and did nothing.

Toward the end of 1866, as a result of Prussia's victory at Sadowa and France's failure in Mexico, Napoleon roused himself. Behind Eugénie's back, he approached Ollivier with the offer of a Cabinet post. Though reluctant to join the government in any capacity before further reforms had been established, Ollivier consented, provided some conditions were met, most notably freedom of the press.

The Emperor literally begged Ollivier to interview the Empress in hopes of securing her approval of Rouher's dismissal, as a first step. Ollivier agreed ("What great things we shall do together if Napoleon really wishes to establish liberty!").

As they say in Brooklyn, he shoulda stood in bed. The intransigent Empress refused to sanction Rouher's removal and refused to discuss any liberal reforms that would follow consequentially. Ollivier felt he had no choice but to turn down the Emperor's offer of a Cabinet post.

This compelled the Emperor to pull himself together—sort of. A week later, he granted the Chamber of Deputies the right of interpellation.* Two months later, the emboldened Emperor took another step. Bowing to the demands of the Senate, he granted that body the right to examine projected laws in detail and return them for further action if deemed necessary—instead of, as had been the Senate's function, merely passing on their constitutionality.

Rouher, abetted by the Empress, organized a secret ring in the Chamber of Deputies devoted to defeating all of the Emperor's reform projects; the group set about with relish to slander Ollivier. Their success was of immense gratification to the Empress.

Also gratifying was the fact that Ollivier's chief supporters, Walewski and Plon-Plon, were both now out of the government. Walewski had been forced by the "Empress's Party" to resign as President of the Corps Législatif (he had succeeded Morny in that post); Plon-Plon, who had been Vice-President of the Privy Council, had been humiliated into private life by the Emperor—at the instigation of the Empress.

It happened while the Emperor was visiting Algeria. Plon-Plon went to Corsica to dedicate a statue of Napoleon Bonaparte and delivered a two-hour harangue that called for a liberalization of the regime far beyond the Emperor's intentions, called for France's championing of the Poles and Hungarians, attacked mercilessly Austria and Russia, condemned the Temporal Power through which the Vatican had become "the center of reaction against France, against Italy, against our society" (he also called for "a crusade to raze this last fortress of the Middle Ages"), demanded that Rome be made the capital of Italy, and condemned the Mexican adventure.

He then sent a copy of his speech to the Minister of the Interior, demanding that it be printed in the next day's *Moniteur*.

---

* *It was, of course, a halfway measure: since every interpellation required the previous approval of four committees, the government majority could forestall any undesired questions.*

Eugénie, in her capacity as Regent, led the Privy Council in suppressing the speech. Then she sent the copy to the Emperor in Algiers, arguing that he could "hardly tolerate such a public utterance, even from a cousin." Accordingly, Napoleon sent Plon-Plon a sharp letter of rebuke, and sent a copy of the letter to the Empress as proof that he had taken her advice. The Empress had it published in the *Moniteur*. Now publicly humiliated, Plon-Plon retired into private life.*

By 1867, the reform-minded, maddeningly vacillating Emperor stood practically alone against the conservative Bonapartists at Court and in the government—and against the Empress.

Envision a magnificently appointed ballroom in which, to an olio of Strauss and Offenbach airs, a legion of gorgeously dressed people, their faces hidden behind domino masks, waltz riotously as the clock approaches the bewitching hour—at which time everyone removes his or her domino to reveal not a face but a skull.

Such a vision characterized the Second Empire in the year 1867—the year of the great *Exhibition Universelle*.

The Exhibition had been planned long before the regime realized it would desperately need a great spectacular to deflect the public's attention from the mounting chaos about them. The timing was perfect. Forgotten—for the moment—was the fact that a series of wars had left France with little save a large dent in the exchequer and black bunting over the doorways of many a grieving family. Prosperity was abounding. "Everyone" was converging on Paris, including a plethora of foreign royals. The royals felt they had nothing to fear in the Emperor who had seemed to pose a threat to their respective sovereignties; the Emperor's physical and emotional in-

---

* *There was a reconciliation of sorts following the Emperor's return from Algeria. Allowing that he had nothing against Plon-Plon personally, Napoleon admitted his unhappiness over the embarrassment this cousin had caused him: "I do not want it to be thought that I have two policies, an official one and a hidden one of which you are the exponent." At Eugénie's urging, he did not suggest that Plon-Plon return to public life, and Plon-Plon let it go at that.*

stability was an open secret. By his latest bumblings, he had proved
to be a paper tiger.

As the historian La Gorce remarked: "Never had France
entertained more guests—and fewer friends."

The most popular visitor, the Man of the Hour, was Bismarck.
Believing that it was in France's best interests to accept the inevitability of Prussia's being the paramount German Power, Paris
succumbed to Bismarckomania. Bismarck Brown replaced Magenta
Red (named after the battle), Eugénie Blue, Mathilde White, and
Nuance Téba (a sort of powdery green that alluded to the Empress's
origins and suggested envy). Bismarck Brown was hardly an
aesthetic improvement over the colors it replaced in popularity (it
reminded Pauline Metternich of "petrified shit"), even though it was
available in varying hues, from the dull *Bismarck malade* through
Bismarck content and *Bismarck glacé* and *Bismarck scintillant* to
the lively *Bismarck en colère*. Still, it became all the rage.

And Bismarck Brown was only the half of it. Elegant ladies literally Bismarcked themselves all over: Bismarck boots, Bismarck
gloves, Bismarck parasols, Bismarck bonnets (a confection of Bismarck straw trimmed with Bismarck lace worn atop Bismarck-dyed
hair fashioned in a Bismarck chignon). Male courtiers and disassoci-
ated dandies sported trousers, coats, gloves and boots dyed in the
Bismarck tones.

Bismarck himself stuck to white, a color he had always favored.

Highlight of the "season" was Offenbach's *The Grand Duchess of
Gerolstein*, a brutal satire on that with which, in the eyes of so
many, the Bonapartist Court was most closely associated: absolute
power and war. The Emperor found it all vastly amusing (as did
everyone else), though he was seen to wind the tips of his moustache
throughout the performance—always a telltale sign of his perplex-
ity.

The Exhibition opened with fanfare on the first day of April.
There were novelties galore: gas or compressed-air engines, mine-
borers, aluminum, railway signals, petroleum oils, and carbolic acid
(destined to be used widely as a disinfectant in those periodic cholera outbreaks). Because the American Civil War had disrupted the
cotton industry and silkworm disease was disrupting the silk industry, milady's attention was now called to the wonders of woolen

goods from the looms of Rheims and Amiens. (Fashion note: Crinolines were "out"; "in" was the Empress's latest innovation—short dresses.) Novelties in furniture included easy chairs from England and, from America, rocking chairs. Standing cheek by jowl with French guns, field kitchens and ambulance wagons were the huge German guns now being turned out by Herr Krupp. In the *Salle des Beaux-Arts*, one could see what had come out of the more notable *ateliers* since 1855: the works of Rousseau, Corot, Millet and Flandrin.

And then there were the international exhibits. One could see Arabs sulking in front of their tents, Mexicans sprawled atop papier-mâché Aztec tombs, Russians galloping in circles on Ukrainian horses, Chinese maidens screeching in their pagodas, Egyptians praying in their temples, Turks picking everyone's pocket. Hawkers offered anything from brassware, fancy cakes, sausages and potted meats to objets d'art stolen from mansions in the Faubourg Saint-Germain. There were "musical cafés," where maidens masquerading as Bavarian or Dutch peasants offered food, drink and gonorrhea.

Adding to the gaiety of the season were the colorful activities that spilled beyond the Exhibition's confines in the Champs de Mars. All the Imperial palaces and foreign embassies were thrown open nightly for banquets and balls. There were "hilarious suppers" at such fashionable restaurants as the Café Anglais, where, more often than not, Princess Pauline von Metternich could be counted on to put in an appearance and dispense a dollop of charming smut.

For the more culturally elevated, there were such novelties as Verdi's latest masterpiece, *Don Carlo*—proof that the titan had not lost his genius—and Dumas *fils*'s sequel to his *Dame aux Camélias*, a dreadful pastiche entitled *Les Idées de Madame Aubray*—proof that one should not attempt to improve upon success.

On June 6, Napoleon staged a great army review at Longchamps for the Russian and Prussian sovereigns. Thirty-five thousand troops marched by. It was a colorful march, intended as a not too subtle reminder that the glory of France—its army—was a force with which to reckon.

Who could have suspected this glory was, like so much of the Second Empire, more shadow than substance?

As the sovereigns were returning to Paris through the Bois de Boulogne, a Polish patriot took a potshot at the Tsar. The bullet wound up in the nose of an equerry's horse. Never at a loss for the appropriate remark, Napoleon, in whose carriage the intended victim was riding, said: "We have been under fire together, so we are now brothers-in-arms."

This attempt on the life of so distinguished a visitor did not put a damper on the festivities.

Nor, for that matter, did the ongoing demonstrations by the students, clerks and shop assistants who had been evicted from their Left Bank hotels to make room for the locust-like invasion of foreigners come to the fair.

Paris had never been gayer than that 1867 Exhibition Season.

It would never be so gay again.

Between the eleventh and sixteenth of June there was a great deal of ceremonial hoopla attendant upon the departures of the Russian and Prussian sovereigns. It was time to welcome yet another potentate, the Sultan of Turkey. He had come, in his words, "to attend the Carnival of Venice."

Barely had the Sultan begun to pinch a few Bismarcked bottoms around town when the carnival was transmogrified into a wake.

Word was received that the Emperor Maximilian of Mexico had been executed.

For Napoleon and Eugénie, it was not so much a matter of waiting for the second shoe to drop as hoping it never would.

Once the French troops had withdrawn, Juárez had gone on the offensive; by April 1867, Maximilian had fled to Querétaro, where he had been captured on May 15.

July 1 was to be the highlight of the Exhibition: it was Prize-Giving Day. The Emperor and Empress were to do the honors in the presence of the Sultan of Turkey, the Prince of Wales, the Crown Prince of Italy, and the mad Empress Charlotte's favorite brother and sister-in-law, the Count and Countess of Flanders.

The evening before, Napoleon was handed a message rushed over from the Quai d'Orsay: a cypher had arrived from Washington advising that the Emperor Maximilian had been condemned to death by Juárez on June 13 and executed three days later.

Napoleon was so shattered by the news, he burst into tears in front of the embarrassed messenger. On regaining his composure, he went to break the news to the Empress. She collapsed.

It was not lost on the superstitious, guilt-ridden Eugénie that the dreadful news had arrived on a Sunday.

Early next morning, after dressing herself in mourning and sneaking off to the Church of Saint-Roche for an hour of prayer, the Empress bedecked herself in white (no Bismarck Brown for *her*) and drove with the Emperor to the prize-giving.

As the ceremony proceeded, the Emperor became more and more nervous, the Empress's fixed smile became more and more labored.

Midway through the festivities, the Empress collapsed and had to be hauled back to the Tuileries. All festivities were canceled, and the Court was plunged into mourning.

A week later, Adolphe Thiers rose in the Assembly to present the balance sheet on the Mexican fiasco. It had cost France 6,000 men killed and 600 million francs. In pointing out the moral, Thiers demanded more effective parliamentary control of the conduct of the government.

The Minister of War replied lamely: "Our soldiers do not count the number of the enemy before the fight; and after they fight, they do not count their dead."

One indignant Leftist interrupted: "No! But here in France there are mothers, daughters and wives who have counted them!"

Also doing a little counting were many Frenchmen who had lost money—in some cases been wiped out—on those Mexican bonds.

Napoleon and Eugénie met at Salzburg with Emperor Franz-Josef to express their official condolences on the death of Maximilian. The journey had an ancillary purpose: much to Eugénie's pleasure, Napoleon was beginning to suspect that perhaps the time had come to draw closer to Austria.

Franz-Josef was not interested; he did not trust Napoleon.

On returning to Paris, Napoleon and Eugénie—but especially Eugénie—were now made brutally aware of the low esteem in which they were held by their subjects. Harboring no illusions, Napoleon confessed as much in a speech he made at Lille. Admitting that "black clouds have arisen to darken our horizon," he appealed to confidence in "the wisdom and patriotism of the government" for the warding off of "imaginary fears."

It did not wash with the public. The Mexican fiasco was the last straw. On the Left Bank, where resided the regime's severest critics—the students, intellectuals, artists and authors—massed demonstrators were arrested for crying, "That Louis, what a horror!" and "That Eugénie, what a slut!"

They had to be released. All swore they were merely demonstrating against some unpopular fellow-students named Louis and Eugénie.

In feuilletons and penny-dreadfuls, the Emperor's legitimacy was called into question. In the more sophisticated satirical journals, the Emperor's political legitimacy was called into question, e.g.:

> It is the Spaniard Eugénie I who governs us under the Presidency of Napoleon III. She is planning Ultramontane expeditions; she presses her political and social plans on the ministers, who bow their bald heads before the wisdom of this prodigy. A famous conference of ministers took place today, in which the Empress participated, bringing all her crinolines with her. Europe watched; but after nine hours, it was clear that the only decision was that the little Prince [Imperial] should not be allowed to eat gingerbread.

The attacks on the Empress were merciless; she was more despised than the Emperor. He was, after all, a Frenchman. His consort, as Persigny never failed to remind one and all, was "a Spaniard." For example:

> She is an angel of gentleness; she is enthusiastic over bullfights; she is bigoted, a confessing child of forty-three; she is the Queen of the crinoline; it is impossible to talk of politics, without her coming in with her dressmaker.

Also ridiculed was her celebrated obsession:

> The Empress has just bought a small piece of furniture that belonged to Marie Antoinette at an auction. We know that the wife of Napoleon III admires Marie Antoinette. . . . In her love for Marie Antoinette's furniture she went so far as to take her throne.

Eugénie sought to dismiss it all as "vulgar jokes." In a way, they were.

But it was no vulgar joke that the Empress's influence in the government was now coming under direct attack by the politicians, who reproached Napoleon for allowing her any voice in the direction of State affairs.

Persigny minced no words: "You allow yourself to be governed by your wife; you are sacrificing your own interests as well as the interests of your son and your country. People think you have abdicated; you are losing prestige, and your friends are discouraged—the few you still have!"

The Emperor accepted without comment this rebuke from the man who had served him loyally since those far-gone days of Strasbourg and Boulogne. (He also acquiesced in Eugénie's insistence that Fould, his most capable minister, be dismissed from the Cabinet.)

A few days later, there was a particularly fierce clash between Persigny and Eugénie at a Cabinet meeting. When Persigny appeared at a Tuileries reception that evening, he was greeted by the vindictive Eugénie before the entire Court with: "It would have been better if you had stayed at home, rather than coming here and making me nervous by your presence!"

Persigny wrote a screed castigating the Empress's evil influences on the Empire and its Emperor, resigned from the Cabinet, and went home to the Loire to await a call to return from the man he had helped to the throne.

The man sent word that he was naming Persigny prefect of the Loire.

Exit Persigny.

Attacks on the Empress continued. Entering the Imperial box one evening for a gala at the Théâtre Odéon, she was greeted with shouts from the audience to "Shut your damn mouth!" The Emperor squirmed. Days later, Eugénie collapsed in a screaming fit upon learning that the Prince Imperial had been booed by a group of students on whom he was bestowing some prizes.

Napoleon—ever the persuasive propagandist—embarked upon a campaign to defend her. He published pseudonymously a psychological portrait of the woman "whom everybody is now attacking." He hoped all of France would "see her in the proper light." He praised her interest in economic and financial questions and her addiction to "serious reading." (Mérimée had suggested Eugénie "undertake some serious reading" as an anodyne to her emotional distress.) He allowed as how "her refreshing comments, the audacity of her ideas arrests one's attention." He conceded that "her manner of expression is at times incorrect," but, conversely, "colorful and animated," and he hoped the reader would appreciate that "in matters pertaining to politics and morals, she rises to true eloquence." He went so far as to admit that "sometimes she likes to discuss too much and allows herself to be drawn into expressions that at times have brought her enemies," but justified it all on the grounds that "even her exaggeration is founded on one motive only, the love of good."

It was a gallant effort, but a futile one. Nothing could convince the French that their Empress was anything other than what they thought her to be.

Worse, the Emperor's attempt to point out the Empress's strengths only succeeded in pointing out his own weaknesses. And of those weaknesses, by far the most pronounced was his inability to shuck "the Spaniard's" deleterious influence—which was seen as the root of his refusal to grant the liberal reforms he had been promising for so long.*

Now remembering his own dictum—"March at the head of the ideas of your century and these ideas will follow you and support you"—the Emperor began to march following the 1868 elections that further increased the number of the opposition in the legislature. On May 11, with the halfhearted consent of the Empress, he promulgated a liberal press law abolishing censorship. A month later, he granted the limited right of public assembly. The Empress thought this should suffice. What more did the people want?

A year later, the legislature let her know. The Third Party demanded the creation of a "responsible ministry." With the coopera-

---

* Plon-Plon got into the act: "The old man is failing rapidly," he wrote for public dissemination. "He is more weary than people realize. There is no controlling hand. The Empress is a fool, incapable of governing except among dressmakers, and yet she aspires to reign. She awaits with impatience the death of the Emperor, in order to become Regent. If he dies, there will be a revolution, and then my hour will come!" Plon-Plon's hour never came. He was too detested, even among those who shared his political and religious convictions.

tion of forty Deputies of the Left, the Third Party (numbering 116) now had a majority. Napoleon had little choice but to yield. In October, he invited Ollivier to visit him in utmost secrecy at Compiègne. Ollivier agreed to enter the government after a number of preconditions had been met, most notably the removal of Rouher and the more obdurate conservatives from the Cabinet—and the banning of the Empress from future Cabinet meetings.

Fortunately, the Empress was away in Egypt, representing France at the opening of the Suez Canal. The Emperor promulgated a *senatus consulta* that made the Assembly and Senate constitutional deliberative bodies, dismissed the entire Cabinet, and formally asked Ollivier to form a new ministry. Stocks rose immediately on the Bourse. Public confidence in the Emperor was restored.

The new Cabinet was finally assembled on January 2, 1870. The next day the ministers went to pay their formal respects to the Empress, who was still bristling over the *fait accompli* with which she had been greeted on her return from Egypt. (The public was told the Empress would cease attending Cabinet meetings "in order that opinions may not be attributed to her which she does not entertain and that she may not be suspected of an influence which she does not desire to exercise.")

The Empress told the ministers that as long as they had the Emperor's "confidence" they could count on her "good will." She wanted them to know they did not have *her* confidence.

During the first week of the new government, the Republicans broadcast their intention to remain in opposition, though they admitted ruefully amongst themselves that there was little future for their hopes to overthrow the monarchy. On January 10, those Republican hopes were restored, thanks to one of the Emperor's cousins, Prince Pierre-Napoleon Bonaparte, the aforementioned "Wild Corsican Boar."

Prince Pierre had of late been engaged in a journalistic duel with the Leftist journal *La Marseillaise*, which had been mercilessly attacking the memory of Napoleon Bonaparte. In hopes of settling the matter, the journal sent two seconds—one of whom was the popular editorialist Victor Noir—to arrange a duel with arms.

Instead of calling on Pierre's seconds, they called on Pierre personally. He received them, as he received everyone else (mistresses included), with a loaded revolver. There ensued a short argument, which Pierre ended by planting a bullet in Noir's brain. (The other "second" fled.)

Though Ollivier acted swiftly, arresting the murderer that very evening, Noir's newspaper published a call to revolution, penned by Henri Rochefort:

> I have had the weakness to believe that a Bonaparte could be something other than an assassin! I dared to suppose that a straightforward duel was possible with this family where murder and snares are tradition and custom. . . . For eighteen years now France has been held in the bloodied hands of these cutthroats, who, not content to shoot down Republicans in the streets, draw them into filthy traps in order to slit their throats in private!

The journal was seized for inciting revolution. (Under the liberalized press laws, it was still illegal to publish any material that insulted the Emperor—though not the Empress—or provoked revolution.) Worse, since the law provided for special criminal jurisdiction in cases involving members of the Imperial family, it was difficult to deny the possibility of a governmental whitewash.

Ollivier sought valiantly to disassociate the government from Prince Pierre. The Republicans, intent upon squeezing all possible mileage from the incident, rallied close to 100,000 people for Noir's funeral.

Had the rally been better organized, there is every probability that a revolution would have broken out. But the Emperor's luck was still holding; his enemies were unable to resolve their own differences.

The rally did, however, convince the people of one thing: it might be difficult to erect barricades in Baron Haussmann's broad boulevards—but it was not difficult to fill those boulevards with humanity.

Rochefort was condemned to six months' imprisonment for provoking civil strife and for "offense to the Emperor's person." Prince Pierre was acquitted on the grounds that he had fired in self-defense; he thought the two seconds (who had called on him unarmed) had come to kill him.

Moving quickly to offset public reaction, the Emperor called for a plebiscite: on May 8 the voters were asked to respond "Yes" or "No" on whether they wanted to live under the constitutional monarchy as now constituted.

With the Republicans of the Right supporting the government, 7.5 million voted "Yes" out of a total of 10.8 million votes cast (there were 1.8 million abstentions).

Announcing the returns to Napoleon, Ollivier said: "In supporting the Empire with more than seven million votes, France says to you, 'Sire, the country is with you; advance confidently in the path of progress and establish liberty based on respect for the laws and the Constitution. France places the cause of liberty under the protection of your dynasty.' "

Responding to the address, Napoleon told the Corps Législatif: "Now more than ever before we can look forward to the future without fear."

The Second Empire had less than four months to live.

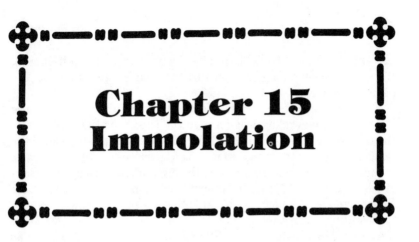

Chapter 15
Immolation

Clever politicians do not create situations; they exploit those created by others. Bismarck was a clever politician. He needed a war with France in order to bring the independent states of the South German Confederation into the Prussian maw and thus complete unification. But France had to be provoked into starting that war; she had to appear as the aggressor in the eyes of Europe.

A vacancy on the Spanish throne—Queen Isabella II was deposed in 1868—provoked France. All Bismarck did was "toss a red flag at the Gallic bull" (his words).

Said Bismarck in retrospect: "If Napoleon had not married, we would never have had a war."

That was the truth, but not the whole truth. Eugénie was guilty by act of commission; but then, Napoleon was guilty by act of omission. Their joint guilt is mitigable, though. Eugénie could never have had "my war" (her words) if the government and nation had not wanted it, whereas Napoleon was too weak—too ill and dispirited—to impose his will when it was most needed.

This neither excuses the French sovereigns' behavior nor absolves Bismarck of culpability. It merely sets the events in their proper perspective.

For two years the Spanish had been hawking their vacant throne around Europe. One royal house after another had turned it down for the same reason no Spaniard wanted it: the Carlists were raising hell on the right, the Republicans were raising hell on the left. In March 1870, a secret council in Berlin decided it was "the duty of a patriotic Prussian Prince" to accept the unwanted crown if offered. Bismarck passed along the word to the Spanish government. The offer was made.

On July 3—a Sunday—it was learned at the Tuileries that Prince Leopold of Hohenzollern-Sigmaringen had accepted the crown, with the required consent of King William I in his capacity as "head of the family." (One interesting item often overlooked by historians: though a Prussian through and through, Prince Leopold was a closer relation to Napoleon than to William, as he shared both Bonaparte and Beauharnais blood with the Emperor.)

Presiding over the Quai d'Orsay at the time was the Duke d'Agénor de Gramont, whom Eugénie adored. Not only was he an ardent papist, he loved Austria inordinately and hated Prussia irrationally.

When, at Eugénie's insistence, he named Gramont to head the Foreign Ministry (May 1870), Napoleon's lack of enthusiasm bespoke volumes: "It does not matter whom we appoint, since we have made up our minds to do nothing." Bismarck called Gramont "the stupidest man in Europe." He probably was.

On learning of Prince Leopold's acceptance, Gramont sounded the tocsin in the Assembly:

> It is impossible for us to allow a foreign power to place one of its Princes on the throne of Charles V and thereby upset the present balance of power in Europe to the detriment of France and the peril of her interests and her honor. To prevent this eventuality we count both on the wisdom of the German people and the friendship of Spain. But if it should turn out otherwise, strong in your support, gentlemen, and in that of the nation, we shall know how to fulfill our duty without hesitation or weakness!

The gentlemen of the Bonapartist Right cheered him to the rafters. They were already counting on war to renew the prestige of the regime and herald a return to the traditions of unenlightened despotism. So far as they were concerned, all this "liberalization" had gone too far.

The gentlemen of the Left appealed to Ollivier to apply the brakes. Ollivier, a strong orator but a weak statesman, replied lamely: "The government would only have peace with honor."

The Empress argued that the time had come "to put Prussia in its place!"

Where was the Emperor throughout all this?

He was in a state of near invalidism. In addition to rheumatoid arthritis and untold agonies from an aggravated kidney and inflamed gall bladder, he was suffering from the added complications of gravel, dysuria, and pus in the urine.

On July 1, a panel of medical experts examined him. What ensued we can only speculate about. Some sources claim the physicians merely recommended "corrective surgery," a recommendation the Emperor turned down on the grounds that now was not the time; other sources, that the physicians feared an operation would be fatal and thus withheld the truth.

From his bedroom, the ailing Emperor could hear pro-war demonstrations on the boulevards, pacifists being hooted and hissed. Steamed up by the Bonapartist press, the people were now demanding a war that would bring France *la gloire* and, into the bargain, avenge their defeat at Waterloo a half century in the past.

With war fever mounting, Gramont—egged on by the Empress—played Bismarck's game of forcing the other side to be the aggressor. On July 9, he ordered Count Benedetti to Ems, where King William was taking a cure, with instructions to prevail upon him to revoke Prince Leopold's acceptance of the Spanish throne.

The King replied that Prince Leopold was free to accept or refuse as he saw fit. He did, however, assure Benedetti that he had advised Leopold of the excitement his candidature had raised in France. William, who was acting independently of Bismarck, did not want a war with France.

Her army was touted as the most formidable on the Continent.

Gramont insisted that Benedetti secure an immediate definite reply from the King himself. "Public opinion," he cabled the ambassador, "is tense with excitement and is getting out of hand in all directions, and we are counting the hours."

The Bonapartist press was getting that excitement out of hand in all directions.

Benedetti saw the King again on the eleventh. With understandable irritation, the King explained that the decision had to be Prince

Leopold's. Any concession to France's demands on his part, he added, would be galling to German public opinion. He also admitted that he had prevailed upon Prince Leopold to think twice before accepting the throne.

Upon receipt of Benedetti's report, Gramont informed the Cabinet: "We call upon the King to *forbid* the Hohenzollern Prince to persist in his candidature. In the absence of a definite reply tomorrow we shall interpret silence or ambiguity as a refusal to satisfy our demands."

(Argued Eugénie years after the fact: "If we hadn't obtained it, France would have been humiliated and insulted in the face of all Europe; there would have been an outbreak of anger in every French heart against the Emperor; it would have been all up with the Empire. . . . No, after Sadowa and Mexico we could not subject the national pride to a fresh trial. *We had to have our revenge!*")

Next day, the Hohenzollern candidacy was withdrawn. Napoleon expressed his approval with a characteristically laconic remark: "Public opinion here in France would have preferred war. The country will be disappointed. But it cannot be helped." The news perked the Emperor up. He realized his army was not in fighting shape.

For the past two years, in fact, he had been attempting to reorganize it along the more efficient Prussian lines. All his ministers greeted the requests for a strengthened army with patronizing smiles of toleration. Did not France already possess the finest army in the world? they argued. How can one improve on perfection? Having gradually resigned all autocratic powers, Napoleon was unable to act alone.

Worn out with disappointment and disease, he abandoned the struggle in despair. A month before the war's outbreak, the army was reduced by 10,000 men. Ollivier proclaimed: "The government has no uneasiness whatsoever; at no epoch was the peace of Europe more assured." Napoleon turned to his Minister of War, Leboeuf, for reassurances. Leboeuf assured him that "the finest military machine on the Continent" was "perfectly supplied in every respect."

Leboeuf was loyal to the Emperor and incompetent to the core. Not until it was too late would Napoleon learn that "the finest military machine on the Continent" was just about the rottenest on the planet.

Though the standing army was composed of 350,000 men, what few crack troops it possessed were for display only. There were no battle plans. Supplies were either in short demand or sitting piled up haphazardly at places other than their intended destinations. What supplies were available were, for the most part, of inferior grade; much speculation in the quartermaster corps over the previous decade and a half had taken its toll. Training was deplorable; many troops could march in perfect cadence, but few could fire the newly developed *chassepots* (and this is presupposing those *chassepots* were available). Most of the senior officers were either ignorant of where their headquarters were, ignorant of what regiments comprised their respective divisions and corps, or just plain ignorant. In the event of mobilization, most of the troops—particularly the reservists—would not know where to report; those finding their way to their units would find themselves unable to draw rations. One out of three cavalrymen could not properly fodder his horse. One out of four cavalrymen did not have a horse to fodder.*

Furthermore, the powers that be in the higher echelons were so convinced that war with Prussia would be a one-week excursion to Berlin, they failed to provide any French maps, only German ones. General Frossard had developed an excellent plan for defending France in the event of a Prussian attack. But no allowance had been made for a French retreat. Were the enemy to mount an invasion, the French army, given its total lack of maps, would not even have known where it was!

Committing the French army to a war against Prussia would have been suicidal. But now, with the Spanish candidature resolved to France's satisfaction, the *casus belli* was eliminated.

All this deplorable inefficiency and lack of military brilliance was obscured by splendid uniforms and embroidered battle flags surmounted by those omnipresent golden eagles.

One day during maneuvers, a young officer led a brilliant cavalry charge against a detachment of infantry spiffily turned out. On being congratulated by his general, the officer confessed that the situation might have been different had the infantry detachment been the enemy, using real bullets.

"Well, then what would you have done?" asked the general.

Replied the officer: "I'd have gotten the hell out of here, sir!"

"I am happy that it has ended so," the Emperor told the Empress as he handed her the telegram announcing Prince Leopold's withdrawal.

The Empress stared at the telegram a moment, reduced it to shreds, and stamped on them furiously.

Against Napoleon's explanation that the Hohenzollern withdrawal had left no excuse for a conflict, Eugénie screamed that France must "take a more energetic, a more Bonapartist stand!" Prince Leopold's renunciation, she argued, was "worthless!" since it did not come from the King of Prussia himself.

In the midst of Eugénie's tirade, Napoleon suffered a fainting fit and fled to Saint-Cloud.

That evening, the Empress drove out to Saint-Cloud and went to work on the Emperor, convincing him more than ever that "a victorious war would consolidate our son's throne."

Wearily, the Emperor ordered Benedetti to demand assurances from King William that Prince Leopold—or any other Hohenzollern, for that matter—would never again seek the throne of Spain.

The King replied, in understandable irritation, that the issue had already been resolved in France's favor; furthermore, he was in no position to make any "guarantees" about the future. After dismissing Benedetti, the King wired to Bismarck a report of the interview.

This was the famous Ems Telegram.

Bismarck had believed—as had everybody else—that war had been avoided; only the previous evening he had wired his wife reluctantly that he would be joining her for a prolonged holiday at their country estate.

Now, as he pored over the telegram from his monarch, Bismarck suspected it could be turned to his advantage.

Reaching for a pencil, he judiciously edited the text—cutting a word here, a word there—so that it read as if Benedetti's interview with the King had resulted in an insult to Prussia as well as to France. He then "leaked" the amended text to the press.

Within twenty-four hours, Parisians were screaming "*À Berlin!*" while Berliners were screaming "*Nach Paris!*"

Napoleon proposed the immediate calling of a European congress to resolve French and Prussian differences. The Empress dismissed the idea, declaring that "the country wants war, Louis!" The Emperor summoned his Privy Council. As he sat squirming painfully, Gramont delivered a ferocious anti-Prussian diatribe, following which the Empress demanded that the Council decide in favor of war. Next day (July 15), the Chamber of Deputies voted a 500-million-franc credit and ordered immediate mobilization.

Four days later, France declared war on Prussia.

The Emperor announced he would go to the front (though nobody knew exactly where it was) and direct overall operations. Princess Mathilde was appalled. "But you are not physically able to command the army," she argued. "You cannot ride any more! You could not even endure the difficulties of travel by coach!"

Replied the Emperor calmly: "You exaggerate, my dear."

"Oh, no! Just look at yourself in the mirror!"

"Yes, indeed; I am not beautiful, I do not look frisky."

Mathilde persisted in her argument until she was waved off with a fatalistic gesture.

During the feverish days leading up to the war's outbreak, Great Britain had made it quite clear that, while wanting to be on the friendliest terms with France, she would favor Prussia. Austria, Italy, the South German Confederation and even Denmark—all fearful of Prussian hegemony—had suggested they would join France as allies after one successful battle.

But Bismarck cannily remembered that document in his safe vis-à-vis Napoleon's designs on Luxembourg and Belgium, and took pains to assure it was given the widest possible dissemination. All of Europe now believed the old Bonaparte leopard had not changed his spots after all.

France stood alone.

Though no one was prepared to come to her aid, no one wanted France to be destroyed. It was felt that the war would be fought to a standstill, at which time a general congress would resolve the issue. Since France boasted the largest, most powerful army on the Continent, the Powers felt confident she could hold her own.

No one dared suspect France would cave in after six weeks—just as during World War II no one dared suspect France, at the time boasting the largest army in the world, would duplicate that incredible feat.

On July 23, the Emperor gave a speech indicating he would "follow the will of the people." Three days later, he appointed Eugénie Regent and issued a proclamation to the Imperial army: "The war which is beginning will be long and painful."

It would be painful indeed, especially for a Commander-in-Chief whose pain was such that he could barely tolerate being lifted on and off his horse, much less sitting it. But it would not be long.

Napoleon III's departure for the war, at ten o'clock in the morning of July 28, was a far cry from his departure for the Italian War in 1859. Then he had been hale and hearty, overflowing with confidence, with the cries of all Paris ringing in his ears. Now he left from Saint-Cloud, seen off by a handful of faithful courtiers, aged beyond his years, lacking in all confidence and pitiably ill.

He insisted on detouring around Paris: "I do not like to be praised before I have won." In truth, he feared what his subjects would think on beholding an invalid Emperor whose rouged cheeks and dyed hair fooled no one, whose lack of confidence was palpably obvious, who was not so much going off to war as being driven off to a ghastly venture, the outcome of which he dared not contemplate.

"In fourteen days, you will be in Berlin!" shouted someone in his entourage.

"No," he murmured. "Don't expect that—not even if we are successful."

Eugénie drove her husband and son in her pony carriage to the Imperial train, which had already been boarded by a suite of aides, equerries—and a medical staff with full kit, prepared, should the necessity arise, to perform the surgery they should have insisted upon three weeks earlier.

The fourteen-year-old Prince Imperial, newly commissioned a Lieutenant of Infantry, appeared small and frightened; he was going off to war at his mother's insistence. ("I think I would rather see him dead than without honor," Eugénie had written to her mother back in Madrid.) In his hands he clutched Eugénie's going-away present: a copy of Thomas à Kempis's *Imitation of Christ*. ("I

know that when men are left among themselves, they are sometimes inclined to behave irregularly.")

The Empress made the sign of the cross over the Prince. The
Emperor's last words were for his favorite valet: "Beaumanoir, I
forgot to say good-bye to you!"

As the train steamed out, the Empress shouted: "I expect you to
do your duty, Louis!" The courtiers all wondered which Louis she
meant, father or son.

Napoleon arrived in Metz, the army's staging area in the north-
east corner of France, at seven that evening, and immediately his
worst fears were realized. There was no end to the shortages: doctors, nurses, wagons, horses, tents, mess gear—and troops. Men
were piling off trains in a state of drunkenness, disarray and total
disorientation. Telegrams were coming in advising that supplies
were sitting piled up on railway sidings all over France—and even
in Algeria. Officers were frantically seeking out the units to which
they had been assigned. Two thousand men of the natty *Garde
Mobile* stood around waiting to share a handful of antique rifles
dating from 1842, while a parrot trained by the Zouaves squawked
"*À Berlin! À Berlin!*"

The Emperor telegraphed the Empress: "There is an utter lack of
everything."

Well, not exactly everything. There was no lack of complete
confidence—and maps of Germany.

A council of war was called at Napoleon's headquarters in the
Hôtel de l'Europe (to which journalists—and spies—enjoyed free
access). Initial strategy called for the Emperor to lead the eight-
corps Army of the Rhine—spread out along a hundred-mile salient
behind the Saar, from the Luxembourg border to the Swiss
border—in an invasion of the South German states.

It was not a bad strategy. Fearing Prussia, the South Germans
would have preferred to throw in their lot with a victorious France.
But, as Napoleon post-mortemed,

> Instead of having, as we had a right to expect, 385,000 men in line to
> oppose the 430,000 of North Germany [Prussia] and the southern states,
> the army numbered only 220,000 men; and even so, not only were there
> gaps in the ranks, but there was a shortage of indispensable equipment.
> The Army of the Moselle had only 110,000 men in place of 220,000; that of

Marshal MacMahon's only 40,000 instead of 107,000. There were great difficulties in making up General Douay's corps at Belfort; and that of Marshal Canrobert was not yet complete; and . . .

The Prussian strategy was to fight a defensive war; they believed Leboeuf's claims that the French army was invincible. This would explain how the French were able to penetrate two miles inside Germany to Saarbrücken when hostilities commenced on August 2.

It was a penetration analogous to *coitus interruptus*. The French failed—or forgot—to cut the bridges in the town or destroy the railway station and telegraph lines before being chased back across the border—thus ending the war's only battle on German soil.

That night, the Emperor suffered a severe attack of nephritis while the Prussians suffered a change of strategy.

Two days later, 500,000 men invaded France. Within forty-eight hours, the French were driven back into Lorraine, Alsace was invaded, and Strasbourg was invested.

And that was only the beginning.

Shortly after midnight of that ominous August sixth—it was now Sunday morning—the Empress was awakened with a telegram from the Emperor: "It is necessary to declare martial law and prepare for the defense of Paris." She summoned a Council for 2 A.M.

A few hours later, she telegraphed the Emperor: "I am confident that the Prussians will soon be driven back beyond their borders. Take courage; with energy, we will dominate the situation. I will answer for Paris."

That day she told Mérimée: "We will dispute every foot of ground. The Prussians don't know what they are in for. Rather than accept humiliating terms, we will keep up the fight for ten years!"

Mérimée admired her courage but questioned her confidence.

Ollivier argued for the Emperor's immediate return to Paris; his experience, his "clever tactics" had often saved a situation; he would be more able "to master the present difficulties" than his consort, who was "too temperamental."

Replied Eugénie: "To leave the army before a battle is to give up one's honor!"

Countered Ollivier: "But no; it will mean the salvation of the dynasty."

Eugénie stared at him a moment. "What care I for the dynasty? I am interested only in the Empire!"

Ollivier persisted; it would prove "fatal" if the Emperor remained with the army.

Said Eugénie: "If I agree to the return of the Emperor, then the Prince must stay with the army."

"What could the Prince do in the army?" asked Ollivier incredulously.

To which Eugénie screamed: "Oh, let him be killed!"

The Empress was not being heartless. Just hysterical.

A deputation from the Assembly, echoing the growing public panic, demanded a change of generals at the front and, at home, dismissal of those who had promised—nay, guaranteed—victory: Leboeuf, Gramont, Ollivier, *et al.* Though as Regent she lacked the power to do so, Eugénie dismissed the Ollivier ministry and asked the Count de Palikao, a dreadful strategist but a good conservative, to form a new Cabinet. The new Cabinet, clerical conservatives all, rallied to the side of the Empress.

Over the next few days, as reports came in hourly that the army was being pushed back in all directions, preparations were made for a siege of Paris. Bachelors and childless widowers were called up and new divisions and provisional regiments formed (on paper); ramparts and forts around Paris were armed (with pickaxes and broomsticks); corn and fodder were collected and stored (much of it fell into the hands of enterprising Parisians), and cattle were collected and put out to pasture in the Bois de Boulogne (many broke their rickety fences and disappeared). Masterpieces from the Louvre were sent to Brest, together with the Crown Jewels and most of the cash from the Bank of France.

Merely as a precautionary measure, the Empress entrusted her jewels to her dear friend Pauline von Metternich.

There were disturbances throughout the country. At Marseilles, a mob broke into the Hôtel de Ville; at Lyons, there were shouts of *"Vive la République!"* and *"Down with the Empire!"* In other cities, gunsmiths' shops were pillaged. There was general looting throughout the provinces.

All were contained by National Guardsmen. But all were an adumbration of things to come.

The Empress conceived the idea of arousing the enthusiasm of the people by riding through the streets. The idea was abandoned, because no one could find her a black riding habit and she refused to wear any other kind. It was just as well. She probably would have been assassinated if she had dared show herself in public.

Already many were adding *"Down with the Spaniard!"* to their litany of public demands.

At the Empress's insistence, Marshal Bazaine replaced the Emperor as overall military commander in the field. Hurt at his wife's interference, the Emperor telegraphed her: "I believe we are going through a revolution."

Back came a telegram: "You do not know the situation. People have confidence only in Bazaine."

The Emperor suffered another nephritis attack.

It was now at the point where surgeons were forced to relieve his pain twice daily by drugs and pressure. Sometimes ignored, sometimes unrecognized, he was shunted back and forth on slow, unscheduled trains, not knowing what was happening at the front or back in Paris and, more often than not, not much caring. At times, he would command that he be lifted onto his horse, and would canter out agonizingly toward the Prussian lines.

He literally hoped to die.

On August 17, the Emperor called a conference at Châlons, whither he had been forced to retreat with what was left of the Army of the Rhine, now commanded by the comparatively capable Marshal MacMahon. In attendance were MacMahon, General Louis Jules Trochu, and Plon-Plon.

Plon-Plon had rushed to his cousin's side—according to some sources, to offer his assistance; according to other sources, to urge abdication in his favor. In order to get Plon-Plon out of the way, Napoleon sent him to Italy on what he knew was a futile errand: seeking Victor Emmanuel's intercession. Before leaving, Plon-Plon urged that Trochu, a popular military figure, be sent to Paris as Military Governor "to check the Empress" and that the Emperor follow. The Emperor agreed.

Arriving at Paris the next day, Trochu informed the Empress of his new assignment and that the Emperor would be arriving shortly. Eugénie, who (along with Palikao) disliked Trochu intensely, told him: "No! The Emperor must not come back! The

Emperor will not return!" Off went a telegram to the Emperor advising him of his Empress's decision.

On receipt of the telegram, Napoleon treated his aides to a characteristically mordant witticism: "I seem to have abdicated."

A few days later, the Emperor decided to retreat with Marshal MacMahon's army to Paris and head the defense of the capital. Back came a telegram from Eugénie: "You must not think of coming back if you do not wish to evoke a dreadful revolution. . . . They will say here that you left the army because you feared danger."

The Emperor was ordered to march with MacMahon's army in an attempt to join up with Bazaine, who was now trapped at Metz. MacMahon decided they should march to the Meuse; it was not deemed necessary to go to Bazaine's aid—he had sent a telegram that he expected to break out of his entrapment "momentarily." (He and his army were still trapped at Metz when the war ended.)

On August 27, Napoleon decided to send the Prince Imperial out of the country. Informed of this decision, Eugénie telegraphed the Prince's equerry, Count Duperré: "For the Prince's safety, ignore orders from the Emperor, as he cannot judge."

Napoleon realized she could not judge either. Duperré was ordered to take the Prince to the comparative safety of Amiens.

Furious on learning this, Eugénie wrote to Duperré: "I consider this retreat to Amiens unworthy of the Prince and his parents. My heart is torn, but resolute. . . . Be sure of one thing: I can weep for my son if he is dead or wounded, but if he flies . . . I shall never forgive you. . . . We shall hold out in Paris if we are besieged, and if away from Paris we shall hold out just the same. Peace is impossible!"

So was victory. A few days later, MacMahon's army blundered into what Von Moltke, the Prussian commander, called "the mousetrap of Sedan."

Actually, it was a shooting gallery. Sedan sits in a valley; the only way to defend it is to occupy the heights. MacMahon failed to do this. Von Moltke didn't. The Germans bombarded the area, now full of refugees and fugitive French soldiers.

The final battle began at 5 A.M. on September 1. As the King of Prussia, surrounded by his suite, watched from the heights ("A view of the battle such as no other commander of an army in Western Europe was ever to see again"), crack Bavarian troops swarmed down into the valley. For five hours, literally strapped onto his horse, Napoleon rode agonizingly up and down the lines, praying that someone would shoot him.

Early that evening, sickened by the sight of the slaughter, he ordered the white flag hoisted and dispatched an aide to the King of Prussia with a note:

> Sire, my Brother,
> Having been unable to die among my troops, there remains nothing for me to do but surrender my sword to Your Majesty. I am Your Majesty's good brother, Napoleon.

Back came a letter from the King:

> My Brother,
> While regretting the circumstances in which we meet, I accept Your Majesty's sword, and request that you appoint one of your officers furnished with the necessary powers to treat for the capitulation of the army which has fought so valiantly under your command. I, for my part, have appointed General Von Moltke to this duty.
> Your loving brother, William

That evening, the Emperor telegraphed the Empress: "The army has been taken prisoner, and I share its fate."

Next day, having surrendered his sword to the man who had been his playmate at Malmaison fifty-six years earlier, he wrote:

> My dear Eugénie,
> I cannot tell you what I have suffered and am suffering. We made a march contrary to all the rules and to common sense: it was bound to lead to a catastrophe, and that is complete. I would rather have died than have witnessed such a disastrous capitulation; and yet, things being as they are, it was the only way of avoiding the slaughter of 60,000 men.
> Then again, if only all my torments were concentrated here! I think of you, of our son, of our unfortunate country. May God protect you! What is going to happen in Paris?
> I have just seen the King. There were tears in his eyes when he spoke of the sorrow I must be feeling. He has put at my disposal one of his châteaux near Hesse-Cassel. But what does it matter where I go? I am in despair. Adieu; I embrace you tenderly.

The château designated for his detention was Wilhelmshöhe, once the palace of his uncle Jerome when that buffoon ruled as King of Westphalia. This might account for the presence of the portrait of Queen Hortense, which Napoleon spotted on his arrival and which led him to recall: "I found my mother waiting for me."

That night, after a light meal, the Emperor read himself to sleep with a book he found in a nearby case.

It was Bulwer-Lytton's *The Last of the Barons*.

The Empress had been dreaming of late that she was insane. She confided to Pauline Metternich that she always wept on awakening to discover she was not. Easily roused to hysteria on the slightest provocation, she was now becoming emotionally unglued. It is testimony to her remarkable recuperative powers that she did not go completely over the edge when the Emperor's telegram of surrender was received.

At three in the afternoon, by which time the news had spread throughout the capital, Filon joined Conti, the Emperor's former secretary, at the Tuileries to wait upon the woman they both adored. Suddenly she appeared at the head of the little winding staircase which connected her apartments with those of the Emperor below.

"Do you know what they are saying?" she blurted out abruptly. "That the Emperor has surrendered, that he has capitulated!" Then, her voice becoming strident: "Surely you do not believe that abomination!" The two men remained mute. The Empress screamed maniacally: "But you could not believe that!"

Conti mumbled: "There are circumstances, Madame, where even the bravest . . ." At which point the Empress threw a hair-raising fit.

Recalls Filon:

> I must confess that I was so overcome at the time that I have remembered scarcely anything of this tragic scene but the sound of her words. I only know that it lasted five long, terrible minutes. Then the Empress left the room and went down the little staircase. We remained speechless, benumbed, like men who have come through an earthquake.

The Empress rushed downstairs to the Emperor's apartments and ransacked his desk, burning many vital State papers, holding onto a few (of which she ever afterward refused to allow publication). This seemed to calm her down a bit.

Through the windows could be heard a distant rumbling. Rioters from the outlying districts were pouring into Paris. Crowds surged down the boulevards screaming "Abdication!" and "Dethronement!" and "Down with the Empress!" and that old reliable, *"Vive la République!"* One mob attacked a police station. Beaten back, they hurried to the Louvre to protest against police brutality.

Rouher came by and informed the Empress that in his considered opinion the revolution would begin on the following day.

Now surrounded by her panicking entourage, Eugénie—still in the black cashmere dress she had been wearing for four days—decided to appeal to Trochu to restore order. But Trochu had been told by Palikao to do nothing. He decided to do just that. While the Assembly met to debate, Eugénie held a series of meetings with her ministers and then had a few hours' sleep. She rose again at six and attended mass.

It was now Sunday morning.

Filon tried to persuade Eugénie to leave Paris. She had another idea. Hurriedly summoning yet another Cabinet meeting, she proposed that the Chamber of Deputies be asked to appoint a Council for the Regency, to be headed by the Empress. Police burst in with reports that the mobs in the streets were becoming ugly. Eugénie ordered out the National Guard. Back came word that the National Guard was already out. A few minutes later—it was now 11 A.M.—a telegram was received: Lyons had declared for a republic. Her ministers urged the Empress to leave Paris.

"No!" she said. "I am like the captain of a ship. I can leave the ship only when everyone else has left."

Some of her ministers snuck out to leave the ship.

Moments later a deputation arrived from the Chamber of Deputies to inform the Empress that a Council for the Regency did not sound too promising. She replied:

> If you and the Chamber feel that I am in the way, if it is abdication that you demand, I shall not complain; I can leave my post honorably, for I have not deserted. But I am convinced that a reasonable and patriotic attitude on the part of the representatives of the people would require that all civil disputes be discounted for the time being, and that you now gather around me to resist the common enemy.

Whereupon, as the deputation stared down at their collective boot
in embarrassment, she surrendered once more to fantasy:

> Perhaps I shall be able to secure a favorable peace treaty. Only yes-
> terday the representative of a foreign Power offered to obtain interces-
> sion of neutral Powers in securing a treaty on the following basis: our
> territory was not to be curtailed, the dynasty was to be maintained.

The deputation stared at her as if she were mad, and then excused
themselves. Eugénie turned to her entourage and threw another
verbal fit:

> I told them I would be no trouble to them, if only I could stay here! On
> the contrary, I would undertake the direction of an organization for the
> assistance of the sick and wounded, would visit the hospitals . . . would
> do anything, even go to the outposts at the front! But they did not want
> to listen! In France, a crowned head must not be an object of misfortune!
> I—

On and on she ranted. One moment she vowed not to "surrender"
a throne that was not hers to surrender; the next moment she would
expatiate for "the sins of France" by becoming a practical nurse.
Her auditors stood in mute stupefaction.

The fit passed. Her entourage was invited to join the Empress for
luncheon. It was like sitting to table on the *Titanic* after the last
lifeboat has gone over the side. From outside could be heard the
crowds shouting *"Vive la République!"* and *"Down with the
Spaniard!"*

A few of her more daring ministers came in to announce that a
mob had invaded the Palais Bourbon and proclaimed a republic.
Eugénie asked what they were going to do now. The ministers
replied they were going to the Hôtel de Ville to see the same thing
done there. The Empress said no one need stay. After a moment of
embarrassed hesitation, most of those present got up from the table
and crept away.

The Empress then went to her private apartments, trailed by a
small crowd that included ambassadors Metternich and Nigra (the
Sardinian envoy; Eugénie liked him, though she cared little for his
country), Madame Lebreton (her reader), and a maid who had had
the foresight to retrieve the Empress's jewels from Pauline Metternich.

On reaching her cluttered drawing room, Eugénie looked about at all the Marie Antoinette memorabilia and repeated what she had often said down through her eighteen years on the throne: "I will not die like Marie Antoinette on a guillotine! I would rather die in the streets!"

She really did not wish to die in the streets either. She wished to flee—but did not know how or where.

As everyone stood about wondering what to do next, the door opened and in walked Thélin, the ever-loyal valet-turned-treasurer who had helped Napoleon escape from Ham. To go through the palace was impossible; the mobs were already beating their way in.

Thélin hurried the Empress and her entourage through the gallery that connected the Tuileries with the Louvre. In the Hall of the Seven Chimneys, Eugénie decided that all but Madame Lebreton and the two diplomats should fend for themselves.

Led by Thélin, the small party rushed through the seemingly endless, dusty, littered corridors. Behind them could be heard the commotion of National Guardsmen evicting the frenzied mobs from the Tuileries.

In the Assembly, at that very moment, Jules Favre rose to declare the overthrow of the monarchy. France was now a republic.

At last Thélin found an exit to the street. Ever afterward, the Empress would remember the last painting she saw as she left the Louvre.

It was Géricault's *The Wreck of the Medusa*.

Now safely out of the palace, Eugénie faced the problem of getting safely out of France.

A crowd had gathered in the little square before the Church of Saint-Germain d'Auxerois into which the refugees had stepped. One young man recognized the Empress and made a threatening gesture. Nigra and Thélin held him off while Metternich rushed to find a carriage. Eugénie ran to a cab that was standing idle, hustled Madame Lebreton (who was carrying the jewels and purloined State papers) into it, and hurried the driver on.

The cab went through the Rue de Rivoli—and smack into a mob crying *"Abdication!"* and *"Vive la République!"*—and *"Death to the Empress!"* Madame Lebreton ordered the driver onto a quieter street. As they passed the corner of the Rue Caumartin and the

Boulevard des Capucines, Eugénie saw two men on a ladder taking down the Imperial coat of arms.

"Already?" she cried, and collapsed in a swoon.*

The driver was ordered to take them to the mansion of one of Eugénie's loyal courtiers on the Boulevard Malesherbes. He was not at home. Then on to the house of another favorite. He wasn't home either. The servants were, though; but they refused to let her in. Eugénie considered seeking the protection of the United States ambassador, but did not know his address.

Then she remembered another American, Dr. Evans, who had been her and the Emperor's dentist. Dr. Evans was home. Eugénie threw herself at him: "My fortunes have suffered a reversal! I am now alone, abandoned by everybody!"

She was carrying several passports that had been provided by Metternich days before this fateful Sunday, in case she should have to cross the French border. One was in the name of a British doctor who was taking a patient to England. Eugénie suggested that she play the patient, Madame Lebreton play the nurse, and Dr. Evans play the British doctor.

Evans decided, instead, that their best bet was to go to Deauville and try to find a private yacht that would take them across the Channel. ("This is no time for charades, my dear Madame. Besides, your face is not an unfamiliar one.")

Next morning at five o'clock, after a fitful night of insomnia on the Empress's part, they set out by coach. Sticking to the back roads, two days later they arrived at Deauville, where a private yacht, the *Gazelle*, was put at their disposal by a sympathetic vacationing British aristocrat. They reached Rhyde at four the next morning after a wretched crossing. ("I was not in the least afraid," the Empress recalled. "I have always loved the sea; it has no terrors for me. If [sic] and when I am to die, I can think of no more wonderful death.")

The first hotel to which they went refused to take them in: the two ladies had no luggage and did not look trustworthy. The most

---

* *Recalled the Empress decades later: "I had no fear of death. All I dreaded was falling into the hands of viragos, who would defile my last scene with something shameful or grotesque, who would try to dishonor me as they murdered me. I fancied them lifting up my skirts, I heard ferocious laughter, for, you know, the tricoteuses have not died out!"*

celebrated clotheshorse of her time was wearing a filthy black cashmere dress, a dark raincoat and a round black hat with dark veil—all soaked through. After several tries, Evans found a dismal country inn where the two ladies were accepted, and then rushed off to buy newspapers, hoping for some news of the Prince Imperial's whereabouts.

When Evans returned to the inn, the ladies had eaten breakfast and Eugénie was sitting calmly, reading a Bible she had found in the room. She was halfway through the Twenty-third Psalm when Evans informed her that, according to the newspapers, the Prince had also reached England. That evening, mother and son were reunited in nearby Hastings.

Next day, when news of the Empress's arrival became known, the British Foreign Secretary, Lord Granville, spoke for his government in applauding her bravery. He added: "Her misfortune is great, although it is much owing to herself: Mexico, Rome, war with Prussia . . ."

Part III:
Exile

Chapter 16
Napoleon &
Eugénie:
1870-1873

On January 18, 1871, William I of Prussia was proclaimed German Emperor in the Hall of Mirrors at Versailles, thus marking the unification and rise of modern Germany. Ten days later, German troops entered Paris. An armistice was signed, and the French were left to wallow in political chaos. Humiliated by the peace terms and disgusted with the composition of the new National Assembly—its majority was palpably unfriendly to the Republic—the radical element of Paris, which had gone underground during the four-month siege by the Germans, surfaced.

Civil war broke out in the capital. The horrors of the Commune need not detain us here. Let it be noted, however, that during a two-day period many of Napoleon III's buildings went up in flames, thanks to the efforts of French radicals. And that was *after* the Treaty of Frankfurt ended the Franco-Prussian War!

Eugénie at first refused to "recognize" the overthrow of the monarchy. Still posing as Regent, she conceived the idea of establishing herself in some town in unoccupied France, summoning the Corps Législatif, entering into peace negotiations with Prussia, and then submitting the peace treaty to the country in a plebiscite.

Napoleon punctured this balloon. "I regret to say," he wrote her, "that I completely disapprove of the ideas in your letter . . ."

Not until Bazaine surrendered his trapped troops at Metz—two months after Sedan—would Eugénie acknowledge, albeit with difficulty, that she had been chasing a chimera.

A week or so after her arrival in England, Eugénie received a letter from Napoleon:

> I know, from the experience of my younger days, that, in our position, we can be happy only in free countries like England or Switzerland. Anywhere else, governmental and ordinary people feel nervous about compromising themselves even when merely showing common politeness. When I am free, it is in England I should like to settle, with you and Louis in a little cottage with bow windows and creepers. . . .

By the end of the month,* Eugénie was settled in Camden Place, Chislehurst, a three-story, tastelessly decorated Georgian mansion in Kent, a twenty-minute train journey from London's Charing Cross Station. Over the porch was hung the motto *Malo mori quam foedari*. Death before Dishonour.

The house had belonged to the Rowles family, whose daughter Emily the Emperor had once hoped to marry. Its current owner, Mr. Strode, a monarchist to the core, leased the house "for whatever Her Majesty the Empress can afford to pay." The Empress allowed she could not afford to pay much, but for Strode it was enough.

Eugénie was not impecunious. Merely cautious. Napoleon had a guarantee of £60,000 per annum from his father's estate. Eugénie had some rather lucrative holdings back in Spain. And then there were her jewels; one lot she sold for £150,000. Eugénie became rather miserly. (She hesitated for years before telling the Prince Imperial he had been left a sizeable sum by one of his Bonaparte cousins.) Through shrewd investments of what she had, Eugénie became over the years a wealthy woman who could indulge herself in such luxuries as a magnificent ocean-going yacht, the *Thistle*. At the time of her death, she was enjoying a yearly income of £25,000 on her capital.

Into Camden Place with the Empress went, in addition to the Prince Imperial and his personal staff, the loyal Filon, Madame Lebreton, a bevy of attendants, and seven or eight servants. Within days, as Bonaparte loyalists began to make their way out of France, the household increased: the aged Dr. Conneau, the Duchess de

---

* *It was, ironically, the very day (September 20) on which Victor Emmanuel entered Rome—thus completing the unification of Italy.*

Mouchy (Princess Anna Murat), and others. Within weeks, even more émigrés settled down in the vicinity of Camden Place. Ere long, the house took on the aura of an Imperial Court-in-exile. All that was lacking was the Emperor.

Napoleon's imprisonment at Wilhelmshöhe was more than tolerable. He was treated with utmost kindness by his Prussian captors, and endeared himself to one and all because of his fluency in German, his perennial charm, dignity and tact, and, above all, his refusal to pity himself or bear any animosity against the Germans. Visitors were permitted. Plon-Plon wrote offering to come; so did Napoleon's mother-in-law, the aging Countess de Montijo. Tactfully he told them to stay away.

There was really only one person he wanted to see. But that person—his consort—found it difficult to face him.

At length, after much importuning on Napoleon's part, Eugénie journeyed to Wilhelmshöhe. The visit lasted but a day; some of the Emperor's generals were coming to share his imprisonment, and Eugénie did not want to face them. Brief as the visit was, though, it reconciled the Imperial couple.

No mention was made of Eugénie's refusal to allow Napoleon's return to his own capital prior to Sedan. Nor was mention made of the many ways in which she had fought him, had overstepped her bounds as Empress-consort, especially in the last years of the Empire.

Eugénie saw Napoleon in a new light. He had made many, often tragic mistakes; but these were mistakes of the head, not the heart. He had wounded her pride by flaunting his mistresses; but he had not done so with the intent of willfully hurting her. He had gambled and lost; but, like a good gambler, he had accepted his losses without recrimination. He had used her and humiliated her; but then, she had brought so much of it on herself.

However, all that was in the past. Now he was an aged, ill, fallen man who needed her.

Eugénie fell in love with Napoleon.

It was hardly a spiritual love, much less an *amour de coeur*. Both were incapable of such love. It was a love rooted in remorse and pity and admiration—and a need on Eugénie's part for self-atonement.

On her return to Camden Place, she confided to Filon: "No one knows the Emperor. They say he is cold, has no feeling, is unapproachable, because he is so cool and reserved in his manner. But they did not really know him. When I arrived, he . . . was in complete control of himself because there were strangers present, but when we were alone . . ."

She wrote him tender letters: "The long days of exile seem so sad. . . . my tenderness and my love for you grow stronger . . ." On January 30, 1871, she wrote:

> Dearest friend, today is the anniversary of our wedding. . . . I want to tell you that I am very fond of you. In good times, the links between us may have grown loose. I had thought them broken, but stormy days have shown me how solid they are. There is nothing more left to separate us. We are united, a hundred times more united, because our suffering and our hopes meet in Louis. Now more than ever, I am reminded of the words of the evangelist: "for richer, for poorer, in sickness and in health, to love, cherish, and to obey" . . .

She meant what she wrote. Never again would Eugénie bad-mouth Napoleon; nor would she allow him to be criticized in her presence. For the remaining two years of their life together, she would subordinate herself to him. For the forty-seven years that separated her death from his, Eugénie would devote herself to Napoleon's memory.

She would even attempt to make the world see him for more than he really was.

Early in December, Eugénie journeyed to Windsor, and Queen Victoria wrote in her journal: "She was very nervous when she arrived, and as she walked upstairs [she] quite sobbed. . . . What a fearful contrast to her visits here in '55! Then all was state and pomp, wild excitement and enthusiasm—and now? . . . The poor Empress looked so lovely in her simple black, and so touching in her gentleness and submission." The next day, Victoria wrote to her good friend Queen Augusta of Prussia: "The Empress bears her sad fate with the greatest dignity. Not one word of complaint or bitterness is ever heard from her, and she accuses no one . . ."

To the courtiers at Camden Place, it was another story. Eugénie found it difficult to adjust to the life of an exile, and impossible to forgive those who had "deserted the Imperial cause." She railed interminably against those who had not stood by her in the last days of her Regency. Prime target of her wrath was Trochu, who threw in his lot with the new Republic. "What time is it?" she asked one day. Replied a courtier wearily: "Madame, it is forty-five minutes past Trochu."

Eugénie's favorite lady-in-waiting, Marie de Larminat, recalled: "She seemed unable to overcome her resentments or to free her mind of its burden of rancor and revolt. . . . She found it difficult to forgive; a caustic article in a newspaper, an odious insinuation, or a mere nothing would wound her to the quick, and sometimes put her completely out of humor, and we would pass some unpleasant hours. Her impetuous, passionate nature must have made her suffer more intensely than others."

Napoleon was released from Wilhelmshöhe on March 19 and arrived the next day at Dover. On hand to greet him, in addition to his wife and son and a number of loyalists, was a cheering mob of English, whose former suspicions of this Bonaparte had been transmogrified into sympathy. As he made his way hesitantly down the gangway, hat in hand, the fallen Emperor stopped halfway upon realizing the cause of the uproar, waved to the crowd, and burst into tears. The dockside reunion with his family was brief; policemen had to clear a path for the man whom so many strangers wanted to touch in empathy.

As the Imperial party was walking toward their train, they spotted, coming from the opposite direction, members of the Orléans family en route to France; with the recent elections having gone strongly in their favor, the deposed junior branch of the old Bourbon house assumed their moment had come. (It hadn't.)

There was an awkward moment of protocol: Who should give way? Gracefully, the Empress—it was one of her finer moments— stepped aside and made a curtsy to the Orléans Pretender. The Emperor and his son moved to her side, lifted their hats, and bowed. The Orléanists nodded, returned the bows, smiled, and continued on to France, while the Bonapartes rushed to catch their train to Chislehurst.

Napoleon's first caller was Lord Malmesbury, who had first met him in Rome four decades previously, during his "harum-scarum" days. Wrote Malmesbury:

> After a few minutes he came into the room alone, and with that remarkable smile which could light up his dark countenance he shook me heartily by the hand. I confess that I never was more moved. His quiet and calm dignity and absence of all nervousness and irritability were the grandest examples of human moral courage that the severest Stoic could have imagined.

A more emotional reunion occurred a week later, when Napoleon was invited to Windsor. Recorded the Queen:

> I went to the door and embraced the Emperor *comme de rigueur.* It was a moving moment, when I thought of the last time he came here in '55, in perfect triumph, dearest Albert bringing him from Dover, the whole country made to receive him, and now! He seemed much depressed and had tears in his eyes, but he controlled himself, and said *Il y a bien longtemps que je n'ai vu votre Majesté.* He is grown very stout and grey and his moustaches are no longer curled or waved as formerly, but otherwise there was the same pleasing, gentle, and gracious manner.

Napoleon's manner would remain pleasing, gentle, and gracious to the end. He led the life not of a recluse but of an exile. He read; he dabbled in some modest experiments (including a Benjamin Franklin–like stove for the poor); he wrote a few pamphlets (all of which went unnoticed and all of which are eminently forgettable). He tried horseback riding—but after the third ride he had to abandon this favorite sport.

At times, when he felt up to it—his pain was constant, and the dreary climate, to which he was not accustomed, did not do wonders for him—he would visit factories and take notes on the latest technological advances; at other times, he visited Brighton and the Isle of Wight. For the most part, though, he did not move beyond the confines of Camden Place. One intimate recalls:

> The Emperor would walk up and down the long corridor of Camden Place with his arm on the young Prince's shoulder, while he talked to the lad of men and things. After the midday breakfast, at which the little Court met for the first time in the day, he would sit in the morning-room in his arm-chair by the wood fire and talk cheerfully with the Empress or

with any visitors who had come. It was but a small circle in which the Imperial couple moved, but it was one of steadfast friends. The Emperor talked willingly and freely of the remote past, but he was only a listener when contemporary politics were under discussion. If he interfered, it was to counsel moderation of speech or to protest against reprisals.

Though she strove to make him comfortable, Eugénie found the confinement nerve-wracking. And monotonous. On Sundays, public entertainers and French émigrés came down from London to pay their respects, only to leave on the evening train.

Otherwise, the Court was on its own. Meals were taken together, after which everyone sat around. When the weather was inclement, which was often, one and all would "exercise" by wandering up and down that "long corridor of Camden Place"—a not very large upstairs front gallery, at one end of which stood a large bust of Machiavelli. Servants, attendants, loyalists, political hangers-on, the Imperial family—back and forth they walked, forty, fifty times a day.

"This is the raft of the *méduse*," the Empress remarked one day. "Every now and then we feel like eating one another."

During that first summer, Napoleon suggested that Eugénie go to Spain to visit her mother, arrange about her property and investments there, and calm her nerves. Her departure had the added effect of calming everyone else's nerves.

There was a reconciliation between mother and daughter. The old Countess had gone blind; her *salon* had gone to seed. Eugénie now felt only compassion and admiration. As she recalled in after years:

> My mother made incredible efforts to hide her infirmity from strangers and from herself. She insisted on directing her own steps as well as those of others, she knocked over furniture, she hurt herself against walls which she could not see, she attempted to walk through closed doors. So great an effort did it cost her to acknowledge herself beaten— even by an infirmity.

Like her daughter, Doña Manuela de Montijo had risen so high and fallen so low.

When Eugénie returned to Camden Place in the autumn, she and Napoleon sent their son to King's College, London. It was a mistake. The other students did not know how to consort with an Imperial Prince, so they ignored him; too, he was unable to follow the courses, which were too technical and advanced for him. A year later he was transferred to the Royal Military Academy at Woolwich, where he fared better and was happier.

Life resumed its monotonous routine at Camden Place. "I can tell what everyone here is doing every hour of the day," Eugénie complained to Marie de Larminat.

Early in 1872, a change came over the Emperor. He began to avoid the company of most of the hangers-on. He preferred to sit in his study, staring into the fire and chain-smoking. He had not fallen into a depression.

He was scheming again.

In the recent elections, Rouher—who had returned to France to organize a Bonapartist party—had been elected to the National Assembly as a member for Ajaccio. Ere long, agents were crossing the Channel in both directions; Bonapartist propaganda was flooding France; the Emperor was grinding out a stream of pseudonymous journalistic propaganda (all of which makes rather embarrassing reading). By the end of the year, a plan had been worked out.

The Emperor would leave England secretly, join Plon-Plon in Switzerland, and head for Lyons, where the garrison commander was a Bonapartist loyalist. From there the small party would set out for Paris. It was to be another Return from Elba. The return was set for March 1873. Everyone agreed that France's only salvation lay in the Emperor's return.

"Yes," he allowed. "I know I am the only solution." Then he added plaintively: "Only it is a pity I am so ill."

He was more than ill. He was moribund.

In December, a team of doctors including Sir Henry Thompson, the leading specialist in diseases of the bladder, examined the Emperor and urged a lithotrity. That the Emperor, given his deteriorated condition and knowing the dangers of such an operation, agreed would suggest he was taking one more gamble. He had to be able to sit a horse.

Napoleon III could not return to Paris on a stretcher.

It was decided that three operations should do the trick. The first two—on January 2 and 6—went well. Queen Victoria sent telegrams daily. ("I am so anxious to hear how His Majesty is today.")

The third operation was planned for the ninth. The night before, Napoleon was given a powerful narcotic to ease his excruciating pain.

At 10:25 A.M. the following day, as preparations for the operation were in progress, the Emperor's pulse suddenly became weak. The Empress was sent for. He did not seem to recognize her. Realizing the end was near, Eugénie telegraphed to Woolwich for the Prince to come at once, and sent for the Chislehurst parish priest.

By the time he arrived a few minutes later, the Emperor had been revived with small doses of brandy, and all the courtiers had filed in to join the Empress in the death watch. After the Emperor was given Extreme Unction, Eugénie approached the bed. The Emperor motioned pitifully that he wanted to be raised up so that he might give her a last kiss. There was a long silence.

Then he murmured his last words; they were to the faithful old Dr. Conneau: "We weren't cowards at Sedan, were we?"

Napoleon died moments later—at 11:15 A.M.—in Eugénie's arms.

On hearing the news, Victoria recorded in her journal: "Was quite upset. Had a great regard for the Emperor, who was so amiable and kind, and had borne his terrible misfortunes with such meekness, dignity and patience." But the true epitaph came from Eugénie herself, decades later:

> I want to tell you how fine he was, how unselfish, how generous. In our happy times I always found him simple and good, kindly and compassionate: he would put up with opposition and misrepresentation with wonderful complaisance. . . . when we were overwhelmed with misfortune, his stoicism and gentleness were sublime. You should have seen him during those last years at Chislehurst: never a word of complaint, or blame, or abuse. I often used to beg him to defend himself, to repulse some imprudent attack or the vile execrations hurled at him, to check once and for all the flood of insults that were endlessly pouring over us. But he would reply gently:
>
> "No, I shall not defend myself . . . sometimes a disaster falls upon a nation of such a kind that it is justified in blaming it all, even unfairly, upon its ruler. . . . A sovereign can offer no excuses, he can plead no extenuating circumstances. It is his highest prerogative to shoulder all the responsibilities incurred by those who have served him . . . or those who have betrayed him."

The six-day lying-in was horrendous. Bonapartist loyalists—including Plon-Plon and his sister Mathilde, who rushed over from Paris—and the just plain curious streamed in and out of the upstairs gallery to get a last view of the Emperor.

He lay in a satin-lined coffin that was all but inundated by count-less bunches of Imperial violets, which gave off a harrowing stench in the fetid air. He was dressed in his favorite uniform; his moustaches had been waxed as in the old days, and his hair combed flatteringly forward. But the embalming had turned his never at-tractive face a distressing chrome yellow. People came and went in droves, and many were sick. Providing a threnody, as it were, the Empress alternately sobbed, moaned and screamed.

The funeral services were held in the little church of Saint Mary's on Chislehurst Common. Diplomatic representatives from all over Europe, loyal courtiers, 4,000 émigrés, and twice that number of the idle curious tried to squeeze into a chapel that seated no more than two hundred. Outside the chapel, the Prince Imperial was acclaimed as Napoleon IV. To his credit, he disclaimed the honor.

Immediately afterward, Plon-Plon outdid himself in sheer un-mitigated nastiness. The cause was the Emperor's will, drawn up in 1865, when the sovereigns had agreed that on the Prince Imperial's accession, Eugénie, as Dowager Empress, would move into the Elysée Palace.*

Napoleon left his entire estate to Eugénie; to his son, who would inherit the Civil List and thus not be wanting for funds, he left a watch seal that had belonged to Queen Hortense. He made "no mention of my faithful servants"; he was "convinced that the Em-press and my son will never abandon them." Plon-Plon was not mentioned. Ergo, his miserable tantrum.

Plon-Plon insisted that there was another will, in his favor, un-less the Empress had destroyed it. He barged into the Emperor's study, where the desk had been sealed on his death, broke the seals,

---

* The document would seem to belie what the Empress subsequently told Paléologue: that she and the Emperor had drawn up an agreement sometime between 1863 and 1866 whereby he would abdicate in the Prince Imperial's favor in 1874, when the Prince reached his majority.

and flung papers in all directions, looking for that "missing will."
(He later claimed a vandal had ransacked the place.)

Eugénie, unaware of Plon-Plon's rampage and hoping to heal the
rift between them, sent for him and said, "Let the past be forgotten." To which Plon-Plon snarled: "Madam, in a short time I will
acquaint you with my intentions!"

In a short time he did. Plon-Plon demanded immediate acclama-
tion as leader of the Bonapartist party and complete and sole guard-
ianship of the Prince Imperial; also he issued a public statement to
the effect that the Empress had destroyed a will naming him the
Emperor's successor, and another public statement to the effect
that Eugénie was morally, intellectually and emotionally unfit to
bring up her own child.

Plon-Plon's behavior spoiled what political chances he had—they
were exiguous in the extreme to begin with—and made him the
Bonapartist pariah. Even his sister Mathilde was forced to repeat
herself: "You are a fool! You always were!" Which is as fitting an
epitaph as any for Plon-Plon.

A few weeks after the funeral, Queen Victoria came to Saint
Mary's to pay her final respects to the Emperor, whose remains now
resided in the small vestry, pending construction of a tomb. Afterwards, the Queen drove to Camden Place for a visit with "the poor
dear Empress. . . . She cried a good deal, but quietly and gently,
and that sweet face, always a sad one, looked inexpressibly pathetic."

To the Prince Imperial, whom she noted was "looking very ill,
very handsome, and the picture of sorrow," the Queen presented
an autographed copy of her mind-warping contribution to belles-
lettres, *Leaves from the Journal of Our Life in the Highlands*.

It was like Moses bestowing a Commandment.

She also threatened to become a Bonapartist on the spot: "The
Queen does *not* think the Bonapartist cause will lose by the poor
Emperor's death," she informed one of her government officials.
"On the contrary, *she* thinks the reverse. *For* the peace of Europe
SHE thinks (though the Orléans Princes are her *dear* friends and
connexions and some relations, and she would not for the world have

it *said* as coming from her) that it would be for the best if the Prince Imperial was *ultimately to succeed*."

Victoria had asked Eugénie ("now we are to each other *chères soeurs*") for a souvenir of the Emperor. Eugénie complied with a small clock which had stood beside his bed.

"It has recorded the happy hours of the old days," she wrote dedicatorily, "and the long hours of moral and physical suffering; years of joy, and years of sorrow—and Oh! how long these last have been!"

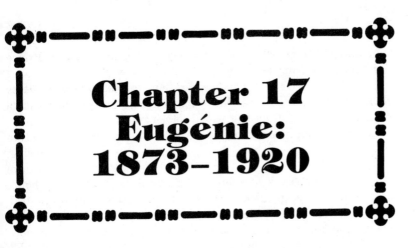

Chapter 17
Eugénie:
1873-1920

Eugénie sank into a lethargic reclusion following Napoleon's death. With the Prince Imperial's coming of age, she "rejoined the human race."

The birthday *fête* (March 16, 1874) was turned into a Bonapartist demonstration at Camden Place; it became what we would today call a media event. British and French newspapers sympathetic to the exiled royals hailed the occasion. British Railways ran special trains from Charing Cross Station to Chislehurst, bedecked with the Bonaparte tricolor and banners proclaiming "Majority of the Prince Imperial." Channel boats covertly shuttled over French nationals who had been forbidden by their government to attend. Throughout Kent, the tintinnabulation of church bells provided a fitting cacophony for the chaos at Camden Place: Bonapartist loyalists and the local gentry mingling with entrepreneurs hawking pictures of the Prince. Three thousand were fed in a tent on the front lawn.

The aging Duke de Padoue, a senile, doddering loyalist with distant Bonaparte family connections, addressed the Prince "on behalf of your loyal subjects," ending with: "Be ready for the fate that Providence may assign you!" Pale and nervous, the Prince replied that he was ready.

The thrust of his speech—written by Rouher and Filon, edited by Eugénie—was that a French plebiscite would raise him to his late father's throne: "I am ready to undertake the responsibility that the confidence of the nation assigns to me." The speech was punctuated with cries from the audience: "Long live the Emperor!" and "Long live Napoleon IV!"

Newspaper accounts of the celebration were all favorable—the young Prince had acquitted himself admirably; the day had been a roaring success. But nothing would come of it. France was not prepared to hold another Bonaparte plebiscite.

The Prince possessed all his father's good qualities—most notably charm, grace, genuine kindness and tact—and none of the bad ones—most notably deviousness and duplicity. Outwardly he was pleasant and likable. Inwardly he was gloomy and without humor. He took his role as Pretender seriously. Unfortunately, Eugénie did not know how to inculcate him in the Napoleonic legend as Queen Hortense had inculcated his father. She turned him into an absolutist and imperialist—and came close to convincing him of the divine right of kings.

Lou-Lou was kept on a tight string by his mother, who literally smothered him with her incessant presence. He obediently followed in Eugénie's wake as she traveled back and forth about the Continent, touching base with Bonapartist co-religionists, who—given the knowledge that France was not amenable to political turbulence of an imperialist nature—found it easy to be a Bonapartist without a Bonaparte.

Like his father, Lou-Lou spoke little but thought volumes. As he moved into manhood, he became a man-about-town. His connections were impeccable. The Prince of Wales was one of his roistering companions. Queen Victoria adored him and kept a friendly eye on his development.

Lou-Lou had inherited his father's talent for flattery, something that worked well with the aging Queen. When, following one dinner at Windsor, a fellow-guest asked if the monarch did not terrify him—she terrified everyone else—he replied: "Good heavens, no! Why should she? We like each other."

It was the truth. On one visit to Osborne, Lou-Lou was treated to that most splendid of honors: a personally guided tour of the meretricious mausoleum Victoria had had built at Frogmore for her "dearest of *all* husbands." Lou-Lou waxed eloquent on inspecting that dreadful pile. The Queen's joy knew no bounds.

Victoria and Eugénie had become even closer. Both spent many an hour commiserating over their common affliction: widowhood. On one occasion, Eugénie was planning to visit Windsor when she learned that members of the Orléans family had asked to visit at the same time. She wrote to the Queen suggesting a postponement of her visit, to save Victoria the awkwardness of having both the rival French royalties at the same time.

"No," Victoria told her daughter Beatrice, "by no means put off the visit. If anyone postpones it, it had better be *they!* The Orléanists are my relations, but the Empress is my *friend*, and that is *much* more sacred to *me!*"

The exiled Imperial family became almost an adjunct of the royal family. A friendship developed between the Prince Imperial and Victoria's youngest daughter, Beatrice ("Dearest Baby"). Soon there was talk of an engagement between the young pair.

The Empress was all for it. She was beginning to entertain private doubts as to Lou-Lou's ultimate success in reclaiming his father's throne. Should, God forbid, he not become Emperor of the French, being son-in-law to Europe's most powerful monarch might not be a bad consolation prize.

Problems supervened, however, not the least of which was the matter of religion. (Said Victoria: "Dearest Baby could *NEVER* become a Roman Catholic!") The betrothal never got off the ground. Lou-Lou made the rounds of the European Courts in consideration of marital prospects.

Like his father, though, he was determined not to marry while still in exile.

As he entered into his twenties, Lou-Lou eschewed the man-about-town life and settled down to seriously planning for his presumed accession. Ever the Bonaparte, he wanted military experience. He sought service with the French and Austrian armies, but was turned down by both governments. Turning to the British army, he was rewarded with a commission in the Royal Horse Artillery. He made periodic trips to the Continent to acquaint himself with Bonapartist loyalists.

Eugénie abdicated her leadership of the Cause in his favor; she even released his funds, so that he might comport himself like a true Pretender. Lou-Lou was convinced that ultimately he must triumph as his father had triumphed.

Eugénie did not share that confidence. "My son has a feeling of responsibility," she admitted, "but at the same time he is not very adventurous. In order to tempt him to do something prudent, one would have to arouse this spirit of adventure in him."

Added to Eugénie's doubt about her son was the fact that her political attitudes were changing. To the old Countess de Montijo, who had written to express joy over the restoration of the Bourbons in Spain, she wrote:

> When one has witnessed in Paris the triumphal departure of the Emperor to Italy and a few years later, in the same city, the embittered masses about the Tuileries, one is prepared to make a correct estimate of the value of both. The world as you see it is that of the Middle Ages . . . kings, princes, and the nobility have been working against each other for centuries, and their alliances will never come to anything. Now one must reckon with new forces. The age of men of destiny is over. In a skeptical society, redeemers become the victims.

Not until she was in exile did Eugénie realize what she should have realized before she was an empress.

The Prince was determined to follow in his father's footsteps and create a military reputation for himself. For him, riding a horse at the Aldershot Tattoo was a far cry from the real thing. In the words of Marie de Larminat, he "anxiously scanned the face of the earth, his sword burning in his hands."

The year 1879 was a replay of the year 1831. In 1831, Napoleon III had gone off to Italy and acquitted himself well against the papal and Austrian armies. In February 1879, "Napoleon IV" went off to Africa to acquit himself well against the Zulus.

Eugénie initially opposed the idea. ("How cruel a son is! How often I have regretted he was not a girl!") Lou-Lou persevered: "As long as there is one man of my battery in England, I could stay here. But . . . how is it possible for me to appear on the parade grounds when all my comrades are in Africa?"

The British government felt quite confident of defeating the Zulus without Lou-Lou's help; opposition derived not from the fact that he was a Bonaparte, but from the embarrassment that might ensue were he to die in battle.

Eugénie reluctantly intervened in his behalf with her *chère soeur*. Victoria acquiesced: "I understand how easily in his position he must wish for active employment." The Cabinet gave its consent. Disraeli would afterwards say: "Well, *my* conscience is clear. I did all that I could to stop his going. But what can you do when you have two obstinate women to deal with?"

On February 27, Eugénie accompanied her twenty-three-year-old son to Southampton, where the pair was feted by local dignitaries: thanks to a sympathetic press and their close relationship with the royal family, the exiled Bonapartes were more popular in England than in France. Eugénie sobbed bitterly as she kissed Lou-Lou farewell; she remained standing on the Southampton dock until the S.S. *Danube*, bearing the Bonaparte Pretender off to glory, disappeared from view.

Eugénie spent the next three months "at the mercy of the telegraph wire," in retreat from the world, barely able to eat or sleep. She took comfort in Lou-Lou's letters: he was enjoying himself, he was "proving" himself, he was popular with his comrades. For Eugénie, it was precious little comfort. "This state of expectation reminds me of 1870," she told one of her attendants.

Her fears gave way to characteristic superstition: in a dream, she envisioned her son's fate. She philosophized: "Defeat is a misfortune in a land in which the wounded are left to die on the field of battle or are surrendered to the enemy."

It was as if Eugénie knew she would never see her son again.

On June 1—it was a Sunday—the Prince set out with a small reconnoitering party under the command of one Lieutenant Carey. A few hours later they encountered some Zulus. Without giving orders to his men, Carey spurred his horse and fled; he was followed by five of his six troopers.

The sixth trooper—the Prince Imperial—was mounting his horse when the pommel gave way in his hand; due to profiteering, the saddle was merely heavy paper under a veneer of leather. Deserted by his comrades, surrounded by Zulus, he put up a courageous fight.

The Prince's fate became known later that afternoon, when his horse wandered into the British camp. (The horse's name, ironically enough, was Fate.) When a search party recovered the body two days later, it was found that the Prince had been

> assegaied in seventeen places, his arms were crossed over his chest, and his face, which was beautiful in death, was disfigured by the destruction of the right eye from an assegai wound. . . . The body was stripped naked except for a gold chain with medallions, which was about his neck. His sabre, his revolver, his helmet, and his other clothes had disappeared, but we found in the grass his spurs with their straps, and a sock marked N.

Due to primitive communications, it was not until June 15—a Sunday—that Eugénie learned of her son's death. She collapsed.

Her courtiers rallied around, but Eugénie was inconsolable. A few days later, Queen Victoria went to Camden Place to offer her condolences in person. To Disraeli, she wrote of the visit:

> The dear Empress Eugénie's conduct is *beyond* all praise. Her resignation, her unmurmuring patient submission to God's will, her conviction that it could not be otherwise, and the total absence of all blame of others are admirable. But her heart is broken and her poor health seems sadly shaken. She can eat nothing and hardly sleeps. But *how* could it be otherwise?

The funeral, at Camden Place on July 11, was a Bonapartist event. Loyalists converged from all directions. Plon-Plon, who had publicly dismissed the Prince Imperial as "an incurable imbecile," came from Italy to act as chief mourner. Queen Victoria ordered her Cabinet to attend, but the British government did not want to offend the French Republic. Victoria raised so harrowing a fuss, the Cabinet relented to the degree that two ministers (War and the Colonies) were permitted to attend, in full dress and medals. The Queen herself came, attended by Beatrice and the Princess of Wales. Rather nastily, the French government refused to allow Napoleon III's chief officers, notably MacMahon, Canrobert and Leboeuf, to attend.

The Prince Imperial was accorded full military honors. Cadets of Woolwich formed an honor guard; pallbearers included the Prince of Wales and his brother the Duke of Connaught, the Crown Prince of Sweden, and the Duke of Cambridge (Victoria's cousin and Commander-in-Chief of the British army). After a mass celebrated by Cardinal Manning, Catholic primate of England, the coffin was

set beside that of Napoleon III in Saint Mary's Church on Chislehurst Common.*

Eugénie hoped the sad occasion would mark a reconciliation with
Plon-Plon and Mathilde. The latter was amenable. So was Plon-
Plon—until the Prince's will was made known. Plon-Plon had been
passed over in the succession; the Bonaparte heir was now his eldest
son, Prince Victor. Plon-Plon threw a predictable tantrum, called
for his carriage, and rode out of Eugénie's life.

In the will, written the day before his departure for Africa, the
Prince had written: "I need not recommend my mother to defend
the memory of my great-uncle and father. I beg her to remember
that so long as a Bonaparte lives, the Imperial cause will be
represented."

The representation was dismal. Prince Victor's ambitions were
only of the social variety: he was quite content to fritter away his
days as a hanger-on in his Italian grandfather's Court. And not even
the most die-hard loyalist would have anything to do with Plon-
Plon—who, true to form, disowned his son. ("I leave nothing to
Victor," wrote Plon-Plon prior to his own death in 1891. "He is a
traitor and a rebel. I do not wish him to be present at my funeral."
He wasn't.)

Bonapartism was dead. And no one realized this better than
Eugénie herself.

To her mother in Madrid, Eugénie wrote: "I am crushed, I no
longer live, I wait for death, for it alone can reunite me with those
who are waiting for me. I hope that calm and solitude will return. I
badly need to be left alone with my thoughts, my memories, and
nothing must come between them and me from the outside . . ."

Her wish could not be totally respected. The death of the Prince
Imperial was for the British government a profound humiliation.
There was a great outcry over Lieutenant Carey's cowardice in
abandoning him; Carey was court-martialed and convicted. It was
only as a result of Eugénie's plea for clemency that he was not
cashiered:

------

* *Victoria sought to have the Prince memorialized with a statue in
Westminster Abbey; when her government vetoed the idea, she had a
small statue erected to his memory in St. George's Chapel at Windsor.*

The only earthly consolation I have [she wrote to the British government] is in the idea that my beloved child fell as a soldier, obeying *orders,* on a duty which was *commanded,* and that those who gave them did so because they thought him competent and useful.

Enough of recriminations. Let the memory of his death unite in a common sorrow all those who loved him, and let no one suffer, either in his reputation or his interests. I, who desire nothing more on earth, ask it as a last prayer.

Eugénie wished to spare the Queen and the British army further humiliation; furthermore, she realized that all the recriminations in the world could not bring her son back to life.

In her last letter to the Countess de Montijo, who died a few months later, Eugénie wrote: "I am without purpose and courage. The weather is cold, I have a fire, but nothing can warm me and my heart is turned to ice . . ."

In the autumn, Victoria insisted that Eugénie accompany her to Balmoral. There in the Scottish Highlands, Eugénie decided to make a pilgrimage to the spot where her son had died. In March of the following year, accompanied by a small retinue, she sailed for Africa.

"What misfortune that the Emperor should have married a Spaniard and I a Napoleon!" she wrote Victoria. "Our son naturally had to be the victim. Through my race I gave him the gift of Quixotism, the readiness always to sacrifice all to the ideal: the Emperor gave him the obligations of his name. And all in the middle of the nineteenth century, when materialism is closing in on us like weeds from all sides. . . ."

Directly on her return, Eugénie disposed of Camden Place. It was too small; it was too filled with memories; and she felt that her husband and son deserved more than the small crypt in Saint Mary's on Chislehurst Common. She purchased an estate at Farnborough in Hampshire and had built a new church to house the remains of Napoleon III and Napoleon IV, a church she named Saint Michael's Abbey, after the patron saint of France.

Eugénie brought her memories to Farnborough. The house (it

eventually became a Catholic girls' school) was aclutter with mementoes: pictures, statues and busts of Napoleon and Lou-Lou; paintings devolving upon the Second Empire and even of many of the Bonapartes she could not have known: Queen Hortense, the ex-King of Holland, the Empress Josephine. The "Emperors' Room" contained a gray coat that had belonged to Napoleon I, a cap that had belonged to Napoleon III, and all of the Prince Imperial's uniforms. The "Prince's Room" contained his books, a large painting of himself, even a statue of Lou-Lou with his dog Nero, standing in a patch of grass the Empress had brought back with her from Zulu-land.

All the walls at Farnborough were adorned with photographs, paintings and framed mementoes of her eighteen years as Empress of the French: the Emperor in his Robes of State, a photograph of the Prince Imperial on horseback, the famous painting of herself surrounded by her ladies-in-waiting by Winterhalter, and the like. There was even a framed color print of the verses Théophile Gautier had composed in celebration of her marriage: "Sweet, pure jasmine of Spain that the golden bee has kissed . . ."

But there were no Marie Antoinette memorabilia. That obsession had been laid to rest with the Second Empire.

She collected a large library, which was impressive if rarely used. She cared not for novels: "The authors that can arouse my feelings and touch my heart are no longer living." Poetry was beyond her: "I do not understand poetry; it makes me tired." She did read news-papers, though, and took an active interest in the politics of Europe and the changing world about her.

By 1890, Eugénie had developed the pattern her life would follow to its end. She indulged an incessant mania for travel: Scotland, Ireland, Scandinavia, Austria (where she was received handsomely by the Habsburg royals), throughout the Mediterranean on her yacht, the *Thistle*. She traveled throughout Asia Minor. She spent six weeks in Ceylon. In Egypt, at the age of eighty, she rode out sightseeing on a donkey. There were numerous trips to Spain; she concerned herself with Paca's grandchildren, who now had children of their own.

She was permitted to return to France, where she purchased a villa at Cap Martin on the Riviera. It was named Cyrnos, the Greek form of Corsica. There she passed the winters.

On her trips to Paris while en route to Cap Martin, she invariably stopped at a hotel that overlooked the spot where the Tuileries had once stood. When asked if this upset her, she replied: "The Empress died in 1870."

When back at Farnborough, Eugénie occupied her time overseeing the servants, inspecting the small working farm on the estate, poring over old letters, rearranging her memorabilia, and entertaining a steady stream of visitors. Two future monarchs of England, Edward VII and George V, visited regularly. She came to know many of the upcoming royals of other countries. And she made new friendships. The first-generation Bonaparte loyalists—Conneau, Filon, Rouher—died off; she took an active interest in the lives of their offspring.

But Eugénie did not confine her friendships to coevals. One of her admirers was the composer Dame Ethel Smyth, who visited Farnborough often and was taken with the Empress's congenital habit of switching from childish joy to self-pitying tragedy in the bat of an eyelash. With Dame Ethel, Eugénie indulged both a girlish pleasure in the gossip of the British Court and a penchant for allowing that she had nothing left to live for, that everyone she had ever loved was gone.

"When I am with her," wrote Dame Ethel, "I feel all the time as if I were reading *Antigone* or *King Lear*."

She carried on a friendship of sorts with the Princess Mathilde. Mathilde had been permitted to remain on in Paris after promising not to meddle in politics. The passing years took their toll: she got fat, took a young lover who did not love her, and holed up with four dogs in a clutter of chinoiserie and Second Empire furniture and bibelots. When Mathilde died in 1904, Eugénie attended the funeral as chief mourner.

There were many trends that to Eugénie were utterly incomprehensible. Paramount among these was the rise of anti-Semitism as a creed, thanks in large measure to the efforts of such evangelists as Gobineau in France and Wagner in Germany. On one voyage through the Mediterranean aboard the *Thistle*, Eugénie landed at Corfu at a time when the libelous charge of ritual murder was imperiling the local Jewish community. Ostentatiously, she went to the ghetto and handed the rabbi a large sum of money for the poor.

The Dreyfus affair in France aroused her passions. She followed the trial assiduously and was one of the first to declare the defendant innocent. It cost her the friendship of one of her oldest and most loyal friends, the Duchess de Mouchy, a confirmed anti-Semite. But Eugénie would not compromise her principles. She had always hated religious intolerance.

There were many trends that to Eugénie were addictive. She learned to ride a bicycle. She purchased one of the first automobiles manufactured. She wanted to learn to fly and always regretted that no one would take her up in an airplane.

When World War I broke out, she established a hospital for officers at Farnborough, and dipped into her own pocket to equip it with the very latest in machines, the very best in food. Despite the infirmities of age, she insisted on personally helping tend the sick and wounded. When the armistice came, Eugénie was euphoric; the Germans she loathed had been "given their just desserts." She could barely wait to get to Paris.

Eugénie's age was taking its toll on her once fabled beauty, yet her physical strength remained constant. Friends became alarmed that she moved about constantly and insisted on sleeping by an open window.

"I am my own doctor and know best what is good for me," she declared with obstinacy.

The only one who had any influence over her was Dr. Evans's successor, Dr. Hugenschmidt. Eugénie thought he bore a remarkable likeness to the Prince Imperial. The likeness is explainable if the rumors surrounding Hugenschmidt's birth are true: that he was the Countess di Castiglione's bastard by the Emperor Napoleon III.

In her last years, the Empress developed crotchets. Mention of her name day was forbidden; it called up too many bitter memories. She refused to allow publication of any of her letters and, as heretofore indicated, would not consent to writing her memoirs; she feared they might be regarded as "an apology for my life." On one occasion she said: "I do not want anything done or said to justify me. I have long ceased to think about it!"

On another occasion, she was sent for comment a series of articles written by Admiral de la Gravière describing her influence as Regent in 1870. Eugénie wrote him:

One remark in your discussion annoyed the Empress. It has to do with her feeling for the Emperor, that feeling of fidelity, which remains unchanged to the end. The idea that she could, even for one moment, have considered the Emperor unworthy of her hurts her deeply. She would rather endure the most cruel insults of an enemy than any appreciation from friends that have failed to recognize how she felt toward the Emperor.

Also in her last years, Eugénie was given over to introspection. She admitted what Napoleon had once said to her: "You never get an idea, Eugénie. An idea gets you!" To Paléologue she said: "Oh, my dear, you should have known him. He was always kind and generous to everyone."

And she was given over to frustration concerning her role as a historical personage: "At the beginning of the regime, I was considered a frivolous woman, who spent her time doing nothing; toward the end, I was a fateful woman, who was blamed for all the mistakes and all the misfortunes!" And: "I ask of God but one thing: that I may live until France has learned to take a more just view of us."

One day, as Eugénie's long life was coming to a close, she was asked by Dame Ethel Smyth: "Does Your Majesty know hatred?"

She replied: "I . . . no—I hate no one." Then she added, after a hesitation: "Besides, they are all dead; I have outlived them all."

In 1919, the Empress was told blindness was inevitable. "I am now a very old bat," she told Paléologue. "But like butterflies, I long for light; and before I die, I would like to see the sky of Castile."

Early in May of the following year she arrived in Madrid. Her advanced years and declining sight notwithstanding, Eugénie displayed remarkable vitality: she went on long automobile rides, received countless visitors, and engaged in extended discussions that ran the gamut from old politics to new advances in science and technology.

On learning of an oculist who claimed he could operate on cataracts without an anaesthetic, she went to see him, insisted on the operation, and came through it with flying colors. She planned to return to Farnborough in mid-July. On the morning of July 10, she felt slightly indisposed.

"It will pass quickly," she said.

It did pass quickly.

Eugénie's last view, as she lay abed in Paca's room in the Liria Palace, was of the three photographs that "go everywhere with me": Napoleon III, the Prince Imperial, and Queen Victoria—and, directly facing the bed, a large portrait of her beloved Paca.

Just before lapsing into a coma, she told her grandnephew the Duke of Alba: "In Spain, I saw the light for the first time; in Spain, my eyes will see it for the last time." The next morning she passed quietly into death, amidst the sound of church bells.

It was a Sunday.

In her last conversation with Paléologue, the old Empress had said: "There is a prayer in the liturgy of death that I have repeated time and again: '*Proficiscere de hoc mundo anima Christiana*'—'Go forth from this world, O Christian soul.' When the priest speaks these beautiful words in the last hour of my life, I shall be thankful and happy."

The priest did.

She was.

Dressed in the white robes of the Order of St. James, and in a simple coffin of Spanish oak, Eugénie was returned to Farnborough on July 18—a Sunday—amidst the panoply due an Empress. Recalls the local curate:

> Just before twelve noon we went in procession from the Church [Saint Michael's Abbey] down to the station. Troops, mounted and on foot, were already in position and holding the dense crowds back. Lord Rawlinson, G.C.O. Aldershot, and his staff were on the platform. As we approached, the cavalry drew and presented arms. The train arrived punctually. There was a guard of Irish soldiers accompanying the coffin and many mourners with Prince Victor [the Bonaparte heir] at their head. The coffin was mounted on a gun carriage and covered with the Union Jack. At the moment the coffin was taken off the gun carriage, the band played the *Marseillaise* . . .

The French Republic made official protests against honors being shown the last Empress of the French; the British War Office ordered that the guns already in position were not to fire their planned salute due a fallen sovereign.

Among the mourners in attendance were the kings of England, Portugal and Spain (Princess Beatrice's daughter Victoria-Eugenia, the Spanish consort, was Eugénie's namesake and goddaughter); other European royals, incumbent as well as dethroned, were officially represented. The rites were celebrated by the Cardinal Archbishop of Westminster.

Interment was in the massive Norman crypt of Saint Michael's Abbey that Eugénie had personally designed. In the transepts to the right and left of the altar are the two sarcophagi containing the remains of her husband and her son.

Her own coffin was set in where the Empress had insisted was to be her final resting place: in the wall above the altar—looking down on the others.

Bibliography

Alba, Duke of (Editor). *Lettres familières de l'Impératrice Eugénie*, 2 vols. Paris, 1935.

André-Maurois, Simone. *Miss Howard and the Emperor*, translated by Humphrey Hare. London, 1957.

Arnaud, René. *Le 2 Décembre*. Paris, 1967.

———. *The Second Republic and Napoleon III*, translated by E. F. Buckley. London, 1923.

Aronson, Theo. *The Fall of the Third Napoleon*. New York, 1970.

———. *Queen Victoria and the Bonapartes*. London, 1972.

Aubry, Octave. *The Second Empire*. Philadelphia, 1940.

d'Auvergne, Edmund B. *Napoleon III, A Biography*. New York, 1929.

Bac, F. *Intimités du Second Empire*, 3 vols. Paris, 1931.

———. *Le Mariage de l'Impératrice Eugénie*. Paris, 1928.

Barshak, Erna. *The Innocent Empress: An Intimate Study of Eugénie*. New York, 1943.

Barthez, A. C. E. *The Empress Eugénie and Her Circle*. London, 1912.

Bellessort, André. *La Société française sous Napoléon III*. Paris, 1932.

Bertaut, Jules. *Le Boulevard*. Paris, 1957.

Bicknell, Anna. *Life in the Tuileries under the Second Empire*. New York, 1895.

Blanchard, Jerrold. *The Life of Napoleon III*, 4 vols. London, 1874–82.

Blanchard, Marcel. *Le Second Empire*. Paris, 1950.

Bleton, Pierre. *La Vie sociale sous le Second Empire*. Paris, 1963.

Bonnin, Georges (Editor). *Bismarck and the Hohenzollern Candidature for the Spanish Throne*. London, 1957.

Boulenger, Marcel. *Le Duc de Morny, Prince français*. Paris, 1925.

Brodsky, Alyn. *Madame Lynch & Friend*. New York, 1975.

Brooks, Graham. *Napoleon III*. New York, 1933.

Buffin, Camille. *La Tragédie Mexicaine*. Brussels, 1925.

Burchell, S. C. *Imperial Masquerade: The Paris of Napoleon Third*. New York, 1971.

Cadogan, Edward. *Makers of Modern History: Louis Napoleon—Cavour—Bismarck*. Port Washington, N.Y., 1970.

Carette, Mme. (Mlle. Bouvet). *Souvenirs intimes de la Cour des Tuileries*, 3 vols. Paris, 1888–91.

Carey, Agnes. *The Empress Eugénie in Exile*. London, 1922.

Case, L. M. *Franco-Italian Relations 1860–65*. Philadelphia, 1932.

Castelot, André. *La Féerie impériale*. Paris, 1962.

Castillo, H. *Le Comte de Persigny*. Paris, 1857.

Cheetham, Frank H. *Louis Napoleon and the Genesis of the Second Empire*. London, 1909.

Chesnelong, Ch. *Les Derniers Jours de l'Empire*. Paris, 1930.

Cowley, Lord. *Secrets of the Second Empire*, F. A. Wellesley, editor. London, 1929.

Dansette, Adrien. *Les Amours de Napoléon III*. Paris, 1938.

Debidour, A. *Histoire diplomatique de l'Europe, 1814–1878*, 2 vols. Paris, 1891.

Decaux, Alain. *La Castiglione, le coeur de l'Europe*. Paris, 1953.

———. *Offenbach, roi du Second Empire*. Paris, 1958.

Delord, Taxile. *Histoire du Second Empire*, 6 vols. Paris, 1869–75.

Des Garets, Marie, Comtesse (de Larminat) de Garnier. *Souvenirs d'une Demoiselle d'Honneur: l'Impératrice Eugénie en exile*. Paris, 1929.

Du Camp, Maxime. *Souvenirs d'un demi-siècle*. Paris, 1949.

Dubeau, Georges. *La Vie ouvrière en France sous le Second Empire*. Paris, 1946.

Evans, Thomas W. *Memoirs of Dr. Thomas W. Evans*. London, 1906.

———. *The Second French Empire*. New York, 1905.

Filon, Augustin. *Memoirs of the Prince Imperial*. London, 1912.

———. *Souvenirs sur l'Impératrice Eugénie*. Paris, 1920.

Fleury, Comte Maurice. *The Memoirs of the Empress Eugénie*, 2 vols. London, 1920.

———, and Sonolet, Louis. *La Société du Second Empire*, 3 vols. Paris, 1911–13.

Forbes, Archibald. *The Life of Napoleon the Third*. London, 1898.

Fuye, L. de. *Louis-Napoléon Bonaparte avant l'Empire*. Paris, 1951.

Gooch, G. P. *The Second Empire*. London, 1960.

Gorce, Pierre de la. *Histoire du Second Empire*, 7 vols. Paris, 1894–1905.

Gramont, Duke of. *La France et la Prusse avant la guerre*. London, 1872.

Gramont, Sanche de. *The French*. New York, 1969.

Guedalla, Philip. *The Second Empire*. London, 1922.

Guerard, Albert. *Napoleon III—A Great Life in Brief*. New York, 1955.

Guest, Ivor. *Napoleon III in England*. London, 1952.

Hales, E. E. Y. *Pío Nono*. London, 1954.

Hallberg, C. *Franz-Josef and Napoleon III*. New York, 1955.

Haslip, Joan. *Imperial Adventurer, Emperor Maximilian of Mexico and His Empress*. London, 1971.

d'Hauterive, E. *Napoléon III et le Prince Napoléon.* Paris, 1925.

Holt, Edgar. *Plon-Plon, The Life of Prince Napoleon.* London, 1973.

Horne, Alistair. *The Fall of Paris.* New York, 1965.

Hortense, Queen. *Memoirs of Queen Hortense,* edited by Jean Hanoteau, translated by Arthur K. Griggs. London, 1927.

Howard, Michael. *The Franco-Prussian War.* New York, 1962.

Hübner, Count. *Neuf ans de souvenirs d'un Ambassadeur d'Autriche,* 2 vols. Paris, 1904.

John, Katherine. *The Prince Imperial.* London, 1939.

Kerry, Earl of. *The Secret of the Coup d'Etat.* London, 1924.

Krackauer, S. *Offenbach and the Paris of His Time.* London, 1937.

Kurtz, Harold. *The Empress Eugénie: 1826–1920.* London, 1964.

Labracherie, Pierre. *Napoleon III et son temps.* Paris, 1967.

———. *Le Second Empire.* Paris, 1962.

Legge, Edward. *The Comedy and Tragedy of the Second Empire.* London, 1911.

———. *The Empress Eugénie, 1870–1910.* London, 1910.

———. *The Empress Eugénie and Her Son.* London, 1916.

Lenôtre, Gaston (Louis Leon Theodore Gosselin). *En France jadis.* Paris, 1938.

———. *The Tuileries.* London, 1934.

Llanos y Torriglia, Félix D. *Maria Manuela Kirkpatrick, Condesa de Montijo.* Madrid, 1935.

Loliée, Frédéric. *Frère de l'Empereur, Le Duc de Morny et la Société du Second Empire.* Paris, 1909.

———. *The Gilded Beauties of the Second Empire.* London, 1910.

———. *Rêve d'empereur.* Paris, 1913.

Longford, Elizabeth. *Victoria R.I.* London, 1964.

Lord, Robert H. *The Origins of the War of 1870.* Cambridge, 1924.

Ludwig, Emil. *Bismarck.* London, 1927.

Malmesbury, Earl of (James Howard Harris). *Memoirs of an Ex-Minister.* London, 1885.

Maupas, C. E. de. *Mémoires sur le Second Empire.* Paris, 1884.

Maurain, J. *La Politique Ecclésiastique du Second Empire.* Paris, 1930.

Maxwell, Sir Herbert E. (Editor). *Life of the Fourth Earl of Clarendon,* 2 vols. London, 1913.

Mercier, Jacques and Dominique. *Napoleon III quitte la scène.* Paris, 1963.

Mérimée, Prosper. *Correspondance générale, établiee et annotée par Maurice Parturier,* 16 vols. Toulouse, 1946–61.

Metternich, Princess Pauline. *Souvenirs 1859–71.* Paris, 1922.

Metternich, Prince Richard. *Mémoires et documents d'ecrits divers de Metternich.* Paris, 1883.

Montesquiou, Robert de. *La Divine Comtesse.* Paris, 1913.

Napoléon III. *Oeuvres.* Paris, 1856.

North Peat, A. B. *Gossip from Paris during the Second Empire.* London, 1903.

Orsi, Count. *Recollections of the Last Half-Century*. London, 1881.
Packe, Michael St. John. *The Bombs of Orsini*. London, 1958.
Paléologue, Georges Maurice. *Les Entretiens de l'Impératrice Eugénie*. Paris, 1928.
Papiers et correspondance de la Famille Impériale, 3 vols. Paris, 1870–72.
Pflaum, Rosalynd. *The Emperor's Talisman*. New York, 1968.
Pinkney, David H. *Napoleon III and the Rebuilding of Paris*. Princeton, 1958.
Poirson, P. *Walewski*. Paris, 1943.
Rheinhardt, E. A. *Napoleon and Eugénie, The Tragicomedy of an Empire*. New York, 1931.
Richardson, Joanna. *Princess Mathilde*. New York, 1969.
Roux, Georges. *Napoléon III*. Paris, 1969.
Rumbold, Sir Horace. *Recollections of a Diplomatist*, 2 vols. London, 1902.
Saint-Amand, Imbert de. *Napoléon III et sa Cour*. Paris, n.d.
Salomon, H. *L'Ambassade de Richard de Metternich*. Paris, 1931.
Schnerb, R. *Rouher et le Second Empire*. Paris, 1949.
Sencourt, Robert. *The Life of the Empress Eugénie*. New York, 1931.
———. *Napoleon III, The Modern Emperor*. New York, 1933.
Simpson, F. A. *Louis-Napoleon and the Recovery of France*. London, 1923.
———. *The Rise of Louis-Napoleon*. London, 1909, 1925.
Smyth, Dame Ethel Mary. *Streaks of Life*. London, 1921.
Soissons, Count de. *The True Story of the Empress Eugénie*. London, 1921.
Sonolet, Louis. *La Vie parisienne sous le Second Empire*. Paris, 1929.
Stacton, David. *The Bonapartes*. New York, 1966.
Thayer, W. R. *The Life and Times of Cavour*, 2 vols. Boston, 1911.
Thompson, J. M. *Louis Napoleon and the Second Empire*. New York, 1967.
Veuillot, Louis. *Les Odeurs de Paris*. Paris, 1867.
Victoria, Queen of Great Britain. *Letters of Queen Victoria: A Selection from Her Majesty's Correspondence, 1837–1910*, 9 vols. London, 1907–30.
Viel-Castel, Horace de. *Mémoire sur le règne de Napoleon III, 1851–64*, 6 vols. Paris, 1883–84.
Villemot, Auguste. *La Vie à Paris*. Paris, 1858.
Vizetelly, E. A. *The Court of the Tuileries*. London, 1912.
Wellesley, V., and Sencourt, R. *Conversations with Napoleon III*. London, 1934.
Williams, Roger L. *Gaslight & Shadow*. New York, 1857.
Wolf, John B. *France, 1814–1919*. New York, 1963.

Index